Intellectual Property and Business

D1427776

Intellectual Property and Business
The Power of Intangible Assets

Rodney D. Ryder
Ashwin Madhavan

www.sagepublications.com

Los Angeles • London • New Delhi • Singapore • Washington DC

Copyright © Rodney D. Ryder and Ashwin Madhavan, 2014

All rights reserved. No part of this book may be reproduced or utilized in any form or by any means, electronic or mechanical, including photocopying, recording or by any information storage or retrieval system, without permission in writing from the publisher.

First published in 2014 by

SAGE Response
B1/I-1 Mohan Cooperative Industrial Area
Mathura Road, New Delhi 110 044, India

SAGE Publications Inc
2455 Teller Road
Thousand Oaks, California 91320, USA

SAGE Publications Ltd
1 Oliver's Yard, 55 City Road
London EC1Y 1SP, United Kingdom

SAGE Publications Asia-Pacific Pte Ltd
3 Church Street
#10-04 Samsung Hub
Singapore 049483

Published by Vivek Mehra for SAGE Publications India Pvt Ltd, typeset in 11/13 Bembo by RECTO Graphics, Delhi, and printed at Saurabh Printers Pvt Ltd, New Delhi.

Library of Congress Cataloging-in-Publication Data

Ryder, Rodney D.
  Intellectual property and business: the power of intangible assets/Rodney D. Ryder, Ashwin Madhavan.
    p. cm.
  Includes bibliographical references and index.
    1. Intellectual Property—United States. I. Madhavan, Ashwin. II. Title.
  KF2979.R94   346.7304'8—dc23   2013   2014018433

ISBN: 978-81-321-1791-9 (PB)

The SAGE Team: Sachin Sharma, Isha Sachdeva, Anju Saxena and Dally Verghese

To

Rebecca, Mark, Gunjan
—Rodney D. Ryder

Sandy: my adorable four-legged brother
Amma and Appa for always believing in me and supporting me
Naani (Saroja Chary) for her unconditional love
—Ashwin Madhavan

LEISURE AND CULTURE DUNDEE	
C00748636X	
Bertrams	18/06/2015
	£19.99
REF	346.73048

Thank you for choosing a SAGE product! If you have any comment, observation or feedback, I would like to personally hear from you. Please write to me at <u>contactceo@sagepub.in</u>

—Vivek Mehra, Managing Director and CEO,
SAGE Publications India Pvt Ltd, New Delhi

Bulk Sales

SAGE India offers special discounts for purchase of books in bulk. We also make available special imprints and excerpts from our books on demand.

For orders and enquiries, write to us at

Marketing Department
SAGE Publications India Pvt Ltd
B1/I-1, Mohan Cooperative Industrial Area
Mathura Road, Post Bag 7
New Delhi 110044, India
E-mail us at <u>marketing@sagepub.in</u>

Get to know more about SAGE, be invited to SAGE events, get on our mailing list. Write today to <u>marketing@sagepub.in</u>

This book is also available as an e-book.

⸱⸱⸱⸱⸱ ঙ)ওঙ ⸱⸱⸱⸱⸱

Contents

List of Illustrations

FIGURES

TABLES

Preface

The idea of writing this book came from various interactions we have had in these past five years on Intellectual Property (IP). The goal of this text is to help people understand and use our IP system as a "force" to further creativity and economic development.

The audience for this text is anyone who is associated with innovation, creativity, and new ideas, in any way—managers, business leaders, advocates, policy makers—irrespective of where they are located or which sector they operate in.

We felt that there was a need for a book that explains the nuances of this unique form of intangible property, which many people did not understand properly. Whenever we conducted training programs and workshops for professionals on ways to protect their IP assets, we could see eyebrows being raised and a sense of ignorance on the very meaning of the term IP.

With this in mind, we began penning down our thoughts on the various facets of this exciting subject of law and management. Many people believe that IP is only for lawyers and in-house legal counsels of very large corporations. What these people do not understand is the fact that having IP gives any corporation big or small a certain financial muscle, which if used properly can reap in immense financial benefits. IP is nothing without law because without legal protection, the value of an intangible asset is minimal, but equally important is the fact that IP is nothing without proper management. We will demonstrate through the pages of this book the reason why managing IP assets is equally important.

When we first conceived of the idea of writing this book, we planned to target it at practicing lawyers and in-house legal counsels. Through our legal experience, we have come across lawyers and in-house counsels who want to understand the concept of IP. As we wrote the book, we realized that the business organizations as well as the student community in India would definitely benefit from this book. A number of business professionals and experts who read the earlier drafts of this book gave us feedback on how to make it more appealing to the business and the nonlegal community. Several chapters including (a) Intellectual Property Approaches and Strategies and (b) Intellectual Asset Management have been inspired by those conversations that we had with our early reviewers.

This book is for all those individuals who want to know more about the power of IP and its various nuances. It has been written in the simplest of language without going into any legal jargon, which many a times puts off people. We begin this book with an introduction on why IP is important and explain the characteristics of the various forms of IP. We then focus on the approaches and strategies to protect IP. We dive deep into how organizations should defend their IP assets.

The following chapters on IP management, brand management, IP licensing, and franchising contain useful information about how companies should use their IP assets with the help of several live example case studies.

As a bonus, we have also added chapters on IP valuation and royalty, which highlight the various ways in which IP is valued and how royalty is paid to various stakeholders.

Throughout the book, we have included case studies, and tips and techniques that will help you in understanding this subject that we love in a much better way.

We do hope you find this book useful!

Rodney D. Ryder
Ashwin Madhavan

Acknowledgments

This book took us five years to write. All books are collaborative efforts and this one is no exception. We owe a deep sense of gratitude to many people who helped us write this book by sharing their thoughts and insights. Writing a book about IP from the management and business perspective while practicing law and running a knowledge business required the patience and support of many individuals.

We could have never undertaken this task of writing on a topic that is new in India without the help and support of Devna Arora, Akshat Razdan, Roshan John, and Kshitij Parashar, who researched for this project. To put it in another way, to have such young and bright individuals to bring about excellent research material for this book is truly commendable and our sincere thanks to all these four. Many thanks to Mr. Rinku Kumar and Mr. Neeraj Bhalla for designing the figures for this book.

We wish to express our special gratitude to our commissioning editor, Sachin Sharma, and Isha Sachdeva, associate production editor, at SAGE Publications for their enthusiasm, insight, and perseverance to get this book published.

Finally, we owe this book to our families who have been incredibly patient and supportive through the process. We are indeed very fortunate to have such families backing us.

1 The Intangible Landscape — Understanding Core Concepts

Intellectual Property is the most important asset for any business organization.

After reading this chapter, you will be able to

- Understand the importance of IP
- Understand the kinds of IP that an organization should protect
- Understand some of the factors on when to protect IP
- Understand the salient features of the traditional forms of IP: (a) patents, copyrights, trademarks and (b) nontraditional, newer forms of IP such as confidential information, plant varieties, circuit layouts, trade secrets, registered designs, and domain names
- Understand the importance of markings and notices

Very often IP is known to be a domain for lawyers alone. But is this true? Do lawyers alone need to know about IP? Is it not necessary for corporate organizations and business managers and the likes to understand the nuances of IP? We begin this book with a question, why is IP important for corporate organizations? Through the pages of this book, we will demonstrate how companies can deploy their IP not just as legal instruments but also as dominant and powerful financial assets and useful arsenal, that can boost their business. In terms of commercial viability, IP in our view is the most vital asset for any business organization. IP is not something that should be left for lawyers to deal within the corporate structure of any company. IP is at the core of any business and it is IP that can propel an organization to reach new heights by creating excellent products and services. As John Palfrey, the author of *Intellectual Property Strategy*, puts it: "IP is what an organization's community knows in the aggregate and what its people can do."[1] IP is often the sole reason for new products; take for example, the Apple iPhone and Research in Motion's (RIM) Blackberry. It is because of Apple and RIM's IP that these two products (iPhone and Blackberry) revolutionized the way individuals in businesses across the spectrum communicated with one another.

> **IP is the biggest asset class on the planet in terms of value, estimated to be at least US$5.5 trillion in the U.S. alone.**

Most of you reading this book would not be aware that IP is the biggest asset class on the planet in terms of value, estimated to be at least US$5.5 trillion in the U.S. alone.[2] Organizations like Microsoft, Apple, and Samsung have all been successful and have raked in billions of dollars because of their vast IP assets. Microsoft has developed a powerful revenue stream by licensing the proprietary patents it holds on the android technology. It has begun licensing android technology to mobile phone manufacturing companies for a royalty, which goes into billions of dollars.[3] IP has played a crucial role in the market capitalization of Microsoft with 90 percent of its capitalization coming from its IP alone.[4]

---

[1] John Palfrey, *Intellectual Property Strategy* (Cambridge, MA: The MIT Press, 2012), 17.

[2] James E. Malackowski, "Intellectual Property: From Asset to Asset Class," in *Intellectual Property Strategies for the 21st Century Corporation*, ed. Lanning G. Bryer et al. (Hoboken, NJ: John Wiley & Sons, 2011), 75.

[3] John Ribeiro, "Microsoft signs two new patent licensing deals covering Android, Chrome" (July 10, 2012) available at http://www.infoworld.com/d/mobile-technology/microsoft-signs-two-new-patent-licensing-deals-covering-android-chrome-197353.

[4] Weston Anson and Donna Suchy, *Intellectual Property Valuation: A Primer for Identifying and Determining Value* (American Bar Association 2005), 232.

Today, IP is one of the driving engines of any high-technology economy.[5] Companies that treat IP as an important and strategic asset will definitely enjoy success over others who do not treat IP as such.

IP is all pervasive and surrounds us in our daily life and business. If you closely observe the environment in which we live, work and do business, you will notice the "invisible and intangible infrastructure" of IP.

What is IP? What are these legal and business concepts? How do these rights flow—from your mind, to the computer screen before you, to influence the world? What role does IP play in generating and driving innovation and economic growth for an individual, a corporation and nations?

All of us must learn the fundamental concepts, dynamics, and strategies of IP.

The chapter introduces the main types of IP—including a detailed summary of the legal basics, how each type of property is created, and importantly, how the exclusive rights empower the owner. The idea behind protection of IP is to secure a monopoly or near-monopoly position. Organizations can achieve this by either protecting their IP assets through legislations such as the Trademarks Act, Copyright Act or Patent Act to name a few or they can invest in a robust IP strategy, which will not only include protection through various legislations of the country but also through several business strategies that will be discussed in great detail in following pages.

We believe that understanding IP is not for lawyers alone. Without proper management and commercialization of a particular IP asset, which in our view can be best handled by business professionals, the basic principles of IP, of giving advantage to the creator to reap in benefits of his or her creations, fail. Protection of IP necessarily involves educating the staff of the organization

---

[5] Karl Rackette, "Patent Revenue Generation Patent Strategic Defense" (Regional Training Program on Intellectual Property Management) available at http://www.ecapproject.org/archive/fileadmin/ecapII/pdf/en/activities/regional/ripma_06/patent_revenue_generation.pdf.

about the principles of IP and the risks of failing to adequately protect the IP. This aspect is probably one area in which Indian organizations fail to implement adequately or nothing at all. IP in companies across India is seen as a legal document that has to be filed and forgotten. But this attitude has to change and this is the main reason that we wrote this book.

The purpose of this book is twofold: (a) to give you a basic understanding of the various forms of IP that organizations need to protect; (b) to analyze and understand IP management and strategy through case studies. Before we go further, let us look at how the IP revolution began in the U.S., where most of the successful companies of the world began their journey of prosperity and innovation. It was not until the middle of the last decade of 20th century that companies started looking at IP as a value asset class of its own.

In the early 1990s, IBM was struggling and was sustaining losses close to US$15 billion. In the year 1992 alone, it lost close to US$8 billion. To bring down the losses and make some money, IBM decided to take advantage of its vast patent portfolio. How did it manage to take advantage of its patent assets? Any guesses? It began licensing its IP assets to various companies for a royalty (more on this in Chapter 7 "Intellectual Property Licensing"). This strategy proved to be a success and within a decade, IBM earned US$1 billion just from royalties alone. This US$1 billion was nothing but free cash flow, which directly reached the bottom line of the company helping it revive from its financial crunch. This resulted in other companies including Xerox Corporation, Dell, Dow Chemical, Microsoft, and Lucent Technologies that earlier did not give too much importance to IP to realize the fact that IP management must become the core competence of the successful organization. Since this last decade, companies within the U.S. have come to realize the importance of IP and are doing everything in their power to protect IP from their competitors. In India, the story is not the same because business managers across the board have not been trained in IP management, which not only results in massive losses to organizations, but also in nontapping of commercially viable assets that can generate huge amounts of revenue. As noted earlier, IP in India is seen as a legal matter best left to corporate lawyers.

This book is divided into 10 chapters, each addressing an aspect of IP management and strategy. The chapters include examples of various companies/organizations in India and abroad on how they manage their IP asset. This chapter explains the various forms of IP and the various steps involved in protecting them. This chapter is divided into two sections. The first section looks into the traditional forms of IP, namely patents, trademarks, and copyrights. The second section looks at the comparatively lesser known IP, namely, plant varieties, confidential information and know-how, circuit layouts, geographical indications, registered designs, and trade secrets.

WHICH IP SHOULD THE ORGANIZATION PROTECT?

Here are some of the factors that the organization should determine while going in for protection:

1. Strategic objectives: The fundamental starting point must be the strategic objectives of the organization and the position the IP in question has in that strategy. Applying this criterion will allow key members of the organization to focus on the role of a particular IP in the existence and future direction of the organization and encourage them to treat the IP in the manner that is equivalent to (if not greater than) other assets of the business. If IP is the foundation for the generation of significant revenue, either now or in the future, then protection of IP is a must and therefore should be done at the earliest without any further debate.

2. The Degree of protection: One question an organization should always consider while going in for protection of an IP is whether is it easy for a competitor to reproduce it,

reverse-engineer it or find a way to work around it, which may not only erode the competitive advantage of the organization but also provide a springboard for a competitor to get ahead and establish its own dominant position.

3. Type of protection that can be obtained: Under some circumstances it may be prudent to treat the technological advance as a secret without going through any formal protection process. Filing a patent application opens the creativity and originality of the organization to the world. If the exploitation can occur without giving away secrets, then a strategy without patents can be effective and cheaper.

4. The value of protection of IP: This will often be driven by the demands of customers and clients. In these circumstances, the organization can benefit from the views of a person who is sensitive to the market. These may be people from the marketing division or a consultant/vendor from outside the organization. In either case, it may prove fruitful to give that person an opportunity to place the "view of the market" into the decision-making process of whether the organization should seek to protect the IP.

WHEN SHOULD THE IP BE PROTECTED?

As with any business activity that involves the use of resources of the organization, the timing of protection of the IP will be affected by the overall strategic objectives and priorities of the organization.

In any event the organization is best positioned if it obtains the advice of an IP professional as early as possible. Knowledge of the IP position and a team analysis of the strengths and weaknesses of the technology will enable the organization to better determine when to proceed with IP protection.

The commercialization of IP is essential to an organization. Therefore, the organization and its management would be better placed if the fundamentals and the nuances of IP protection are understood and applied effectively. It is very essential for the management of any organization to understand IP in today's day and age. An organization, which knows how and when to call upon IP experts, will gain some confidence that the organization is heading toward productive territory.

Each form of IP has its own distinctive and strategic characteristics. In fact, each is a volume of learning in itself. Ask any student of IP law and he or she will be able to point you to a bookshelf full of texts that study the development of this area of law and its interpretation by the courts. Adding to this complexity is the impact of globalization and the treaties India is a signatory to ensure that Indian organizations are not left behind in the global marketplace.

The following pages will look at all the important forms of IP and their unique characteristics. The first three forms of IP, namely patents, copyright, and trademark form the traditional IP, which hold immense value in today's world. The other forms apart from these three are the nontraditional forms of IP or the new forms of IP that have become popular only in the last decade in India. Let us first look at traditional IP followed by the nontraditional IP (see Figure 1.1).

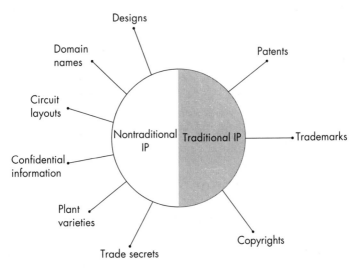

Figure 1.1 Types of Intellectual Property

TRADITIONAL IP

Patents for Invention

What is a Patent?

A patent is a right granted to an individual who has invented something. Just as, households across India have a "safe" within the house or in a bank, where the valuables are kept safely, the same way, a patent for an invention or PATENT in short is more or less a "corporate safe." Patents in today's day and age are used as a business and legal tool to generate immense revenue to the corporate organization. In the course of this book, many case studies have been dealt with, where companies all over the world have used patents for their business strategies and have succeeded immensely.

In order to encourage progress in the field of science and technology, governments of nations through patent laws have given exclusive rights to inventors who have invented new technology. In India, this protection is granted for a period of 20 years, which means that if a company patents an invention and does not commercialize the invention in the 20-year protection period, the invention becomes worthless. In the words of Bill Gates, IP (patents) have a shelf life of a banana.[6] This means that more the delay in commercializing the invention, the more the invention would become obsolete and useless for use by the organization, just like the banana, which if not used within a couple of days, would start decaying and become useless for consumption (see Table 1.1).

The protection for an invention in the form of a patent is granted if and only if the invention is novel, useful to the public and nonobvious. Novel means that it has not been invented before. Novelty has to always be understood in conjunction with "Prior Art"—which means that any art that is already known to the public. Useful to the public means that the invention should be of some use and help the public at large. Nonobviousness means that the invention is not obvious to the person who is

---

[6] John K. Borchardt, "Keeping Secrets" (June 6, 2011) available at http://www.labmanager.com/?articles.view/articleNo/4770/article/Keeping-Secrets.

Table 1.1 Patents

Protectable Subject Matter	Useful, new, non-obvious processes and products (machines, mechanical devices, articles of manufacture and compositions of matter, chemical compounds).
Government Registration	Patent Application—consisting of specification and claims—disclosing the invention, filed by the inventor in each country's patent office (for example, the Indian Patent Office), examined and issued as patent.
Scope of Rights	Exclude others from making, using, selling, offering to sell or importing the patented invention, based on the definitions in the claims granted in a particular jurisdiction.
Duration	From issuance of the patent to 20 years from the date of the filing of the national application.
Legal Basis	National Law (Indian Patent Act, 1970), consistent with TRIPS Section 5, Articles 27–34.

skilled in the subject matter of the invention. This is the most challenging and conceptually the most complex requirement for patentability. In order to prove nonobviousness, "the invention must not be merely a combination of elements of 'prior works' such as would be apparent to a person of ordinary skill in the art, who was seeking to solve the problem to which the invention is directed."[7] The last element, which is essential for a patent to be granted protection, is enablement, which means that sufficient and detailed information about the invention must be provided so that any trained person, who is skillful to an extent is able to make the invention. A patent cannot be granted on merely an idea; it has to be operational.[8]

A Six-player Chess Game: A Case Study

The Indian Patent office recently granted a patent to a nine-year-old wheelchair-ridden boy suffering from a rare genetic disease for his invention of six-player circular chess. Hridayeshwar Singh

---

[7] Alexander I. Poltorak and Paul J. Lerner, *Essential of Intellectual Property* (Hoboken, NJ: John Wiley & Sons, 2011), 3.

[8] Anurag K. Agarwal, *Business and Intellectual Property* (Noida: Random House India, 2010), 15.

Bhati, a class IV student suffering from duchenne muscular dystrophy, a progressive degenerative muscular disorder, has invented an innovative version of circular chess for two, three, four, and six players for which he filed a patent. The patent was granted making him the youngest disabled person in the world to get a patent for invention.[9] The reason for granting the patent was because the idea of a six-player chess game was novel; it was useful to the public as several players could play chess instead of just two players. This meant more interest would be generated for the game in India, which has produced greats like Viswanathan Anand. It was also nonobvious to the person who was skilled in the game of chess and finally it also fulfilled the criteria of enablement as the inventor provided details of the invention on how it can be made operational. Hridayeshwar gets a patent for a period of 20 years under the Indian Patents Act.

Tips and Techniques

To be patentable, an invention must fulfill the following elements:

1. Novel
2. Useful to the public ("utility")
3. Nonobviousness
4. Enablement

Why Seek a Patent? Hewlett-Packard's (HP) Rationale

HP has described its rationale for obtaining patents as follows:[10]

1. To protect the company's ideas and innovations from being copied or infringed

---

[9] "Disabled boy gets patent for 6 players' chess," *The Indian Express*, March 29, 2012, available at http://www.indianexpress.com/news/disabled-boy-gets-patent-for-6-players-chess/930118.

[10] See S. P. Fox, "How to Get the Patents Others Want," *Les Nouvelles* (March, 1999), 4.

2. To obtain design freedom through patent license agreements with other companies
3. To preclude others from patenting inventions first developed within the company
4. To generate optimal return on the company's research and development (R&D) expenditures

These reasons are compelling if the organization is concerned to generate revenue from its IP and secure a position of competitive advantage. The points that an organization needs to consider include the following:

1. Possible alternative forms of protection which include less complexity, cost and resources. For example, software may be adequately protected by copyright, particularly given the high rate of development in this technology, which may make the costs and time incurred in obtaining a patent inadequate.
2. Other possible barriers to entry to the target market which a patent may not overcome. This would be of particular importance in a highly regulated market where legislation or high infrastructure costs prevent the organization from obtaining a competitive advantage, no matter how many patents or other forms of IP it may have.
3. The possibility that the disclosure of the idea or invention through the patent process may outweigh the monopoly position that will eventually be gained by the organization particularly if the lead time for the development of the technology is short.
4. The fact that patents require a lot of time and money, especially if the Indian organization is focused on driving business from foreign markets where IP protection will be an essential part of its strategy.
5. The realization that obtaining a patent is only one part of the game. Effective IP management means that the organization will also need to devote time, money and resources to the detecting and management of infringements of the patent.

If the organization is not willing or able to commit to this aspect of IP management then the effectiveness of the protection afforded by a registered patent may be minimal.

Practical Elements for Patent Protection

The patent application is both a legal and a technical document. Getting it wrong can be disastrous. Applying the right strategy can be invaluable. Therefore, getting the advice of an expert IP lawyer is prudent. The following principles will assist an organization to cooperatively develop a patent strategy with its IP advisers.

Provisional Applications and Provisional Specifications

The submission of a provisional application is probably the most common form of patent application. Provisional application will lapse after 12 months at which time the public may inspect it. An applicant must make a complete application that is "associated with" the provisional application within that 12-month period. If it does so then the provisional application will not be published. The provisional application merely describes the invention and does not set out the "claims" that the applicant desires.

A provisional application will allow the applicant to obtain more details concerning potential impediments to obtaining a patent including time to undertake searches. This will not only strengthen any patent eventually obtained but also, in the long run, prove to be more cost effective. The greatest difficulty is to ensure that there is a sufficient description in the provisional application to fulfill the test that the complete specification is associated with the provisional application. Ultimately, the complete specification must be "fairly based." The meaning of "fairly based" has been the subject of extensive judicial consideration and it is beyond the scope of this book to delve into that topic.

Important Formalities

Protection of patents involves some important formal steps.

1. Annual renewal fees must be paid (referred to as Patent Annuities). Patent protection is lost if they are not.
2. The application must be accompanied by an abstract, which summarizes the technical field, the technical problem, the substance of the solution and the principal uses of the solution.
3. The patent attorney for the organization will, as part of his or her work for the organization, ensure that these requirements are met.

Searches

Prior art searches are essential prior to the filing of an application. This may be costly and it has been suggested that applicants should budget for 10 percent of the overall preparation and filing costs for those searches.[11]

When to File—a Commercial and Legal Evaluation

The description of issues contained in this section on patents is merely a summary of the law related to the protection of inventions. How then can an organization sift through this quagmire of legal and commercial detail to provide its staff with a simple test to determine whether the results of their work could be the subject of a patent?

HP developed a useful set of tests. It suggests that the staff should ask themselves the following questions and if they answer "yes" to anyone of them then there is a potential candidate for a patent that may deserve further scrutiny.

[11] J. L. Brandt, "Capturing Innovation—Turning Intellectual Assets into Business Assets", in *Ideas to Assets*, ed. Bruce Berman (New York: John Wiley & Sons, 2001), 75.

The following questions need to be looked upon:

1. Has the inventor (here inventor would mean an individual or an organization) kept "the idea"[12] confidential?
Answer 1: The disclosure of an idea to others under a confidentiality agreement is broadly no bar to patenting, which means that the particular idea is patentable. If the inventor has described "the ideas" in print or verbally or shown it at an exhibition, then patent protection cannot cover what is disclosed in the exhibition.
2. Is "the idea" a new product (a tangible object), a new material (e.g., a new plastic), a new process for making something (e.g., a cheaper way)?
Answer 2: If the idea is a new product then it may be patentable. If the idea is a business plan or an aesthetic creation or a way of presenting information, it is not patentable. If the idea is a computer program, it is not patentable. To seek protection of a computer program, the organization should seek protection under the Copyright Act 1957. The computer software can also be protected by a confidentiality agreement.
3. Is "the idea" a variation in a product or material or process for which a patent has already been granted?
Answer 3: If the idea is a variation in a product or material or process for which a patent has already been granted, then a patent may be granted for the variation and this is known as patent of addition[13] unless the variation is just a mere duplication or a rearrangement of earlier patented products/processes/materials.[14]
4. Is there a written description of "the idea"?
Answer 4: To apply for a patent, a written description is required to prepare a patent application. A working model is not necessary, but it is advisable that application should contain more

[12] An idea for the purposes of this chapter would mean an invention that is new and original.
[13] Section 54, Patents Act 1970.
[14] Section 3(f), Patents Act 1970.

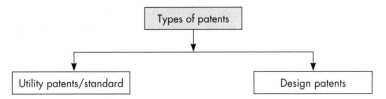

Figure 1.2 Types of Patents

technical information along with sketches or drawings to make the application more explanatory and understandable.

5. Who generated "the idea"?

Answer 5: If an employee makes an invention, the rights often belong to the employer. This principle has been derived from two landmark English court cases.[15] It is also important to note that the inventor is always named as such, even if it is the company/organization that applies for the patent.

Types of Patents

Patents are of various forms and at times, it becomes really confusing and difficult to know which patent should be applied for and which one should not be applied for. Broadly, there are two types of patents in India (see Figure 1.2).

What Is a Utility Patent?

This is the most important form of a patent, and organizations and individuals while dealing with a functional aspect of an invention, should have their inventions protected under a utility patent. "A utility patent may cover a device or an article, a composition of matter, a method or a process of doing or making something or less commonly a new application for an existing device or material or a product."[16] This kind of a patent requires immense paper

---

[15] *Worthington Pumping Engine Co. v. Moore* (1903) 20 RPC 41; *Triplex Safety Glass Co. Ltd. v. Scorah,* (1938) Ch. 211.

[16] Alexander I. Poltorak and Paul J. Lerner, *Essential of Intellectual Property* (Hoboken, NJ: John Wiley & Sons, 2011), 2.

work and a lot of skill in drafting claims. The functional element of the invention is protected under a utility patent. A utility/standard patent may be either provisional or complete.

What Is a Design?

This protection is granted for design and ornamental appearance of the invention. If the design has a functional aspect attached to it, then it is not granted protection. For example, the design of a fighter aircraft made by Lockheed Martin, U.S. cannot be given design protection in India because the design and shape of the aircraft is very crucial for the proper functioning of the fighter aircraft.

Who Is the Owner of the Patent?

To identify the inventor is a fundamental and an important step in commercializing inventions. The process to identify the inventor would generally involve the organization, with the assistance of IP advisers, getting as much information as possible about the contributions by various persons involved in the project that resulted in the innovation.

The rules as to ownership have a range of other factors. There can be joint owners of a patent who, without any other agreement to the contrary, will own the patent as "tenants in common" and share equally in the proceeds of exploitation. Co-ownership as enshrined in Section 50 of the Patents Act presents added complexities to the commercialization of IP Under Indian law a co-owner is able to exercise the patent rights himself or herself, without seeking the consent of another co-owner, such as selling the patented product or manufacturing it. However, a co-owner cannot bestow the monopoly rights to a third party, such as through assignment or license, without the consent of that co-owner.

The implications for commercialization are obvious. A disgruntled co-owner can apply effective guerrilla tactics on the organization's commercialization strategy and can have significant bargaining power even though his or her inputs to the invention and the commercialization may have been minimal. In these circumstances, the best approach is to secure full ownership. If that is not possible, the next best step is to secure as many rights from the co-owner as early as possible when the bargaining power of the disgruntled co-owner is at its minimum. The closer the project gets to successful commercialization, the greater degree of power will be able to be exercised by the disgruntled co-owner.

Time Duration for Protection of a Patent

The time period of protection depends on the type of patent. It is also complicated by the recent amendments to the Patents Act 1970, which extend the period of protection for a standard patent from 15 years to 20 years, depending on when the grant of patent was made or when the application was lodged. In essence, if an application for a standard patent were to be accepted and granted today, the invention would be protected for a period of 20 years from the date of lodgment of the application as enshrined under Section 53 of the Act.

Monopoly Rights to the Owner

Given all of the effort and complexity involved in obtaining a patent, it would be reasonable to think that the Patents Act would set out a long list of rights to the owner of the patent. In fact, the statement is short and brief. The owner of a patent has the exclusive right, during the term of the patent, to exploit the invention and to authorize another person to exploit the invention. The magic here is that the word "exploit" has a broad meaning. It covers hiring, selling, licensing, importing, and using a process to do any of those things.

Disclosure to the Patents Office: Disclose Everything!

The most important aspect in obtaining a patent is disclosing the invention to the patents office. The disclosure of all information pertaining to the invention to the patents office is a trade-off for receiving monopoly rights from the state. A patent disclosure must disclose the best mode of practicing the claimed invention, which means that a person of ordinary skill in the art must be able to practice the patented invention with only reasonable amount of experimentation. Another important aspect that the patentee (a person who files a patent application) should disclose at the time of filing the application is what he or she considers is the best mode possible to practice the invention. Therefore, it is extremely imperative to disclose all the facts to the patent attorney who would be drafting the patent application. Nothing should be withheld or concealed because any withholding of information or concealment may backfire on the patentee if the patent goes into a legal dispute. A patentee should also not take the risk of not disclosing Prior Art, because it will then come back and haunt the patentee in the future. Nondisclosure of Prior Art would lead to rejection of the patent application.

A patent examiner while examining a patent application may not challenge everything written in the application. He or she may not even notice a missing detail that defeats the enablement aspect of a patent, but the opposing counsel in a patent dispute would not miss anything and will challenge everything and will likely have all the resources including discovery procedures available. Therefore, if the patentee believes that by not disclosing certain aspects of the patent, he or she has attained victory, then he or she is mistaken because this victory of not disclosing everything is only temporary.[17]

Patent Filing: A Fundamental Business Decision

The disclosure of a patent to the patents office is a fundamental business decision to make for any organization. If it discloses, then its competitors would know about the invention and they would

[17] Alexander I. Poltorak and Paul J. Lerner, *Essential of Intellectual Property* (Hoboken, NJ: John Wiley & Sons, 2011), 2.

eventually try to work around the invention and seek a similar patent protection for themselves. If the organization does not disclose the invention, the organization risks losing the advantage of inventing something first to a competitor, who may invent the same thing and file for patent protection first. Therefore, the organization is in a dilemma on what to do?[18] In our view, if an organization/individual invents something, which would commercially bring immense benefit, in that case, a patent protection is a must and should be pursued upon.

General Patent Procedure: A Checklist for Documents Required

The documents required during the initial filing process are as follows (Figure 1.3).

1. The application in the prescribed Form 1, in duplicate, as modified to suit the application.
2. Provisional specification describing the nature of the invention (Form 2) or the complete specification, in duplicate, describing the essential and complete details of the invention.
3. Drawings, if necessary, to illustrate the invention should accompany the specification.
4. Statement and undertaking on Form 3 in appropriate cases if the applicant intends to file the corresponding application outside India.
5. Abstract of the invention in approximately 150 words in duplicate. This is not required when filing a provisional application.

Types of Technology for Patentability

There are some types of technology, which raise issues in relation to protection through patents. The following is a summary of some of the issues that are gaining or have gained particular prominence.

---

[18] Roger E. Schechter and John R. Thomas, *Intellectual Property: The Law of Copyrights, Patents and Trademarks* (U.S.: Thomson/West, 2003), 528–529.

PROCEDURE FOR THE FILING OF A PATENT
(Relevant Sections and Rules)

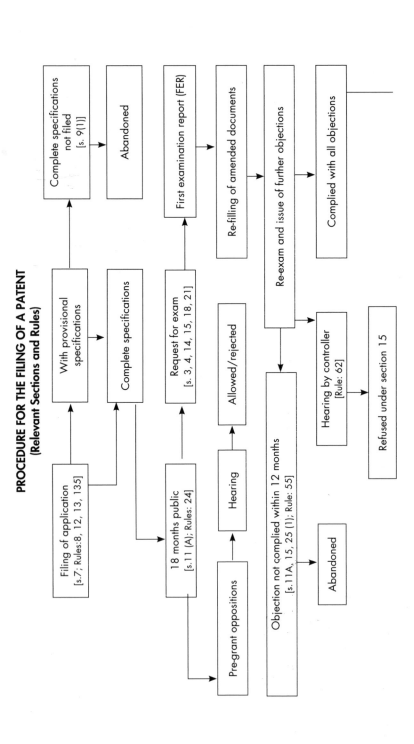

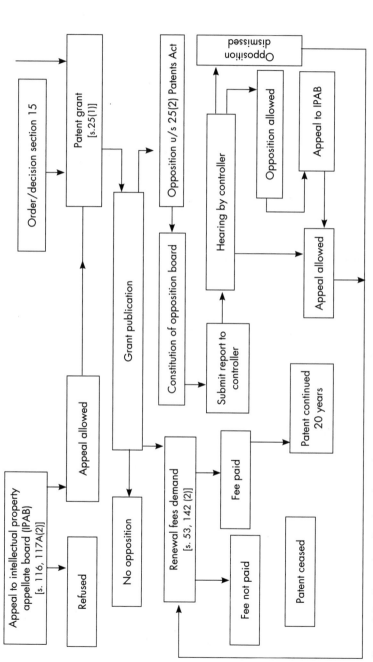

Figure 1.3 Procedure for the Filing of a Patent (Relevant Sections and Rules)

Biotechnology

Genetic invention and discovery have raised the issue as to whether the alleged innovation is merely a discovery or actually an invention. The method of isolating a substance is patentable and the characterization of the structure of a substance and applying a use to the substance is also patentable. However, the mere discovery of something occurring naturally in nature is not patentable. Similarly, a living organism will not, by itself, be patentable.

> **A biological entity may be patentable if the technical intervention of man has resulted in an artificial state of affairs, which does not occur in nature.**

A biological entity may be patentable if the technical intervention of man has resulted in an artificial state of affairs, which does not occur in nature. The isolation and cultivation of naturally occurring microorganisms, which have some new use, satisfy the requirement of technical intervention.

Biological processes, not being microbiological processes, for the production of animals or plants are also not eligible to be an innovation patent as provided in Section 18(3) of the Patents Act. There have been some discussions as to whether there is any real difference between a microorganism that leads to the development of a food ingredient (which is patentable) as opposed to the use for production of a plant. The Advisory Council on IP is examining the implications of excluding plants and animals (including the biological processes for the generation of plant and animals) from the innovation patent system.

Plant and animal varieties are excluded but are covered by the Plant Varieties Rights Act; however, microbiological processes and products of such processes are patentable as innovation patents. The Patents Act requires an applicant for patent involving microorganisms to deposit the microorganisms with the prescribed depository institution.

Now if someone wants to know whether methods to treat the human body are patentable? The answer is yes, they can be patented subject to limitations.

Biocon: Building a Sound IP Foundation

Biocon, a leading biotechnology company based out of Bangalore, India, has taken up the challenge of patenting biotech research. Over the years of its coming into existence, it has focused on developing IP that acts as a value differentiator in the market. Biocon's patent portfolio includes 1,210 applications worldwide with over 291 granted patents, which cover technology areas such as fermentation, protein purification, drug delivery systems and biotherapeutic molecules. Biocon reached the world stage in the 1990s when it invented a new fermentation technology to replace tray-based culture of microorganisms. Fermentation of enzymes is at the foundational core of biotechnology and is a required process in the advancement and development of biopharmaceutical products to make them suitable for human use.

The company developed PlaFractor, a cost-effective bioreactor that enables all the different stage processes involved in the nurturing and pulling out of microorganisms to be carried out within a fully enclosed system and under precise computer control.

> One of the characteristics of PlaFractor is that it makes fermentation repeatable, predictable and reliable. It requires less equipment and floor space than older solid substrate fermentation technologies, conserves energy, and is not labor intensive. All of these qualities translate into a cost-effective product that meets international standards and yields the same quality results as more conventional and expensive technologies. The innovation of PlaFractor served as a technology bridge, allowing Biocon to cross from industrial enzymes into biopharmaceuticals. With it, Biocon was able to begin R&D in other areas such as immunosuppressants (used to reduce rejection risks of organ transplants), which are particularly difficult organisms to cultivate using conventional tray culture. In 1999, Biocon filed its first international application with the Patent

Cooperation Treaty (PCT) system for the company's PlaFractor innovation, with protection granted by the European Patent Office (EPO) in 2005.[19]

Business Methods

Bronwyn H. Hall of the Department of Economics, University of California, Berkeley, writes "that there is no precise definition of a business method patents, and in reading the literature, it becomes clear that many scholars make little distinction between business method patents, internet patents, and software patents more broadly, at least when making policy recommendations."[20]

Methods of conducting business were generally considered not to be patentable because they lacked novelty or usefulness. However, they have gained increased importance due to decisions in the U.S. granting patents for business processes in the late 1990s including one of amazon.com. Now the U.S. courts have struck down the business methods patent obtained by amazon.com for its one-click checkout system.[21]

There have been instances where the U.S. courts have granted business methods patents. For example, in *State Street Bank and Trust v. Signature Financial Corporation*,[22] the signature patent at issue was a "pure" number—crunching type of application, which implemented financial accounting functions. Street Bank had filed a patent application on a "hub and spoke" software programme for managing an investment structure for mutual funds. The software facilitated the administration of mutual funds (the "spokes")

[19] "Building on a Foundation of IP" available at http://www.wipo.int/ipadvantage/en/details.jsp?id=2602.

[20] Bronwyn H. Hall, *Business Method Patents, Innovation, and Policy,* (May, 2003) available at http://www.law.berkeley.edu/institutes/bclt/ipsc/papers/attendees/IPSC_2003_Hall2.pdf.

[21] Eric Krangel, "U.S. Court Strikes Down 'Business Method' Patents (Like Amazon's 1-Click) For Now", (October 30, 2008), available at http://www.businessinsider.com/2008/10/us-court-strikes-down-business-method-patents-like-amazon-s-1-click-for-now-amzn-

[22] 149 F.3d 1368.

by pooling their investments into a single portfolio organized as a partnership (the "hub").[23] The software determined changes in hub investment assets and allocated the assets among the spokes. The U.S. Federal Circuit Court decision stated clearly that Section 101 of the U.S. Patent Code is unambiguous where the word "any" means ALL. Therefore, mathematical algorithms are nonstatutory only when "disembodied" and thus lacking a useful application. The court went on to make sure that the decision was precedent setting by stating that with regard to the business method exception, "we take this opportunity to lay this ill conceived exception to rest."[24]

In another case in the U.S., that is in *AT&T Corp. v. Excel*,[25] the patent at issue contained a method claim about adding a data field to a record for use in a billing system, the U.S. Federal Circuit Court confirmed the State Street decision, saying that a physical transformation was not required for a method claim to be statutory and that mathematical algorithms were patentable if "embodied" in an invention. That is, the State Street decision applies to methods as well as to machines. The success of the patent holder in these two cases has clearly emboldened others who hold patents on Internet based methods of doing business.

Recently in 2010, the U.S. Supreme Court decided a very famous case, which made headlines in the IP world. In *Bilski v. Kaposs*.[26] Mr. Bernard L. Bilski and Mr. Rand A. Warsaw had applied for a patent application concerning the method of protecting buyers and sellers against the risk of price fluctuations in commodities trading. The key claims were one and four. Claim 1

---

[23] Sirkka L. Jarvenpaa and Emerson H. Tiller, *Protecting Internet Business Methods: amazon.com and the 1-click checkout* (Center for Business Technology and Law University of Texas at Austin) available at http://btl.mccombs.utexas.edu/IBM%20Course%20modules/bizmethpatents1.pdf.

[24] 149 F.3d 1368.

[25] *AT & T Corp. v. Excel Communications, Inc.*, 172 F.3d 1352.

[26] *Bilski v. Kappos*, 561 U.S. (2010).

enlisted a chain of steps on how to hedge risk and Claim 4 gave a mathematical formula for the same.

Bilski's application was rejected by the patent's office and the next higher court, that is, the Federal Court affirmed the same. The question that came before the Supreme Court was whether intangible business methods are patentable or not?

The court rejected the contention that the machine-or-transformation test was the sole test of process patent eligibility. With regard to Bilski's patent, the court agreed that he sought to patent an abstract idea and held that abstract ideas are unpatentable. However, the court rejected the complete exclusion of business method patents from the definition of the term "process." The court held that under Section 100(b) of the U.S. Patent Code consists of the word "method," which can be interpreted to include some forms of business method patents.

Bilski case was a balanced judgment, which excluded patenting of abstract ideas but by interpreting the term "process" widely has left scope for patenting of business methods on case to case basis.

As far as India is concerned, ultimately it is a question as to whether the criteria set out in Section 18(1) (*Powers of Controller in cases of anticipation*) of the Indian Patents Act are met or not. Indian courts have entertained the prospect of business methods being patentable under Indian legislation. In *We/come Real-Time SA v. Catuity Inc* (2001) 51 IPR 237, the process and device for operation of a smart card concerning trader's loyalty programs was considered to be patentable and the court applied the test expressed in the *National Research Development Corp. v. Commissioner of Patents* (2001) 51 IPR 237, which is the following: "Is there a mode or manner of achieving an end result which is in an artificially created state of affairs of utility in the field of economic endeavour?"

It remains to be seen just how far the Indian courts will permit protection of business methods under the patent regime. There is already an inconsistency developing between Indian law and the patent law as applied by the courts of India's major trading partners.

Copyright

What Is a Copyright?

A copyright is a form of protection given by the state to authors and creators of "original works," such as literary, dramatic, musical, artistic, and certain other forms, both published and unpublished as well as things which are not "works" that include sound recordings, films, and broadcasts. The Indian Copyright Act, 1957 addresses the regime for copyright in India. Among the various forms of IP, "copyright" is considered to be the simplest to register because the formal registration process of a copyright is optional. Given the breadth of copyright, this book does not deal with the commercialization of copyright in sound recordings, films or broadcasts. These areas have their own rules, both from a commercial and legal perspective, which have been addressed by other authors (see Table 1.2 for an overview on copyright).

Under Copyright Law only the expression of the idea can be protected and not the idea itself.[27] The Copyright Act does not

Table 1.2 Copyright

Protectable Subject Matter	Works of authorship, including writings, books, papers, photographs, music, art, movies, recording, software and the like, reduced to a tangible medium of expression.
Government Registration	Not mandatory once the work is fixed in a tangible medium of expression. Judicial enforcement generally requires a copyright notice, and in many jurisdictions, registration at the Copyright Office.
Scope of Rights	Prevent others from reproducing or distributing copies, preparing derivative works; performing or displaying the work publicly; and transmitting sound recordings.
Duration	At least 50 years from publication—TRIPS Agreement. In India, for new works, life of the author plus 60 years or 60 years from the date of publication for works made for hire.
Legal Basis	National Laws (Indian Copyright Act, 1957), consistent with TRIPS Part II, Section 7, Articles 9–14; and the Berne Convention.

[27] "There can be no copyright on an idea" *R.G. Anand* v. *M/s. Delux Films & Ors.*, AIR 1978 SC 613; (1978) 4 SCC 118; *William Hill (Football)* v. *Ladbroke (Football)*, [1980] RPC 539 (CA Lord Denning MR).

give monopoly rights in relation to the end result of the material expression, which means that it is possible for a person/organization to create the same software or an individual to write a book independently of any other organization or individual, respectively. If this occurs, the same work may exist and have two separate copyright owners.

One of the major beneficiaries of the copyright regime is the entertainment industry across the globe including India. Musicians such as Bryan Adams, Michael Jackson, and MC Hammer have made millions of dollars by creating songs that are protected under Copyright law. Authors such as J. K. Rowling of the *Harry Potter* series has also benefitted immensely because of Copyright law, which gives her immense benefits and protections. We will see in Chapter 2 (Intellectual Property Approaches and Strategies) how J. K. Rowling has used the derivative strategy to reap in the benefits of copyright that has made her the richest author on the planet.

Tips and Techniques

The key elements of the test to establish the existence of copyright will vary according to the following:

1. What is the residency of the creator?
2. Whether the work has been published?
3. Where such publication has occurred?
4. When the work was created?

Before going for any test, one essential point for determining the existence of a copyright would be whether the work is original. This means that there must be a sufficient degree of skill, labor, judgment, and expertise used in the creation of the work. Ultimately, this is a question of fact and not a question of novelty.

Who Owns the Copyright?

The basic premise for copyright is that the author will be the owner of the copyright. This is the person who actually makes the work and was the source of originality. A person who is merely acting as a scribe would not be considered to be the author. A person who used the computer to generate a work would not be the author if he or she were acting slavishly under direction.

The usual exceptions to this basic premise apply, which include employment, i.e., if the author is an employee and the work was created in accordance with the terms of employment then the employer will own the copyright.

It is possible to have joint ownership of copyright, in which case the joint owners will share the copyright equally. This is subject to any agreement between the co-owners. A co-owner can commence infringement action without joining the other co-owner, although each co-owner may have to account to the other for any benefits received arising from that infringement action.

Registration of a Copyright

The general rule in copyright law is that a copyright subsists over a piece of work, when it is created. It is not mandatory to register. But for the software and entertainment companies, it is necessary that they register their copyrights because it might prove useful if such companies are involved in litigation where the dispute is related to who owns the copyright for a piece of software and when was it actually created.

> **The general rule in copyright law is that a copyright subsists over a piece of work, when it is created.**

The procedure for registering a copyright is as follows. Once a work has been completed, companies and individuals alike can file a copyright application in the copyright office. They have to give notice of their application to every person who claims or has any interest in the work, which has been filed for protection. If the Registrar of Copyrights receives no objection within 30 days of the receipt of the copyright application, then the registrar will enter such applications in the register of copyrights and the copyright would be granted (see Figure 1.4).

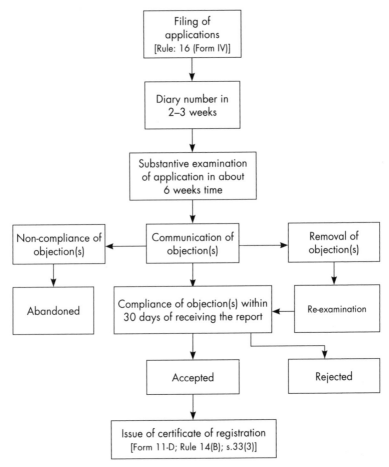

Figure 1.4 Procedure for Filing of a Copyright (Relevant Sections and Rules)

Duration of the Copyright Protection

The general rule is that the owner of a copyright is entitled to the relevant monopoly rights for a period of 60 years plus the life of the author. There are exceptions to this, relating to whether their work has already been published (60 years after publication), which have been laid down under Section 22 of the Copyright

Act. Specific rules related to protection of different types of copyrightable works are laid down between Sections 21 and 29 of the Copyright Act of 1957.[28]

Monopoly Rights

The owner of a copyright has monopoly rights to do the following in relation to a literary, dramatic or musical work:

1. Reproduce the work in a material form
2. Publish the work
3. Perform the work in public
4. Communicate the work to the public
5. Make an adaptation of the work

In relation to an artistic work, the copyright owner has the exclusive right to

• reproduce the work in a material form;
• publish the work; and
• communicate the work to the public.

The right to "communicate" the work is designed to enable exclusive rights to be exercised in the era of the Internet.

Moral Rights

The Copyright Act was recently amended to enable an author to exercise his or her "moral rights" in relation to any literary, dramatic, musical or artistic work and cinematograph films created by him or her. These moral rights belong to the individual author. They cannot be transferred to another person, although the author may elect to consent to another person infringing his or her moral rights.

---

[28] Sections 21–29, Copyright Act of 1957.

There are three essential moral rights bestowed by the Copyright Act:

1. The right to be attributed as the author of a work (*droit a la paternity*)
2. The right not to have authorship of the work falsely attributed to someone else
3. The right for the work not to be subject to derogatory treatment (*droit au respect de louvre*)

In essence, the moral rights regime is aimed at giving the individual author a "noncommercial" benefit. Many authors will, having become aware of their moral rights, nevertheless choose not to make a scene about those rights in a way that would upset a commercial environment. An organization would be foolish to disregard the power that the Copyright Act gives an individual author to exercise those moral rights.

Software: Can It Be Protected under the Copyright Act?

Computer programs are expressly addressed in the Copyright Act and comprise a "literary work." Computer programs are defined as "a set of statements or instructions to be used directly or indirectly in a computer in order to bring about a certain result."

Generally, the copyright in relation to computer programs is expressed in the source code. A source code is a computer program written in any of the several programming languages employed by computer programs. Indian courts have yet to decide as to whether the "look and feel" of the results of a computer software application would be protected by copyright or not.

Fair Dealing

Not all unauthorized use of a copyrighted work can be termed as infringement. Some use of a copyrighted work is allowed without the approval of the copyright owner, which is known as "fair dealing" and the factors that are considered in determining whether a particular use of a copyrighted material amounts to fair use are enshrined under Section 52 of the Copyright Act.[29]

Trademarks

Trademarks are the principal form of IP that is used in the branding or marketing of an organization and its products or services. In many respects, the trademarks can be of greater value to the business than the actual services or products supplied. The value of the trademarks of Coca-Cola, Microsoft and IBM are US$65 billion, US$59 billion and US$57 billion, respectively. The value of the Coke brand is nearly half of the company's market capitalization. In the words of Roberto Goisuetta, the former chief executive officer (CEO) of Coca-Cola, "if all of Coca-Cola's physical assets went away, they could still go to the bank and borrow more than US$60 billion because they own the Coke trademark."[30] See Table 1.3 for an overview on trademark.

Trademarks can be protected without recourse to the formal registration process under the Trade Marks Act, 1999 if the organization has established a reputation in relation to its trademarks. In these circumstances, the organization can also rely on the Competition Act, 2000 or the tort law on passing off. The great

---

[29] "(a) A fair dealing with a literary, dramatic, musical or artistic work [not being a computer program] for the purposes of—

    (i) private use, including research;

    (ii) criticism or review, whether of that work or of any other work;"

    (iii) "the making of copies or adaptation of a computer program by the lawful possessor of a copy of such computer program, from such copy—

        (i) in order to utilize the computer program for the purposes for which it was supplied; or

        (ii) to make back-up copies purely as a temporary protection against loss, destruction or damage in order only to utilize the computer program for the purpose for which it was supplied."

[30] Scott W. Cooper and Fritz P. Grutzner, *Tips and Traps for Marketing Your Business* (U.S.: McGraw-Hill Professional, 2008), 38.

Table 1.3 Trademarks

Subject Matter	Words, names, letters, numerals, figurative elements, colors or combination of colors, symbols or other devices used to distinguish goods or services.
	Trademarks include service marks, certification marks, and collective membership marks.
National Government Registration	Trademark applications depicting the mark and the goods or services are filed in a "national" trademark office (for example, the Indian Trademarks Registry in India).
	In India, no registration is required to claim common law rights based on the use of a trademark.
Scope of Rights	To exclude other from using the mark to cause a likelihood of confusion to the consumer (passing off or infringement— depending on whether the mark is registered or unregistered).
	For famous marks, prevent others from "diluting" the mark.
Duration	Generally, 10 years from registration, renewable in perpetuity, for additional 10 year terms, as long as the mark is used property and not abandoned.
Legal Basis	National Law (Indian Trademarks Act, 1999) consistent with TRIPS Part II, Sections 15–21.

advantage of registering the trademarks is that when seeking to enforce its rights the organization is not required to present evidence of reputation. It can rely upon its certificate of registration. This has significant implications in terms of costs and time in protecting its position.

The trademark regime is focused on a mark that designates the origin of the goods or services that are branded with the mark. The mark can be a "sign" of any description and now includes shapes, colors, sounds, and forms of packaging (trade dress).

Choosing a Trademark

The most important element that should be taken in to consideration while choosing a mark is the function that the mark is intended to perform, namely source identification. It is not the function of a trademark to describe the goods for which it is being protected.

Domain names are registered for the purpose of identifying a domain web site and its registration does not provide any rights per se against third parties using the trademark without the authorization of the owner of the mark.

It is advisable to go in for coined words rather than generic words for trademark protection. Figure 1.5 will help you understand the probability of a mark gaining protection and securing it from being misused in the marketplace. In general terms, the choice of a name or logo can assist the organization to achieve its commercialization goals. Distinctiveness is often the key. Use of a logo in connection with a name will also assist in being able to distinguish the mark from the designated goods or services.

> **It is advisable to go in for coined words rather than generic words for trademark protection.**

Criteria for Protection

The trademarks examiner must accept registration unless the grounds for rejecting the application are met as required under the Trade Marks Act, 1999.

The grounds for rejection of an application are as follows:

1. The mark is not able to be represented graphically.

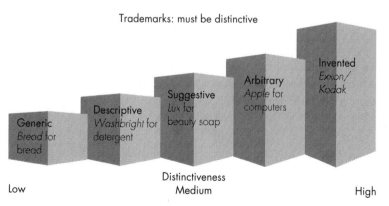

Figure 1.5 What is "Trademarkable"?

2. The mark is not capable of distinguishing the applicant's goods or services. This is the most common form of objection. Essentially the examiner must establish whether the mark is distinctive. Nonetheless, it is possible to overcome this objection if the organization presents sufficient evidence for the registrar to decide that the mark is in fact distinguishable from the designated goods or services.
3. The mark is scandalous or its use is contrary to law. This has been clearly stated in Section 9 of the Trade Marks Act, 1999.
4. If it is likely to deceive or cause confusion. In applying this test, the examiner must compare the mark against any existing registered trademarks and any general information that may arise from a search such as through the Internet.
5. Whether the trademark is identical to any prior registered mark or earlier application for registration of a trademark in respect of similar goods or closely related services? If this objection is raised, it is nevertheless still possible to have the application accepted if the organization can show that it honestly and continuously used its mark from a time before the priority date of the other trademark.

Case Study: Apple iPod

Apple iPod music player is one of the best selling products being manufactured by Apple Inc., headquartered in Cupertino, California. The product is designed and marketed entirely by Apple Inc. The product was launched back in 2001 and since then has occupied the peak position in the premium segment of music players. The product competes with major rivals such as Creative Zen, Microsoft Zune HD, Philips Go-Gear, Sony Walkman, and Samsung Galaxy range of music players.

But what sets it apart from these other music players?

In October 2001, Apple filed its application for the traditional trademark for the unique product name iPod at the Patent and Trademark Office. At the first stage, Apple sought a trademark for a two-dimensional iPod symbol, then for a mark for co-branded products and finally for the three-dimensional shape of its players. The product immediately after its launch was termed as a pioneering innovation and an example of harmonious design. The company thereafter, shielded their utility and took design patents over their product.

When for the first time Apple applied for registration of the iPod's three-dimensional shape in July 2006, it included a drawing of an iPod seen from an angle. The drawing emphasizes not only the overall rectangular shape of the player, but the viewing screen and circular interface control. Predictably, the case examiner rejected Apple's application, giving as one of the reasons that its trademark description was too broad and could refer to any music player. However, Apple promptly submitted, among other evidence, data reporting that the market share for the iPod of more than 70 percent in 2005, showing widespread consumer familiarity with the product, statements from consumers who attested to the iPod's "distinctive" design and unique "uncluttered" feel when compared with other media players, and an accounting of the advertising budget in "hundreds of millions of dollars" specifically crafted to build an association between the iPod's shape and Apple.

In January 2008, the Patent and Trademark Office granted Apple the nontraditional trademark it desired, along with the following more specific description of the approved mark: "The design of a portable and handheld digital electronic media device comprised of a rectangular casing displaying circular and rectangular shapes therein arranged in an aesthetically pleasing manner."

Thus, they followed a fourfold strategy to protect their IP.

1. They took a unique name and a traditional trademark.
2. They secure utility and design patents to start building a defensive wall against competitors.
3. They created advertisements that spotlighted/highlighted the vital attributes namely—shape, sense and motion, and copyright them.
4. They applied for the nontraditional trademark and persuaded the authorities to negotiate.

Tips and Techniques

The criteria for granting a trademark are as follows:

1. Graphically represented
2. Capable of distinguishing the applicant's products/services
3. Is not scandalous and contrary to law
4. It is not likely to cause confusion in the public

Registration of a Trademark

The registration of a trademark is usually very swift. Here are the steps that an organization or an individual should follow while filing for a trademark application at the trademark registry.

1. Step 1: It is advisable to conduct a trademark search in the trademark registry to make sure that there are no identical trademarks or similar trademarks to the one that is being filed for trademark registration.
2. Step 2: After the trademark search, the trademark application should be completed by the organization with the help of a trademark lawyer and filed at the trademark registry. Once the application is filed, the trademark registry conducts a preliminary examination of whether there is a fulfillment of all the criteria for a trademark registration. If the answer to this question is a yes, then the trademark registry publishes the trademark for the world at large and a time period of 90 days is given for any opposition to be filed by any third party who opposes the publication and registration of the trademark. If the trademark registry objects to the trademark application, then the organization/individual filing the trademark, through a lawyer has to explain the reasons for the trademark registration and explain how unique the mark is and that the mark has been in use in the market in order to gain a registration. If the registry is satisfied with the explanation, then it publishes the mark and a time period of 90 days is given for any opposition

to be filed by any third party who opposes the publication and registration of the trademark.

3. Step 3: If a third party does not oppose the application within the 90-day period but wants to oppose the registration, another 30 days of extension is provided to the third party. If the Trademark registry rejects the opposition, the Registrar of trademarks issues the trademark registration. The total time taken for the registration of a trademark takes between 6 and 12 months depending on the objections, oppositions, and the number of applications pending with the trademark registry.

Figure 1.6 shows the procedure and required time frame for filing a trademark application and grant of trademark in India.

International Issues

The adoption of the Madrid Protocol of which India is a signatory now enables an applicant to register with ease in the European Union. This will have the advantage of saving time and money. Nevertheless, the acceptance of the registration still depends on the domestic laws of each of the international jurisdictions.

Ownership of a Trademark

An applicant for registration of a trademark must claim to be the owner and must have an intention to use the mark or an intention to authorize somebody else to use the mark.

Duration of Protection

A trademark is registered for a period of 10 years and can be renewed in perpetuity after every 10 years.

Monopoly Rights of the Owner

The owner of a registered trademark has the exclusive right to use the trademark as a trademark in respect of the goods or services in

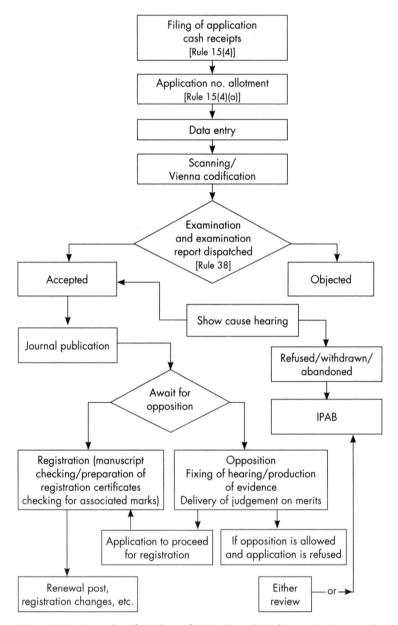

Figure 1.6   Procedure for Filing of a Trademark (Relevant Sections and Rules)

which the mark has been registered. The trademarks register contains 45 classes of goods or services. When submitting its application, the applicant must describe the nature of its goods or services against which the mark is, or will be, applied. The monopoly rights extend to only those goods or services. Accordingly, the description of those goods or services and the choice of classes is a critical element in establishing protection and forming a basis for subsequent commercialization.

The advent of the Internet presents some special issues in relation to enforcement of a registered trademark particularly in respect of domain names, meta tags (a meta tag is coding statement in the Hypertext Markup Language (HTML) that describes certain aspects of the contents of a Web page. It is a kind of an Internet trademark) and hyperlinks.

Important

How to Manage a Trademark Portfolio for Your Company

1. Secure the appropriate and necessary rights: The most important step is to determine which marks are important to your company and develop a strategy to protect them and acquire rights by filing for protection. The second step is to determine which jurisdictions are important to your company from a marketing as well as business perspective.

2. Note important dates and take appropriate action: Always remember that the timing is very crucial for registration of a trademark in most jurisdictions. The first to file takes priority over subsequent filings in respect of identical or similar trademarks. Another important step is to note the registration date and the date on which the trademark has to be renewed. In India, the time duration for protection of a trademark is 10 years and this protection can be renewed indefinitely at subsequent 10-year intervals upon payment of requisite fees. If renewal date is missed, then you may end up losing your right over the trademark.

3. Use of trademarks: The use of a trademark is very much essential to gain rights. It is not necessary to register a trademark as long as it is being used in a trade.[31] In India, the rights to use a trademark will elapse, if the trademark is not used for five years from the date on which the trademark was actually registered.[32] This means that the trademark registrar can remove from the register the trademark owner's mark. It is important to implement programs that ensure continued use, seasonal use, or rotational use of the marks to guard against cancellation.

It is also very necessary to divide the trademark portfolio under three separate heads: (a) strategic trademarks; (b) supportive trademarks, and (c) tactical trademarks.

4. Periodic review of trademark portfolio: Periodic auditing of the company's trademark portfolio is very much essential. Auditing can reveal unused trademarks, as well as defects in the applications of the trademarks that are being used. This helps in taking remedial actions and avoiding future problems. Auditing can also help identify those marks that are no longer aligned with the business and assist the company from taking appropriate action on how to deal with such marks.

Trademark Dispute: A Case Study

Apple Inc. found itself in trouble when it was ordered by Chinese Court to stop selling its popular device, iPad, in China. The reason being that it did not have trademark rights over the word iPad and that the company that had the rights, that is Shenzhen Proview Technology, had asked for an injunction against Apple claiming

[31] Section 47, Trademarks Act 1999.

[32] *Century Traders v. Roshan Lal Duggar Co.* on April 27, 1977: In this case, Century Traders had appealed to the Delhi High Court that the respondent Roshan Lal was using their trademark on textile goods. The Delhi High Court came to the conclusion that the use of a mark is very important to gain rights under trademark law. It is not necessary to register a trademark to gain rights. The Delhi High Court found that Century Traders were using the trademark since a very long time and had interest in the disputed trademark.

that it had the sole rights to use the word iPad as a trademark. When a higher court in Shanghai took up the matter, the injunction was rebuffed and Apple was allowed to sell its iPad in China. The roots of the dispute went back to 2009 when Apple signed an agreement with Shenzhen Proview Technology to transfer ownership of iPad trademarks in countries such as Taiwan. But Shenzhen Proview Technology's Chinese arm contended that there was no agreement to transfer the iPad trademark rights in China therefore it could own the rights in China.[33]

Both, with Apple agreeing to pay Shenzhen Proview Technology US$60 million, finally settled the dispute out of court to use the trademark iPad and avoid litigation. This episode shows how Apple made mistakes in owning its trademark rights in a market such as China. "Apple could have avoided the dispute had it taken crucial steps necessary for companies striking such agreements."[34] Apple should have done their homework properly as explained in the section "How to Manage your Trademark portfolio" above.

Now let us look at the nontraditional forms of IP that have gained popularity in India in the first decade of the 21st century, because some of the legislations dealing with these nontraditional forms were enacted in 2000.

NONTRADITIONAL IP

Circuit Layouts

There is no formal registration process for the protection of circuit layouts. The Semiconductor Designs Act of 2000 defines "circuit layout" to be a "representation fixed in a material form of the three-dimensional location of the active and passive elements and interconnections making up an integrated circuit."

---

[33] Sean Buckley, "Apple Pays $60 Million in iPad Trademark Dispute, Makes Peace with Proview" (July 2, 2012) available at http://www.engadget.com/2012/07/02/apple-pays-60-million-in-ipad-trademark-settlement.

[34] Loretta Chao et al., "Apple Pays Small Price in China Case" (July 2, 2012) available at http://online.wsj.com/article/SB100014240527023042118045775016812336 76036.html.

To achieve protection:

1. The circuit layout must be original. The legislation deals with this aspect by saying "what is not" original. It will not be original if the making of it involved no creative contribution from the maker or it was commonplace at the time it was made.
2. The circuit layout must be made by an Indian citizen or be first commercially exploited in India or a country that is designated by the regulations. It must be "commercially exploited," which is defined as if the circuit layout is sold, let for hire or otherwise distributed by way of trade or imported or offered for sale and the like.

Like the Copyright Act, there is no formal registration system required to obtain the protection under this Act.

Who Owns the Rights?

The person who makes the circuit layout is nominally the person who will be the owner of the monopoly rights. Exceptions to this are where the eligible layout (or "EL rights" as it is known in the Act) is made in the course of employment, in which case the employer will own the EL rights. If the circuit layout made is commissioned by another person then the person who commissioned the making of the circuit layout will own the EL rights.

Tips and Techniques

To get protection, a circuit layout must be

1. original
2. made by an Indian citizen
3. first commercially exploited in India/a country designated by regulations

---

Duration of Protection

The "protection period" varies depending on whether the circuit layout has been commercially exploited. The general rule is that protection applies for 10 years.

Monopoly Rights

The Act gives the owner of the EL rights exclusive right to

1. copy the layout in a material form;
2. make an integrated circuit in accordance with the layout or a copy of the layout; and
3. exploit the layout commercially in India.

Plant Varieties

The development of plant varieties, particularly in an era when genetic modification is becoming prevalent, is a growing form of IP. Its importance is emphasized by the recognized shortage of food in Third World countries and the increasing demand for obtaining high yields in the production of agricultural products. Ingenuity in dealing with plants can attract the protection of patents and plant variety rights (PVR). "PVRs" protect the plant variety, not the process or products resulting from the use of the plants. The rights can extend to varieties predominantly derived from another variety.

The legal regime for PBRs in India is set out in the Protection of Plant Varieties and Farmers Rights Act, 2001. It implements the International Convention for the Protection of New Varieties of Plants to which India is a signatory. It should be worth mentioning that the Protection of Plant Varieties and Farmers Rights Act, 2001 has not come into force in India even though Parliament of India has enacted it.

Who Owns It?

The "breeder" means a group of persons or a farmer or group of farmers or any institution, which has bred, evolved or developed any variety, which is nominally entitled to apply for PBRs. If the variety has been bred or discovered and developed during the course of employment the employer will be the breeder. As with other forms of IP, there may be co-owners of PBRs.

Criteria for Protection of a Plant Variety to a Breeder

The criteria for registration of a plant variety under the Protection of Plant Varieties and Farmers Rights Act, 2001, are novelty, distinctiveness, uniformity and stability. (a) Novelty means that the plant variety has not been sold or otherwise disposed off in India for a period of one year or outside India for a period of six years in case of vines and trees and four years in any other case. (b) Distinctiveness means that it is clearly distinguishable by at least one essential characteristic from any other variety whose existence is a matter of common knowledge in any country at the time of filing of the application. (c) Uniformity means that it is sufficiently uniform in its essential characteristics. (d) Stability means that the essential characteristics remain unchanged even after repeated use.

Duration for Protection

A grant of plant variety will entitle the owner of the plant variety to exercise monopoly rights for a maximum period of 18 years after the date of the registration, in case of vines and trees. A protection of 15 years is granted for extant varieties from the date of notification of that variety by the central government. A protection of 15 years is also granted for other varieties from the date of registration of that variety. However, it is not possible to renew registration.

Monopoly Rights

The grant of a plant variety gives to the owner the exclusive rights in relation to the propagating material for the plant variety to

1. produce or reproduce the material;
2. condition the material for the purposes of propagation;
3. offer the material for sale;
4. sell the material;
5. import or export the material; and
6. stock the propagating material for any of the above purposes.

Unlike patents, the registration of a plant variety is exhausted when the propagating material is sold, unless the purchaser uses the propagating material to further produce the resulting crop. This exhaustion of rights is confined to one production cycle. The "exhaustion of rights" principle will also not apply if the propagating material is exported to a country, which is not subscribed to the convention relating to PBRs and the propagating material is to be used for purposes other than final consumption.

There are certain express exemptions specified in the Protection of Plant Varieties and Farmers Rights Act. These include:

1. The private noncommercial use of the propagating material or use for experimental purposes or breeding of other plant varieties
2. If the farmer harvests a crop and saves the propagating material and uses it for conditioning that propagating material for reproductive purposes or reproduction
3. Use of propagating material as food, food ingredients or fuel

Reasonable steps must be taken by the owner of the PBR to ensure there is a reasonable access of the plant variety to the public. Reasonable steps include making of plant variety available at cheap prices and in sufficient quantities to meets its demand.

Registered Designs

The regime for registration of designs is aimed at protecting the "appearance" of an article. In India, the legal regime that governs designs is the Designs Act, 2000. There is a formal registration process to obtain the monopoly rights bestowed by the Designs Act. That process is similar to that set out in the Trade Marks Act.

The designs regime concerns features of "shape, configuration, pattern or ornamentation." The Act is designed to protect the appearance of an article, not its function, although the article may well have a function, such as a jug. There is a significant overlap between designs and copyright. The policy intended to be reflected in the Copyright Act, 1957 is that copyright protection should not apply where a copyright work that would otherwise qualify for registration as a design is applied to an article for industrial purposes. Unfortunately, it is not easy to interpret the Copyright Act to determine whether in fact copyright protection is lost or not.

A design is defined as the features of shape, configuration, pattern, ornament or composition of lines in two-dimensional or three-dimensional or in both forms by any industrial process or means.

Protection Criteria of a Design

The Designs Act, 2000 states that the design must be applicable to an article and be apparent to the eye. In addition to this, it must be new or original as at the relevant priority date. This is to be judged against articles of an analogous character and must be more than an immaterial difference. The Designs Act allows for a grace period for disclosures at officially recognized exhibitions provided that an application for registration is lodged within six months of that disclosure. Publication without the consent of the designer will not destroy eligibility to obtain registration but it must be shown that the designer has used all reasonable diligence to seek registration once he or she has become aware of the prior publication.

As is with other formal registration systems for IP, a process applies in relation to obtaining registration.

Ownership of a Design

The author of the design is the person who is entitled to apply for registration. This is the person who conceives the design and reduces it to material form. Exceptions to this rule are:

1. If the design is created for valuable consideration
2. If the design was made in the course of employment
3. If the design is transferred by way of assignment

As with other forms of IP, it is possible to have co-owners who hold the registered design as tenants in common. However, a co-owner may license the registered design without the consent of other co-owners.

Tips and Techniques

The criteria for protection of a design are as follows:

1. Must be applicable to an article
2. Be apparent to the eye
3. Must be original at the relevant priority date

Duration for Protection

Registration of a design entitles the owner to exercise monopoly rights for a period of 12 months and to renew for three terms, each of which accrue five years from the date of lodging the application. This means that the maximum protection available for a registered design is 15 years. The exposure draft designs bill proposes a maximum period of 10 years' protection for a registered design, which is consistent with the protection for designs in other countries.

Monopoly Rights

The owner of a registered design has the exclusive right to apply the design to the article in respect of which it is registered, import such an article or sell or hire such an article or authorize a person to do any of those things.

Confidential Information

There is no act that has been enacted by parliament to govern confidential information. The law relating to confidential information has been built up over many decades and emanates from Common Law principles and there is no registration regime for registering confidential information.

Confidential information may be the only way of protecting an idea. Although colloquial use often involves stating that confidential information is "owned," Indian law has concluded that this is so. It is essentially a question of who has the ability to control the release of the information. Nonetheless, English cases have held that it is possible to have "co-ownership" and that each co-owner is entitled to use the information for his or her own benefit.[35] The great advantage for the commercialization process is that there is no limit to the period of protection. If the organization can maintain secrecy then it essentially holds monopoly rights in relation to the use of that confidential information forever. Of course, the downside is significant. Release of the information into the public domain, even if done in an unauthorized manner, means that protection is lost forever. For this reason, the mechanisms and processes employed by the organization to retain confidentiality are critical.

---

[35] *Murray v. Yorkshire Fund Managers Ltd.,* [1998] 2 All ER 1015.

Criteria for Protection

Confidential information is one such area that still does not have any legal regime for its protection. The principles that have been laid down for the protection of confidential information have arisen from a large plethora of case law, both in India and the United Kingdom. An excellent criterion has been laid down in a well-known English case,[36] which more or less explains what confidential information means in the field of IP. The criteria are as follows:

1. The information must be of a confidential nature. There are no limits to the type of information but generally, it must be ascertainable.
2. The circumstances in which the organization discloses the information must have been such to impart an obligation of confidence upon the recipient of that information. In these circumstances, it is relevant to look at the extent to which the information was known within and outside the organization, the steps taken by the organization to guard the information and the value of the information to the organization. The inventiveness of the information is generally not relevant.

It is possible to place a limitation on the use of the confidential information or its further disclosure. Disclosure of the confidential information outside those conditions can give the organization grounds to obtain remedies from a court. It is yet to be settled whether a criteria for establishment of protection of confidential information requires the organization to suffer detriment if the defendant were to use or threaten to use the information.

The nature of the information may also trigger other laws. For example, if the information is personal information about an individual then privacy laws may also apply.

---

[36] *Coco v. A. N. Clarke (Engineers) Ltd.* [1969] RPC 41).

Tips and Techniques

Criteria for confidential information are as follows:

1. Information must be of a confidential nature.
2. The recipient of the information is under an obligation to keep it confidential.
3. Steps taken by the organization to protect such information

---

Practical Issues

There are crucial practical steps—that can be considered to protect confidential information, such as

1. ensuring nondisclosure agreements (NDAs) with employees. The NDAs would spell out confidentiality obligations that have to be adhered to by the employees;
2. implementing a system that clearly identifies information that is considered confidential and the level of security within the organization that applies to the information;
3. clearly setting out to employees and third parties the information that is considered to be confidential and the purposes for which that information can be used;
4. marking sensitive documents as confidential and keeping records of the use and disclosure of confidential information.

Nondisclosure Agreements

It is important to know when to use NDAs. Although they provide a first base for protection, they are commercial agreements and the terms need to be understood in a commercial environment.

In some circumstances, the organization should also consider whether a contractual or other agreement for securing the confidentiality of information is really necessary. The scope of the restraint under an NDA also needs to be carefully considered. If too wide, it could amount to an unreasonable restraint of trade as per Indian Contract Law, and be unenforceable.

The NDAs need to be carefully structured so as not to give too much away to the recipient. The NDAs are normally intended to set up the walls or screens behind which the "real" information will be given to the recipient. If it is set out in the agreement, particularly in drafts of the NDA, the legal impact of the NDA may be severely diluted.

Emails and the Internet

The Internet presents particular challenges for maintaining confidentiality and control over private data. Organizations should have appropriate policies in relation to the use of emails and in particular attaching files to emails. The standard email texts, usually the footer, should include a warning about confidentiality of information.

Now if we look at the Internet as a whole, we find that there are a few problems posed by it in relation to protecting confidential information.

1. By the means of Internet, confidential information of an organization would disseminate instantaneously. The recipient who posts this information on the web world may find himself or herself in a court case filed against him or her by the organization (the plaintiff) for disseminating that particular information.
2. Third parties who would further disseminate the information, who may be in different legal jurisdictions, might use this information readily. This means that it may be difficult for the plaintiff to bring an action against third parties who use the information. If an action can be brought against the original recipient, however, this is not an overwhelming problem.

The organization should take necessary steps to ensure that confidential information of the organization does not get published on the Internet. As a matter of precaution, the organization should allocate passwords to senior level employees to access the confidential information.

It should be noted that once confidential information is part of the Internet, then it becomes public and will cease to be confidential. Protection of confidential information is generally based on trust and employer–employee contracts.

Staff

It is prudent for the company to have policies that set out the expectations of the organization so far as handling of that confidential information by staff. This can extend to educating staff about the principles of confidentiality. This can be done by holding in-house seminars on confidential information, training of staff members on how to protect information from leaking out.

The senior management of the organization should be allowed to access the information and no one else should be allowed. The senior management should be given cards and passwords to access information. The organization should have a secure information system put up in place, which should be monitored 24/7.

Trade Secrets

Trade secret is one of the most difficult concepts of IP. But we have come up with a simple way to explain what a trade secret is? We all are aware of the Coca-Cola Company and its popular drink—"Coke." The ingredient or the formula that the company uses to make the drink is locked up in the company headquarters in the U.S. and nobody except the top management knows about the ingredients used to make the drink. This ingredient used by Coca-Cola is a *trade secret* (see Table 1.4 for an overview on trade secrets).

Trade secret is a legal term for confidential business information. It is an intangible asset of which the organization is the sole lawful owner. No other organization or individual can use the trade secret without the prior permission of the sole legal owner. A trade secret may consist of a formula, a pattern or a device, confidential data of an organization's customers, and so on. A trade

Table 1.4 Trade Secrets

Protectable Subject Matter	Information that has commercial value and is not generally known or readily accessible in the trade, for which there is evidence of efforts to protect secrecy (product formulas, chemical compounds, blueprints, dimensions, tolerances, customer lists, suppliers, financial information, so on and so forth).
Government Registration	Generally none available.
Scope of Rights	Prevent disclosure or acquisition by dishonest means, or use of the secret or confidential information without permission.
Duration	As long as information remains secret (potentially forever).
Legal Basis	National Laws (Rights under Common Law), consistent with TRIPS Section 8, Article 39.
	In India, protected by common law rights, principles of express or implied contracts, laws relating to unfair competition and in some instances, criminal law.

secret is a form of IP that the organization wants to protect from being stolen or copied by its competitors.

> ## Tips and Techniques
>
> The criteria for determining a trade secret are as follows:
>
> 1. The information must not be generally known or ascertained through proper means.
> 2. The information must have an independent economic value due to its secrecy.
> 3. The right holder must use proper means to protect the secrecy of the information.

Protection in India

The protection of trade secrets in India is based on Common Law principles. However, if we look at the Indian Contract Law, some sort of protection has been given to trade secrets. Section 27 of the

Indian Contract Act provides that in the eventuality of a contract, a person is barred from disclosing any information that may be privileged to him during course of employment with a particular organization.

Domain Names: Trademarks on the Internet

We have addresses for our homes and offices, the same way domain names are nothing but simple forms of addresses on the Internet. These addresses enable users to locate web sites on the Internet in an easy manner. Domain names correspond to various Internet Protocol numbers, which connect various computers and enable direct-network routing system to direct data requests to the correct addressee. In other words, a domain name is a "uniform source locator." Domain names are of two types. Figure 1.7 would give a better idea.

Besides locating sites, domain names also have a function of identifying businesses and their goods and services on the Internet, which gives them an edge over their competitors. The Internet landscape has recently undergone considerable change with respect to both the identifiers that are used upon it (including multilingual domain names and keywords), as well as issues related to the organization, management, and coordination of the domain naming system (DNS) including the introduction of new generic top-level domains (gTLDs), emergence of multiple roots, and the Internet Corporation of Assigned Names and Numbers (ICANN) reform.

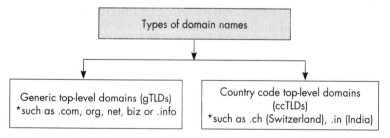

Figure 1.7 Domain Names

The introduction of new gTLDs to complement those already existing (.com, .org, .net, .edu, .gov, .mil, and .int) has been the subject of intense debate for a number of years. The ICANN has played a very important role in getting these new domain names passed. The domain names can be registered by approaching any ICANN accredited registrar.

In the recent past, there have been developments to allow the registration of domain names written in non-ASCII characters such as Arabic, Chinese, and so on.

Domain Names in India

It is a general practice where companies desire to obtain such domain names, which can be easily identified with their established trademarks. This helps the public to identify the company, as there is no physical contact between the two of them.

Domain names and trademarks are connected with each other. Under Indian law, domain names are entitled to trademark protection.[37]

Registration of a Domain Name

It is very simple to register a domain name. To obtain a domain name, an organization or an individual has to approach a registrar of domain names and buy the domain name from it. There is no criterion for registering a domain name.

MARKING AND NOTICES

A common feature of IP regimes is to notify the world at large of the ownership of those intellectual property rights (IPR). Generally this is for the purposes of ensuring that any alleged infringer of the IPRs has constructive "notice," which may enable the organization to overcome any defense of innocent infringement. This is the case

---

[37] *Rediff Communication Limited v. Cyberbooth* 1999 (4) Bom CR 278.

with respect to patents (Protection of Plant Varieties and Farmers Rights Act of the Plant Varieties and Farmers Rights Act) as well as circuit layouts. With respect of trademarks, there are a number of defenses that require the defendant to establish that the trademark was used in good faith (Section 122 of the Trade Marks Act). With respect to copyright, the use of the relevant marking also enables reciprocal rights to be exercised in foreign jurisdictions.

Table 1.5 sets out the nature of the markings that should be applied in respect of each form of IP.

It is optional and a sound practice when dealing with a copyright work to insert "all rights reserved" on the article to designate that no license is implied by the publication or provision of the IPR.

Care should be taken in using the above markings. Some of the IP statutes have specific provisions making it an offence for persons to represent that they are the owners of a registered form of IP when they are not, or that the IP is registered (for example, the Indian Trade Marks Act, 1999). Such conduct may also amount to misleading or deceptive conduct contrary to the Competition Act.

Table 1.5 Intellectual Property: Markings and Notice

Form of IP	Marking or Notice
Patents	"Indian Patent Number xxx" "Patent pending" for applications for patents filed with the relevant patent office
Copyright	"© [name of copyright owner] [country] [year of first publication]" as per the Universal Copyright Convention, [UCC], 1952
Trademarks	"®" for trademarks that are registered—it is an offence to use this symbol for a mark that is not registered "TM" for marks that are the subject of an application for registration that is still pending before the Trademarks Registry
Designs	"Registered Design number xxx"—this is a matter of convention and is not required or regulated under the Designs Act, 2000
Plant Varieties Act	No official standard exists although there has been commentary advocating a uniform international marking
Confidential information	"Confidential" or "commercial not to be disclosed"

2 Intellectual Property Approaches and Strategies

After reading this chapter, you will be able to

- Understand the value chain of IP from innovation to commercialization
- Understand the three different approaches toward innovation, that is research push, market pull, and open innovation
- Understand the importance of protection in the IP value chain
- Know the different IP strategies and case studies of different companies from all over the world.

Until the last decade of the 20th century, IP was looked upon as a nonserious subject. But today, this is not the case. What really happened? What made companies think about IP as a valuable asset? Through the course of this chapter and the chapters ahead, we will demonstrate how some of the well-known and successful companies of India and the world have started leveraging their IP assets. In the 21st century, without IP, the future of your company is bleak. IP according to John Palfrey, author of *Intellectual Property Strategy*, "is not a legal backwater best left by CEOs to their lawyers at a big outside law firm. It is at the core of what drives businesses and many other types of organizations forward."[1]

Many organizations develop excellent ideas and innovations but do not take steps to commercialize them due to a lack of

---

[1] John Palfrey, *Intellectual Property Strategy* (Cambridge, MA: MIT Press, 2012), 17.

business skills, financial resources, market knowledge and time.[2] Commercialization of IP will be facilitated, and prospects are more likely to be achieved, if the organization has given thought to commercialization issues as early as possible, during the development of the technology.

DEVELOPING YOUR IP STRATEGY

The importance of IP should not be underestimated. It should be understood by organizations that IP is a key factor in the worth of a company and is increasingly given a substantial value in acquisitions, disposals, securitizations and enforcement litigation. These days IP also needs to be identified and managed if companies are to maximize shareholder value.[3]

Commercialization is the process where an organization takes its innovation to the marketplace. Commercialization often requires the coordination of inventors, financiers, labor, management, advertisers, and marketers.[4] It is important to note that to commercialize an innovation, a company has to explore all options, assess them in the light of professional and other circumstances to ensure maximum profitability. As Mike Herd, executive director of the Sussex Innovation Centre,[5] puts it "to

> **Commercialization is the process where an organization takes its innovation to the marketplace.**

[2] Mike Herd, "Commercializing your IP: turn ideas into assets, 2006," available at http://www.mybusiness.co.uk/YQLibKNoAI8d7Q.html.

[3] Pricewaterhousecoopers and Landwell, "UK Intellectual Property Survey 2002" available at http://www.landwellglobal.com/images/uk/eng/custom/uk_downloads/ip%20survey.pdf.

[4] Professor Scott Kieff of George Washington University explains the meaning of commercialization. This work has been cited in *From Assets to Profits*, Ed. Bruce Berman, (Hoboken, New Jersey: John Wiley & Sons 2009), 32.

[5] The Sussex Innovation Centre (SInC) is one of the premier technology business incubators in the United Kingdom. Opened in 1996, it provides support for

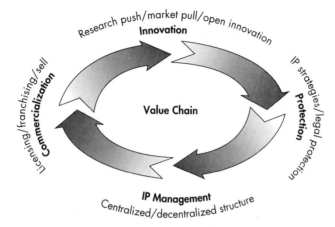

Figure 2.1   The Intellectual Property Value Chain

turn IP into a commercial asset for your company you must look beyond the confines of your own business and explore potential marketing and partnership opportunities with other parties."[6]

To commercialize an IP asset, an organization should have a robust plan in place. Vinod V. Sople, Professor, ITM University, Mumbai, has proposed a value chain (see Figure 2.1), which if followed can generate immense benefits for the organization in terms of commercialization of its IP assets.[7]

---

the creation and growth of technology- and knowledge-based companies. SInC provides excellent facilities and is a thriving business incubation environment for over 70 high-growth companies working within the IT, Biotech, Media and Engineering sectors. Other companies cover fields such as biotechnology, design media, artificial intelligence, laser development and games technology. These businesses are working in fields as diverse as new drug discovery and games technology. Working very closely with the University of Sussex, the SInC is a unique collaboration between the public, academic and business sectors committed to harnessing the economic potential of the extensive education and research resources available in the Sussex area. For more information, visit its web site at http://www.sinc.co.uk.

[6] Ibid.

[7] Vinod V. Sople, *Managing Intellectual Property—The Strategic Imperative* (New Delhi: Prentice Hall of India, 2006), 22.

The IP value chain as we know today is divided in to four stages: (a) innovation, (b) protection, (c) management, and (d) commercialization.

INNOVATION

Innovation means invention, which also means creation. Without innovation, a company cannot progress in this competitive world and will eventually be left behind by its competitors. Every job within the four walls of a company revolves around innovation, creativity, and commercial distinctiveness. Commercial distinctiveness can only be achieved if there is innovation.

Companies such as HJC, a Korean motorcycle helmet manufacturer, holds 42 patents worldwide for its innovative helmets and has enjoyed enormous success in export markets where it sells about 95 percent of its products. The company reinvests 10 percent of its sales in R&D and attaches great importance to innovative design as a key factor of success in the helmet industry.

Innovation and IPR

Tata Steel was incorporated in 1907 and by 1939, it was able to operate the single largest steel plant during British rule in India. The company has been instrumental in incorporating new modernization and expansion programs ever since its inception. In 1990, the company expanded into U.S. market by setting up it subsidiary Tata Inc. in New York. Ever since, their urge to develop and grow has never stopped and they are growing exponentially day by day.

With liberalization and globalization and an increasing scale of operations, technological self-reliance has become a vital prerequisite. In keeping with global ethics of IP, it has become necessary for companies to have their own wings of R&D. Outsourcing R&D is becoming increasingly difficult, as it endangers upon IP and ownership rights. Hence, self-reliance in technology has become necessary for sustainable innovation and growth.

Tata Steel took three steps during 2000–2005, which helped itself establish as a leader in the chosen technologies.

1. Formalized the continuous improvement and innovation process under the powerful program of ASPIRE.
2. Identified the key thrust areas of strategic technology development.
3. Established a sound mechanism for capturing new developments and filing them as IP.

The company set up its own in-house Patent Cell in 2001, as a major step in establishing a sound IP mechanism. This gave focus and fillip to the IP movement in Tata Steel. The results followed immediately. The initiatives taken over the years have helped Tata Steel increase its total IP portfolio (filed and granted patents and copyrights) from 32 in fiscal year (FY) 2000 to somewhere around 500 presently. Out of these, 133 patents have been granted; the remaining 360 have been filed and are at different stages of being granted.

Tata Steel, because of its ethical and sound policies, serves as a benchmark in the Indian manufacturing sector. Given the fact that Tata Steel Europe (earlier Corus Group) already has 864 patents granted since 2003, the Tata Steel Group could well be on its way in achieving technological self-reliance.

Challenges Faced by Tata Steel

There are predominantly two main challenges that will be addressed in the years ahead.

1. The first challenge is the commercialization of IP, involving the marketing of granted IPs, finding prospective customers and negotiating licensing conditions. Efforts are on to benchmark with international best practices and to take professional help from specialists who provide IP licensing and commercialization services. Currently, one patent and 12 copyrights

have been identified for commercialization as pilot cases. Seven companies, globally, have shown interest in the patent, with 78 companies showing interest in the copyrights for e-learning packages.

2. The second challenge that will be addressed is dealing with IP sharing in the case of collaboration with major manufacturing partners. As Tata Steel's indigenous new technologies are growing in scale, it has become necessary to partner with suppliers and other industries. Maintaining claim on its own IP while also sharing the developmental knowledge with others is a fine balance that needs as much understanding of technology as of legal negotiation skills. Again, efforts are on to benchmark against international best practices on this front.

> **Intellectual Property is the oil of the 21st century.**

The vision of the future in IP is to continue to grow the IP portfolio of Tata Steel and to continuously unlock the value through licensing and commercialization. As Mark Getty, CEO of Getty Images says, "Intellectual Property is the oil of the 21st century."

According to Vinod Sople, the products of an organization's creativity are its innovations.[8] A firm has many options to choose on how to innovate, which it believes would benefit it monetarily. In the innovation stage, an organization invents, develops, modifies, acquires, outsources and collaborates to create and increase its IP portfolio. There are three different approaches to address the linkage between innovation and commercialization. This linkage can also be termed as the Innovation Stage. In today's corporate structure, innovation is practiced in three different ways namely: (a) technology push/research push, (b) market pull approach, and (c) open innovation approach. We have tried to incorporate a few case studies of leading international companies that have followed one of these approaches.

---

[8] Vinod V. Sople, *Managing Intellectual Property—The Strategic Imperative* (New Delhi: Prentice Hall of India, 2006), 23.

Technology/Research Push

In the "technology/research push" approach the organization initiates on a research program that is designed to address a scientific or a technological problem in the marketplace without an available commercial application (see Figure 2.2). In this scenario, the organization may achieve its objective of developing a solution, but converting that solution into an applied form that can be commercialized may not be easy. Let us take the example of Google Glass—a spectacle that behaves like a computer. It has an in-built Optical head mounted display, which displays information to the naked eye using a hands free format. Although the technology is revolutionary, Google has not yet been able to commercialize this revolutionary technology.

Although there has been increased focus on the lack of commercial benefit arising from a "research push" approach, it would be incorrect to consider this approach to be illegitimate. As any scientist will tell you, quality research requires quality time. As any business person will tell you, "time is money." Balancing these tensions is the dilemma for the commercialization process.

This approach describes a situation where an emerging technology or a new combination of existing technologies provide the

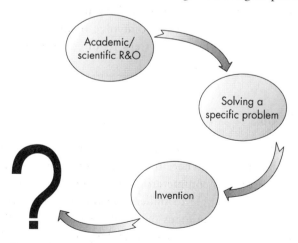

Figure 2.2 Research Push Approach

driving force for an innovative product and problem solution in the marketplace. In certain cases, it is even possible that the new technology, when it is transformed into radical product or process innovations, achieves it own market position. This new technology or technology combination could come into being in a R&D unit, an application orientated development unit, a combination of both or a cooperation extending beyond the confines of a single company's R&D unit.

Important

Applying this approach, the organization needs to ask itself the following questions:

1. Does it have any IP? This may require an IP audit.
2. Does that IP have any actual or potential utility? Determining utility necessarily involves an assessment of the IP in light of the objectives of the organization, both in a broad business context and also in relation to the specific project at hand.
3. Does the organization own and control the IP? This will involve an assessment of the creation and ownership of IP that would be picked up by an IP audit.
4. Should the organization do something to protect the IP or gain control of it? This will also involve an assessment of the usefulness of the IP and the steps required to gain control of it.

Market Pull

The alternative to a technology/research push approach is the "market pull" approach where the research program is driven by one or more identified commercial opportunities (see Figure 2.3).

Let us take an example to understand this approach. A pharmaceutical company may focus on an illness or disease and apply a research program that analyses the biology associated with that illness or disease. In this approach, the pharmaceutical company, in

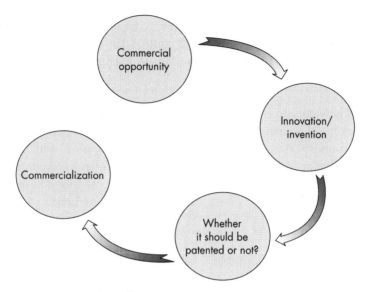

Figure 2.3 Market Pull Approach

deciding to undertake the research program, will have calculated the following: (a) the potential demand for any drug that may be developed through the research program; (b) the costs that a market might bear in paying for that drug; (c) potential revenues that might be earned and (d) an analysis of all the input costs required to get the drug to the market.

Important

The market pull approach involves asking the following questions in relation to IP and commercialization. This concept has been brilliantly summarized in *Intellectual Property Commercialisation: A Business Manager's Companion* by Paul McGinness.

1. Does the organization need to initiate the research and development process?
2. If so, what are the prospects of IP being created?

3. If those prospects are reasonable, what should the organization do to protect, own, and control that IP?
4. What should the organization do to maximize the strategic deployment of the IP?

These questions are essential to know an assessment of the target market. Of course, there is always a prospect that research will lead to an unexpected result as was the case with "Aspirin," which was first developed by German chemist Felix Hoffman in response to his father's rheumatism. It is now one of the most common drugs used in the world for a wide variety of physical maladies.

Case Study

Infosys and Innovation

Many companies in India have adopted innovation strategies to stay ahead in the race; they need to speed up on innovation. Infosys is one such company that believes in innovation and has built its IP portfolio on the intellectual capital of its employees through rigorous training. To achieve higher innovation targets, the company has created the world's largest employee training facility. Infosys believes that innovation is a vital element in a company's growth trajectory and helps it differentiate itself from the competition. The three main elements of Infosys's innovation strategy are (a) products, (b) platforms, and (c) new engagement models.

Infosys began focusing on innovation in 1999, when it set up Software Engineering and Technology Labs (SETLabs). The purpose of SETLabs is to build Infosys's IP portfolio by co-creating with top producers under the age of 30, who are invited each year to meetings with the senior management at Infosys. Under a strategic initiative termed "Infosys 3.0," the "under 30" age bracket producers that include customers, employees, partners, suppliers, investors, regulators, volunteers, citizens and others develop innovative products. The company is expecting to achieve one-third of the revenue from Innovation, which in itself is no small feat to accomplish.

This concept of co-creating with various stakeholders is based on the book *Future of Competition: Co-creating Unique Value with Customers*. Infosys, since early 2011, has been co-creating with various partners, clients. One such example is the collaboration between Infosys and British Telecom where both companies have collaborated by involving researchers conducting joint R&D and prototyping, which has led to new creation of IP that both companies can leverage jointly.[9]

The co-creating initiative has not only created products and services for Infosys, but it has also gained reputation and good will. The brand image of Infosys has also increased with it being ranked #15 in the Forbes List of the World's Most Innovative Companies.

Innovation: The Research Stage

Irrespective of whether a research program is the result of a "market pull" or "technology/research push" approach, the organization will undertake the research program on the basis that the research is consistent with strategic approach for the business and that the results will further its objectives.

The following points need to be considered in the research phase. As with any major undertaking, the research program should be planned and implemented, applying standard project management principles that

1. Identify who is responsible for various tasks.
2. Set budget programs for each anticipated stage through to commercialization.
3. Identify clearly the objectives, the outcomes, which include any IP. These outcomes should be within the strategic direction of the organization.

---

[9] Innovation @ Infosys—Case Study (November 24, 2011) available at http://analysiscasestudy.blogspot.in/2011/11/innovation-infosys-limited-case-study.html.

4. Identify the source of the funds required to support the research program. This will include identifying opportunities for third party funding such as through grants or joint ventures.
5. Undertake a risk analysis that looks at not only the successful completion of the project but also the application of the results in a commercial environment.
6. Set out a timeline for the planning and implementation of the project.
7. Establish and apply an appropriate and effective document management system. This will assist in identifying and assessing IP as is derived.
8. The risk analysis should identify whether there are likely to be any impediments in the research as well as commercializing the outcomes of the research.
9. From an IP perspective, this entails identifying other organizations that may have already secured monopoly rights in the field in which the research is based.
10. IP searches, particularly of patents and plant varieties rights, are an important tool.

It is pertinent to note that IP searches may well disclose impeding patents to a particular project of a company; therefore, it is then open to the organization to try to "work around" those patents. A danger in this approach is obvious. The consequences can be destructive for the organization because of the risk of a court awarding damages and injunctions in the event the court finds that the patents have been infringed. In some jurisdictions, punitive damages may be payable if the organization knowingly infringed another's IPRs. A graphic example of this was the dispute in the U.S. between the Polaroid Corporation and Eastman Kodak concerning the development and sale by Kodak of its instant cameras.

Kodak and Polaroid Clash in the Courts

Kodak had established itself as a monolith in the photographic industry; Polaroid had secured dominance in the instant photography market. In 1976, Polaroid Corporation filed a complaint charging that Eastman Kodak Company had infringed 12 Polaroid patents relating to integral instant cameras and film. Over the next five years, the parties engaged in extensive discovery on the issues of liability and infringement.[10] Kodak obtained legal advice from respected patent experts on the patent position. After receiving this advice, the Kodak technical staff were instructed that they "should not be constrained by what an individual feels is potential patent infringement." Kodak applied a strategy of relying on the assumed invalidity of Polaroid's patents. Not surprisingly, Polaroid sued Kodak and obtained a judgment that Kodak pay US$925 million in damages. Kodak was forced to close its manufacturing plant and lay off hundreds of workers as well as having to spend approximately US$500 million to buy back the instant cameras that it had sold over a 10-year period. The legal fees were reported to be over US$100 million.[11]

This case study should be an eye opener to an organization on how to go about researching in the market for identifying patents of their competitors, which would have already secured monopoly rights in the field wherein the research of the organization is based (see Table 2.1).

Open Innovation

Open Innovation is the third approach that industries, corporate houses and the like are applying to commercialize their internal innovations and to obtain a huge plethora of external innovations to commercialize them as well. In this approach, firms work and interact with external partners and create newer and better technologies and products and thereby benefitting from this interaction. Commons-based peer production is the term coined by Harvard Law School Professor Yochai Benkler to portray a new model

---

[10] *Polaroid Corp. v. Eastman Kodak Co.* U.S. District Court District of Massachusetts 16 USPQ2d 1481 10/12/1990 Decided October 12, 1990 No. 76-1634-MA available at http://www.bustpatents.com/kodak0.htm.

[11] Ibid.

Table 2.1 Timeline for Kodak–Polaroid Litigation

Year	Event
April 26, 1976	Kodak was sued for infringement of 12 Polaroid patents
October 5, 1981– February 26, 1982	A trial was conducted by the district court. It lasted for 75 days involving several motions and pre-trial conferences.
October 11, 1985	District court issued its judgment holding that Kodak had infringed certain claims and a permanent injunction was granted to that effect.
November 4, 1985	Kodak moved to the Federal Court to stay the injunction, pending completion of its appeal. After the oral arguments the court denied that motion.
September 1988–1990	Discussion in court on the quantum of damages to be awarded. Polaroid sought three times damages for loss of market share amounting to US$12 billion.
October 1990	Judge ordered Kodak to pay damages of US$909 million, which was later amended to US$873 million.

of economic production, in which the resourceful energy of a large number of people both within and outside the four walls of the company is coordinated with the aid of the Internet into projects without the usual hierarchical organization. Open innovation actually means connecting external and internal ideas/technologies.

The basic premise of open innovation is the following: Keep your valuable proprietary to yourself and leave everything else to external innovation. Innovation is less about inventing new or building new things and more about coordinating good ideas for commercialization (Figure 2.4).

Why Open Innovation?

The idea behind open innovation is that in the world there are millions of people who have widely distributed knowledge.

Figure 2.4 Open Innovation

Industries and companies do not have the manpower or the resources to create everything on their own and nor can they rely on the research of their respective R&D departments. Therefore, companies open their R&D laboratories and research centers to the people outside their organization to tap into this vast distributed knowledge for their own benefit.

One of the basic principles of open innovation is that "we should profit from others use of our IP and we should buy others IP whenever it advances our own business model."[12] By adopting such a method, the organization manages its IP portfolio to improvise its business model and profit from its competitors use.

The success of open source software is a key milestone of open innovation. One might argue that by allowing people from outside the four walls of the organization to develop software would dilute the very existence of IP, because contributors of any open source project do not retain IPRs to their work. This argument is incorrect since open source software stands as an example of how maintaining a strong, predictable IP regime can support open innovation. People might find it surprising to know that open source has a very strong IPR protection with the coming up of the GNU public license (GPL),[13] which governs the legal regime of many open source software projects.

It is rightly said that we are living in a world where a particular idea becomes old within minutes because there is someone in a different part of the world who would have improvised on that idea and moved on. Open innovation has gained momentum

---

[12] Henry Chesbrough, *Open Innovation—The New Imperative for Creating and Profiting from Technology* (Boston: HBS Press, 2006), xxvi

[13] The GNU Public license was written by Richard Stallman, a software freedom activist. GNU Project is a free software, mass collaboration project. It governs the legal regime of various open source software projects including the well-known Linux Kernel, by contract (a public license) subordinates the IPR of any one individual to the collective rights of the group. Participants who contribute the source code to the open source project agree that their source code when contributed to the project becomes part of and subject to the terms of the GPL.

because of the Internet that has changed fortunes for so many companies the world over.

Internet sites such as zyrist.com, innocentive.com and yourencore.com are providing a platform for many individuals to create, innovate and discuss ideas. In this era of globalization, companies need unique capabilities to leverage benefits faster and more effectively than its competitors. This can only be done if they adopt a policy where they welcome people from outside to generate new ideas, which would not only benefit the people who are bringing these ideas in terms of remuneration, but also the companies that would reap in huge benefits and save a lot of money by not spending it in-house.

The approach in an open Innovation model should be to prioritize an organization's IP into proprietary and nonproprietary IP. Those IP that are proprietary in nature should be kept within the four walls of the company while the nonproprietary ones should be given out to the public at large for further innovation.

To adopt this new and fast-growing approach, the organizations need to dispel some deeply rooted thoughts from within their organizations. "The conventional wisdom says that sharing IP and other sources creates a public good where everyone shares in the benefits, and there is no way to generate private returns."[14] On the contrary, sharing of knowledge can help drive innovation and create wealth. Here is a list of key benefits of open innovation and peer production[15]:

1. Bind external talent: These days the speed and complexity of change in technology is so immense that no company can create all innovations that are needed to compete with competitors under a single roof. We are witnessing a vast sea change in technology and science, which are advancing fast and companies are using and deploying new knowledge in unanticipated ways. Many intelligent firms understand this

---

[14] Don Tapscott and Anthony D. Williams, *Wikimonics—How Mass Collaboration Changes Everything* (U.S.: Atlantic Books, 2006), 93.
[15] Ibid., 94.

innovation by using peer production and open innovation to involve more people in developing newer ideas.

2. Boosting demand for complimentary offerings: Firms that encourage open innovation and peer production can boost demand for complimentary offerings and provide new opportunities to create added value and IP. Just as Wikipedia is gaining popularity, which has convinced its Founder Jimmy Wales that there may be a market for a Wikipedia-branded line of books.

3. Reducing costs: With open innovation and peer production companies can save a lot of money. In this chapter, we will see how IBM and other big companies have saved millions of dollars by adopting this model.

4. Shifting the locus of competition: "Publishing intellectual property in non-core areas that are core to a competitor can undermine your rival's ability to monopolize a resource that you depend on. In the software industry, publishing code has enabled IBM and Red Hat to migrate the locus of competition from operating systems to applications, integration, and services."[16]

Another important principle of open innovation is that the organization should profit from others' use of its IP. The organization should also buy other organization's IP when that particular IP advances its own business model.[17]

Case Studies

IBM and Open Innovation

Open innovation has compelled smart companies to review their strategic management. They are learning how to coexist with and profit with the open innovation phenomenon. "And if there is one company which exemplifies this potential—along with the

---

[16] Don Tapscott and Anthony D. Williams, *Wikinomics—How Mass Collaboration Changes Everything* (U.S.: Atlantic Books, 2006), 93.
[17] Ibid.

deep, wrenching transforming it entails—its IBM, whose early foray into open source provides lessons for anyone seeking to harness peer production in their business."

IBM has embraced open innovation is such a way that many organizations of its stature have dared. IBM did not join the open innovation model from a position of dominance. The company was having a rough time as many of its operating systems were failing and the company was having a tough time in competing with its long-time archrivals such as Microsoft and Sun Microsystems.

IBM in a move which was termed quite unorthodox, started showing interest in open source software by donating huge sums of money and proprietary software code and establishing teams to help open source community-based web servers such as Apache and Linux (operating systems).

> **Today IBM saves billions of dollars per year over what it would cost to develop an operating system similar to Linux on its own.**

Today IBM saves billions of dollars per year over what it would cost to develop an operating system similar to Linux on its own. In the same way, Linux services and hardware represent billions of dollars in revenue because of IBM's investment. IBM's support to open source has enabled IBM to leap forward from its competitors such as Microsoft and Sun Microsystems who charge for operating system software.

The benefits, which IBM gets from helping Linux, are many. Let us now look at how does it help IBM. We all know that IBM business model is selling its hardware for servers, software and services. Linux on the other hand offers operating systems (a competitor to Microsoft), which are more or less complimentary products to IBM's goods. Now if we look carefully at the principles of Economics:

> If the price of a complementary product goes down, one can price one's own product higher and sell more of it. Here, by helping

Linux acquire or use intellectual property, IBM can help Linux gain an advantage over Microsoft and encourage more people to use Linux. Since Linux is nearly free, this will lower the average price of the operating system, which will benefit IBM as a seller of complementary products such as hardware, software, and service. Intel uses the same strategy when fostering competition among hardware manufacturers of hard drives and RAM in order to lower the price of products that are complementary to microprocessors.

Google and Open Innovation

We all are familiar with the product Google launched in the early part of this decade, which is Google Map/Google Earth. Google Maps with its high-quality satellite imagery of the world makes it easier for people to locate places. Google found out to its surprise that individuals all over the world were using creative ideas and reverse engineered the Google Map application for their services.

Google was in a dilemma, whether to sue these individuals or open its doors for more creativity. It decided to open up its application programming interface (APIs) to harness external ideas, talent on a mass scale. By doing this, Google has embarked on a journey where it can develop innovations faster than companies who have a centralized internal structure of operations.

Before Google opened the Maps API, several mashups had been created, including the famous individual Paul Rademacher's housing map, who developed an API that layers the popular Craigslist (www.craiglist.com) housing ads onto Google maps.

Google was delighted when it found the housing maps application doing well in the Web 2.0. It was free publicity and free product prototyping and they saw in Paul Rademacher a promising new talent whom Google promptly hired. By taking this move, Google has acquired an idea (housing maps), which is now in its IP portfolio. Also, Google has saved a lot of money in its internal R&D to develop a technology to counter Paul Rademacher's housing maps.

Amazon and Open Innovation

Amazon.com has also joined this wave, which is creating a revolution in all spheres of the corporate sector. The question in everyone's mind is how does an Internet-retailing company benefit from open innovation? The answer lies here!

Amazon has opened up its APIs to its e-commerce engine to invite external participants to become co-programmers and co-developers on its platform. Nowadays, Amazon's internal ingenious applications ranging from web sites that organize catalogs of CDs according to the top songs in rotation at major radio stations to an instant messaging application that enables MSN and AOL users to ping an Amazon BOT (a software that runs automated tasks on the Internet) with a request and have it message back to the person with links to relevant products, are all developed by people who are not within the four walls of Amazon.

Now another question would come up; that is, why developers develop such programs for Amazon? The reason is simple: Amazon is the biggest online retailing company in the world, with customers numbering millions. For a software developer it makes a great customer. One may think that Amazon would safeguard most of programming interfaces developed by the external talent. The answer is just the opposite. By not protecting, more data would be able to be put in the hands of the developers, and by doing so, more and more interesting tools and applications would be built. This in turn would help Amazon eventually as it sees more traffic coming to its web site, more clicks and ultimately more purchases.

PROTECTION

The second stage in the value chain is protection, which has been discussed in some detail in Chapter 1 of this book; although that discussion was only pertaining to legal protection. Legal protection is essential to guard an organization's IP from its rivals. Rivals can either infringe the organization's IP or work around the creation and benefit. IP protection can be achieved by combining legal as well as marketing/business strategies of the organization. In today's business, a legal department of an organization does not function in isolation from the rest of the company. To reap in the maximum advantage of an IP asset, the marketing/business development team as well as the legal team must work as a single unit.

A classic example of not protecting a company's IP assets is that of Xerox, which was the first technology company to invent the graphical user interface (GUI) that later formed the foundation of the Apple Operating System as well as the Microsoft Windows Operating System. Because of not patenting the GUI, Xerox lost out to rivals Apple and Microsoft.[18] It was a terrible blunder to make, as a patented GUI technology would have brought billions of dollars of revenue to Xerox.

> **A classic example of not protecting a company's IP assets is that of Xerox, which was the first technology company to invent the graphical user interface (GUI)**

To protect IP, companies use the combination of IP and marketing strategies to create entry barriers to their rivals and infringers. Apart from entry barriers, organizations also go in for strategies such as the Patent Wall Strategy, which will be discussed in the following pages under Patent Strategies. Some organizations go in for IP insurance (discussed in Chapter 6 Intellectual Property Risk Management) to cover the costs of lawsuits.[19]

> **To protect IP, companies use the combination of IP and marketing strategies to create entry barriers to their rivals and infringers.**

---

[18] Kevin G. Rivette and David Kline, *Rembrandts in the Attic* (Boston: HBS, 2000), 99.

[19] Vinod V. Sople, *Managing Intellectual Property—The Strategic Imperative* (New Delhi: Prentice Hall of India, 2006), 28.

Companies such as Dell have tried to leverage their competitive advantages and have succeeded. Dell has secured close to 42 patents on its famous innovative business model: "build to order," direct sales business model. Dell's advantage lies in its innovative system of selling, distributing and providing after sales support for the personal computers (PCs) that it produces. Dell's patents cover the customer configurable online ordering system, which include the method by which this system is integrated with Dell's constant flow of manufacturing, inventory, distribution and customer service operations. In the recent past, Dell has leveraged its strong business method patent portfolio to strengthen its market advantage. It has done this by using these patents as collateral for a US$16 billion cross-licensing deal (Chapter 7 Intellectual Property Licensing), with IBM for the low-cost components for its PC manufacturing business. This move has freed Dell from paying millions of dollars in royalties to IBM, which eventually helps in making Dell's products more price competitive. [20]

IP MANAGEMENT

An organization may have a large IP portfolio; but if it is not managed properly, then the organization will not be able to generate all the benefits that a large IP portfolio has to offer. Xerox is one such company that although had a large IP portfolio, but could not reap the benefits of the same. Not many know that Xerox in the 1960s and 1970s

> invented virtually every aspect of today's personal computer, including the graphical user interface, on which Windows and Apple are based, along with the mouse, the laser printer, computer networking, internet protocol, bitmapped graphics and e-mail. Despite these profound achievements in computer technology,

---

[20] Kevin Rivette and David Kline, *Discovering New Value in Intellectual Property* (Boston: Harvard Business Review, 2000), Reprint R00109, 5.

Xerox is still known as the copier company because it failed to commercialize or protect these new technologies.[21]

Xerox failed because the management of IP was not very strong. Although it tried to take steps in the right direction in the 1990s, still no one in the company could say with assurance that out of the 8,000 patents in its portfolio, how many had a commercial value or a strategic value. The IP management at Xerox was so poor that its executives failed to take steps to stop infringement of its patents knowing fully well that such illegal activities were taking place.[22] (More on IP management in Chapter 4: Intellectual Asset Management.)

COMMERCIALIZATION

Selecting IP to Commercialize

It is not unusual to find an organization that has an IP portfolio but without a strategy to maximize the utility of that IP portfolio. The organization should assess the various forms of IP like any other assets, before going in for commercialization. The fundamental question that an organization should ask itself is which of the IP in its portfolio will enable it to achieve its objectives? These questions may include:

1. Will the commercialization of the IP enable the organization to achieve and maintain a competitive advantage? Will the IP enable the organization to distinguish itself from its competitors?
2. Will it enable the organization to acquire market share?
3. Will the IP enable the organization to position itself for further strategic moves?

---

[21] Xerox—Strategic Mistakes by CEO http://www.beknowledge.com/wpcontent/uploads/2011/01/a87ffXerox%20%E2%80%93%20Strategic%20Mistakes%20by%20CEO.pdf.

[22] Kevin G. Rivette and David Kline, *Rembrandts in the Attic* (Boston: HBS, 2000), 60.

4. Does it have the best cost/risk/benefit analysis?
5. Will it enable it to achieve a broader public policy objective such as being for the benefit of India?

Indeed, in some circumstances, it may not be better to commercialize the IP at all but to hide it away until other technologies that may present new opportunities are developed. Alternatively, keeping quiet about IP may help the organization maintain a competitive position if it believes its competitors would be able to quickly catch up in the technology race once they become aware of the new development engineered by the organization.

The selection of IP assets for commercialization must be undertaken against clearly defined criteria. Those criteria may vary over time as the strategic direction of the organization evolves. It may vary according to the nature of the IP. It may depend on the success or failure of previous commercialization activities or on the budgetary constraints of the organization.

If the objectives of commercialization are broader than the 'mere' generation of revenue, then the above criteria may need to be revisited. In particular, public sector organizations will have other influences to consider because their roles are designed to deliver outcomes for the "public good." For such agencies, the following criteria may be relevant:

1. Applying the technology for the benefit of the community
2. Application of the technology by the industry or community
3. Facilitation of alliances with other organizations.

Many of the above criteria can be assessed by the organization itself. The criterion most often posing a difficulty will be assessing the market potential for the technology. This assessment ordinarily involves an understanding of the factors that will influence the demand for the technology, including and understanding the factors that may influence the supply of the technology. Obtaining the information to assess these factors can be difficult because for most businesses, access to accurate information is the Holy Grail.

Accordingly, the organization will need to use its networks and may need to engage consultants to investigate the relevant markets, particularly overseas markets.

It may be appropriate to apply weightings to the IP evaluation criteria to enable a ranking of the IP assets for commercialization objectives. The criteria should then be assessed against an estimate of the costs that may be involved in achieving the commercialization objectives including further development, consultancy, legal and accounting services, protection of IP or dealing with IP litigation. Finally, the organization should assess the risks of commercialization of the IP asset, which may include threat of competitive actions such as litigation, failure to retain key staff, failure to secure the IPRs in the technology or the opportunity being lost due to delay.

IP Commercialization: The Unidyne Case Study

Before we go to the next section of this chapter, which deals with IP strategies, let us look at Unidyne Energy Environment Systems, a company engaged in manufacturing various industrial thermal energy systems. In 1999, Unidyne signed a Memorandum of Understanding (MoU) with Indian inventor, Dr. Milind Rane, who developed the design of Matrix Heat Recovery Unity (MHRU). This invention was used for recovering heat from hot gases and/or vapors from engines, boilers or furnaces. Unidyne saw value in this patent application, which was still not granted the status of a patent by the patents office. Dr. Rane, through the MoU licensed his technology to Unidyne to manufacture and sell MHRUs. The patent was granted in 2004 and is now being used in more than 45 companies in India. For Unidyne, the agreement acted as a tool to boost its product portfolio. For Mr. Rane, the license provided an avenue to commercialize the invention. The revenues that were generated from the down payment and the royalties have helped for the development of other inventions.

IP STRATEGIES

Most organizations have multiple IP strategies to gain the maximum benefit from there intangible assets. Let us look at the various strategies that organizations follow or should follow. This section is divided into three separate headings:

1. Patent strategies
2. Trademark strategies
3. Copyright strategies

Patent Strategies

Patents can be used in a variety of ways to exclude others from competing in the market or from developing competitive technologies. These strategies have sometimes been referred to as a "patent blitzkrieg" and can include:[23]

1. "Umbrella patents": Patents that are so broad so as to prevent the development of similar products. This strategy is used in the pharmaceutical industries, where pharmaceutical companies develop a particular drug and obtain patent protection for the general compound of that particular drug and also obtain protection for a method of using the compound in the treatment of a particular disease or condition. Often, additional patents can be obtained to effectively extend patent term and market exclusivity. It should be noted that once a compound has been granted a patent, then it becomes prior art and must be considered by the organization when seeking additional patent protection around the compound. As a result, the new patent protection generally encompasses narrow improvements or new uses for the pharmaceutical not disclosed or

---

[23] See Dunford, 123, citing B. J. Stern, "Science and War Production" (1943) 7 *Science & SOC* 97, 100–101.

suggested in the original patent.[24] The pharmaceutical giant Lilly adopted this strategy for its blockbuster antidepressant drug named Prozac. Lilly was faced with expiration of the patent for Prozac, therefore the company adopted a umbrella patent strategy and developed and obtained a patent protection for a once weekly, sustained release "fluoxetine" formulation.

Additional patents were also obtained by GSK for its migraine treatment drugs, which bring in more than US$1 billion in annual sales for GSK. The original migraine drug was set to expire in 2006; therefore, GSK developed a new formulation for the drug and was granted patent protection.[25] This kind of strategy is also known as evergreening where the brand name manufacturer generates patent protection by obtaining separate 20-year patents on multiple attributes of the drug. In evergreening, the management of the organization does not wait until the last moment to begin the process of patenting the different attributes of the drug. To maximize revenues from their products, the management begins to evolve not only patent strategies but also an entire range of practices aimed to limiting competition or delaying the entry of competitors.[26]

2. "Bottle neck patents": A strategy that controls the use of invention without which the industry cannot operate. This strategy was adopted by Amazon.com in the late 1990s when it was the granted the famous 'One Click' Patent. The One Click technology of Amazon.com helped customers buy products with just one click of a button rather than filling up different forms on the retail web site. The patent was written so broadly that "competitors were prevented not only from imitating the code, but also from adding a single click feature on

[24] Spruill W. Murray, "Strategies for Extending the Life of Patents" (May 1, 2005) available at http://www.biopharminternational.com/biopharm/article/articleDetail.jsp?id=150834.

[25] Ibid.

[26] Vinod V. Sople, *Managing Intellectual Property—The Strategic Imperative* (New Delhi: Prentice Hall of India, 2006), 32.

their websites, regardless of how they made it happen."[27] Bottle neck patents are not just for commercialization purposes, but they are used to keep competitors out of the market.

> **Bottle neck patents are not just for commercialization purposes, but they are used to keep competitors out of the market.**

3. "Patent wall": If the organization develops multiple designs that achieve the same or substantially similar function the organization may choose to patent them all even though its production may rely on only one of them. The patent that is exploited may be the patent which is the most difficult to work around. Gillette over the years has implemented this strategy ever since it developed the twin blade sensor shaver.[28] Building a patent wall around a particular product is sometimes referred to as clustering.

According to John Bush, vice president, corporate R&D at Gillette—seven versions were designed by Gillette for its twin blade sensor and a full patent search was made on all the seven designs which was a difficult task, but eventually Gillette decided to go with the design that potential competitors would have difficulty getting around. [29]

We agree with authors Rivette and Kline, who authored *Rembrandts in the Attic* when they write that "if you (organization) want dominant products, buttress them with dominant patents." Only then would an organization be rest assured that the products would do well in the market.[30] By creating a patent wall, companies feel protected from any lawsuits and its gives them the advantage to counter sue in the eventuality

[27] Richard L. Brandt, *'One Click' Jeff Bezoz and the rise of amazon.com* (U.S.: Portfolio Penguin, 2011), 13.

[28] Kevin G. Rivette and David Kline, *Rembrandts in the Attic* (Boston: HBS Press, 2000), 109.

[29] Ibid.

[30] Ibid.

of litigation. This is what Gillette has done over the years by creating a patent wall of more than 20 patents for all its razors including the Twin Blade Razor, Mach 3, and so on. The Gillette Fusion, which was launched a few years back, has a patent portfolio of more than 70 patents alone.[31]

> **The Gillette Fusion, which was launched a few years back, has a patent portfolio of more than 70 patents alone.**

Some people might say that patent wall is not the correct word to be used in relation to protecting patents. By securing large number of patents for a single invention, organizations are creating a moat around themselves. This way the organizations competitors might want to get hold of that technology, but since a moat has been made around the technology or invention, it would be impossible for them to do so.

The market itself can present opportunities for patent strategies. Feedback from the market on a prototype of existing patented products can present opportunities for improvements to the innovation, which in turn can result in an ability to extend the patent wall or, if there is a sufficiently new invention, to create a new patent foundation.

4. "Bracketing": Sometimes patents can also be used to get an edge over the competitor's market lead, through the process, which is known as bracketing. Bracketing refers to developing and delivering a disruptive technology by jumping ahead of time as well as competition. An example of bracketing can be seen in the telephone industry, where cordless telephones bracketed phones that were attached with wires to their base units. In such an instance, companies that were involved in

---

[31] Anders Sundelin, "Business Model Example: Gillette—The Razor and Blade Business Model" (December 10, 2009) available at http://tbmdb.blogspot.in/2009/12/business-model-example-gillette-razor.html.

bracketing strategies focused on developing disruptive technology to stop competitors and render their products obsolete.[32]

5. "Kill strategy": There are companies that protect their IP, by using a strategy, which we call as the "kill strategy." In this patent strategy, a company introduces a more sophisticated or enhanced version of a product that had already been launched in the market. By doing this, the company introduces a better version of the product that reduces the threat of other competitors from launching similar products. By launching a better product in the market, the company gets a monopoly over the market for a few more years. Technology companies such as Apple adopt this strategy. Apple launches, a newer and a better iPhone every 8 to 10 months to be at the top in the touch screen smartphone market. It does not allow other companies to bring about better and faster products within a particular timeframe, thus gaining market monopoly.

6. "Patent shopping": Organizations in today's day and age have also gone into patent shopping. In the recent past, companies have gone all the way and bought companies just because they have a large patent portfolio and that portfolio would benefit them in the long run. One such company is Google, which recently bought Motorola Mobility for US$12.5 billion gaining more than 17,000 patents and expanding itself in the hardware industry. According to analysts, this strategy by Google is the next step in building its position in the mobile phone world, so that they can distribute Google products and services through mobile phones and tablets.[33] There are other mobile phone companies, which are in the fray of buying patents from various companies. A consortium including Apple, EMC, Ericsson and RIM bought bankrupt telecommunications gear

---

[32] Lindsay Moore and Lesley Craig, *Intellectual Capital in Enterprise Success: Strategy Revisited* (Hoboken, NJ: John Wiley & Sons, 2008), 127.

[33] Brian Womack and Zachary Tracer, "Google to Buy Motorola Mobility for $12.5 Billion to Gain Wireless Patents" (August 16, 2011) available at http://www.bloomberg.com/news/2011-08-15/google-agrees-to-acquisition-of-motorola-mobility-for-about-12-5-billion.html.

maker Nortel's remaining patent portfolio for US$4.5 billion in June 2011 in an auction. Microsoft and Sony were also part of the consortium that included the sale of more than 6,000 patents and patent applications spanning wireless, wireless 4G, data networking, optical, voice, internet, service provider, semiconductors and other patents.[34] This kind of patent strategy benefits companies in the long run as it provides them with the leverage to expand in areas, which can provide immense revenue generation. It must also be noted that not all companies can follow this strategy. Organizations that have financial muscle can only follow this strategy, because the purchase of patent portfolio is an expensive proposition as seen in the examples mentioned earlier.

Another example of patent shopping strategy would be that of Facebook's current acquisition of patents from IBM and America Online (AOL). This acquisition will help Facebook to counter any of the claims put forth by Yahoo Inc on patent infringement as seen in the recent past. This kind of patent shopping of older patents provides leverage for Facebook in the event of a patent infringement suit. The patents that Facebook bought from IBM and AOL are also a telling statement on where Facebook is heading toward in terms of online business. The patents bought from IBM are rumored to be in the networking and software space, whereas AOL's patents are related to email, instant messaging, web browsing, search ads, mobile and ecommerce.

Facebook's acquisitions of these patents show us that organizations also shop for patents because of their long-term business plans and that they want to protect their IP in the event of an infringement claim by its competitors. A large patent portfolio would make it difficult for any competitor to file infringement claims against the organization and also make the competitor vulnerable to infringement suits by Facebook itself. Such

---

[34] "Apple, RIM in Consortium Buying Nortel's Patent Portfolio" (July 1, 2011) available at http://www.itnews.com.au/News/262378,apple-rim-in-consortium-buying-nortels-patent-portfolio.aspx.

patent acquisitions help Facebook, which sees itself in close competition with Google in the future in relation to social networking, mobile, and ecommerce.

7. Protective patents: In a protective patent strategy, an organization to protect its main inventions, files a large number of patents that shut off alternative routes to invent similar functionality products by competitors. This kind of a strategy can also be termed as "offensive." Protective patents or blocking patents as they are sometimes called are those patents of inferior technology that might threaten the main inventions within an organization's patent portfolio if not protected properly. It often happens that an organization has tried a variety of alternatives to develop a technology and therefore has immense knowledge on the likely approaches other competitors can take. Protective patents strategy is to identify enabling technologies for each of the alternative routes and then protecting them with patent protection. Xerox was instrumental in adopting this strategy to protect its flagship copying inventions.[35]

8. Defensive patents: In this kind of strategy, the complete analysis of an organization's competitor is required. The organization should find gaps and loopholes in the patent portfolio of its competitor and then innovate to fill those gaps and file for patent protection. In this way, an organization can either destroy a competitor's advantage or insist on being a partner in a new product launch. An example of defensive patent strategy is that of HP, when it filed a suit against Xerox for patent infringement in user interface technology. This was done just two weeks after Xerox had filed a suit against HP for inkjet patent infringement. For a defensive patent strategy, an organization should have a good patent portfolio that can serve a useful purpose of creating a lawful standoff, so that both sides can settle without incurring huge costs.[36]

[35] R. Preston McAfee, *Competitive Solutions: The Strategist's Toolkit* (Princeton, NJ: Princeton University Press, 2002), 84.

[36] Ibid., 85.

We can safely conclude this subsection with the words of Rivette and Kline when they write that "if patents are the smart bombs of tomorrow's business wars, then companies that fail to develop offensive and defensive patent strategies for their use will do so at their own peril."[37]

Trademark Strategy

Trademarks are not like patents, if an organization does not use its trademarks properly, then it is destined to lose the rights on its trademarks. Usage is an essential element in trademark law. Therefore, a strategy involving trademarks must always ensure that the trademark is used and the registration is renewed every 10 years. Here are some of the trademark strategies adopted by various companies across the globe:

1. Complimentary strategy: There are firms that use both patents as well as trademark strategies, both complimenting each other to protect their IP assets. For example, Aspirin was developed as a drug, which lost its patent protection long time back in the early part of this century. However, Bayer AG, created a strong brand image, (more about brand image in Chapter 6) and got trademark protection for the word Aspirin. Since trademark can be extended indefinitely, this was a boon for Bayer AG, which even today earns enormous revenues as a result of its strong brand image value around Aspirin. In 2010 alone, Aspirin generated 766 million Euros for Bayer.[38]

2. Blitzkrieg strategy: Organizations that have immensely popular brand names use the blitzkrieg strategy to protect their trademarks. In this kind of a strategy, organizations register their trademark in as many classes as possible. Facebook Inc. has

---

[37] Supra note 27, 12.

[38] Alain Strowel. "Bayer's Aspirin: A Lasting Success Without Patent and Strong Trademark Protection" (October 28, 2011), http://www.ipdigit.eu/2011/10/bayers-aspirin-a-lasting-success-without-patent-and-trademark-protection.

adopted this strategy in China, where although it is not permitted to operate, but is already preparing for a major push in the booming Chinese Internet market. Facebook has applied for more than 60 trademarks in Chinese or English in China.[39] As you can see from Table 2.2, Facebook has applied for trademarks in various categories including software under Class 9, Clothing under class 25, and so on. Facebook not only has registered its mark in the English market, but has also registered in the Chinese (Mandarin) language as well "脸书." This strategy is unique because not many companies pay attention on localized trademarks on their existing trademark portfolio before entering a market. But Facebook's trademark strategy shows that foreign companies have realized the importance of brand localization.[40]

Table 2.2 Facebook Inc. Portfolio in China[41]

No.	Name	Class	Applicant
1	Facebook	9、25、35、38、42	Facebook Inc.
2	Facebook	9、35、36、38、41、42、45	Facebook UK Ltd
3	F	9、35、38、41、45	Facebook Inc.
4	The Facebook	35、38	Facebook Inc.
5	脸书 (one of the translations of Facebook in Chinese)	9、35、36、38、41、42、45	Facebook Inc.
6	面书 (one of the translations of Facebook in Chinese)	9、35、36、38、41、42、45	Facebook Inc.
7	飞书博 (the homophic translations of Facebook in Chinese)	35、38、42	Facebook Inc.

[39] Luo Yanjie, "Facebook's Trademark Strategy in China, Sounds Smatter than Apple," (February 26, 2012), available at http://technode.com/2012/02/26/facebooks-trademark-strategy-in-china-sounds-smarter-than-apple.

[40] Ibid.

[41] Ibid.

3. Single trademark strategy: In this kind of a strategy, organizations use their most vital and most popular trademark, which can be their own name. This strategy helps the organization to develop a brand image around all of its products. Intel is one such company that has adopted a single trademark strategy for all its products. [42]

4. Family trademark strategy: There are companies around the world, which use a common trademark to associate all of their products. This is done to link products with the single most powerful trademark in the organization's portfolio. McDonalds follows a similar strategy in the fast food industry, where it uses trademarks such as "McCafe," "McChicken" and "McPuff." The trademark "Mc" is used as a common element to link with other products such as the ones mentioned above.[43] Recently McDonalds had success by implementing this strategy when it successful won a legal battle against Comercial Losan, which had applied for a trademark "McBaby." The courts found that such a trademark would likely cause confusion in the minds of the people who might confuse "McBaby" with an earlier similar mark (McKids) for identical or similar goods and services owned by the fast food giant.[44]

5. Umbrella trademarks: In this kind of a strategy, a corporate entity that has many businesses uses a single name in many different trademarks. It is similar to family trademark strategy; the only difference is that the single name is used across various industries, which are not allied to each other.[45] For example, "Virgin," Richard Branson's company, uses the word "Virgin" in all of its companies such as Virgin Mobile, Virgin Atlantic, Virgin Games.[46]

[42] "DLA Piper's Intellectual Property Critical Issues," available at www.nvca. org/index.php?option=com_docman&task.

[43] Christine Greenhalgh and Mark Rogers, *Innovation, Intellectual Property, and Economic Growth* (Princeton University Press, 2010), 165.

[44] *Comercial Losan SLU v. Office for Harmonisation in the Internal Market (OHIM)*, (Case T-466/09, July 5, 2012).

[45] Supra note 52.

[46] See Virgin's trademarks on its web site http://www.virgin.com.

6. Trademark complimentary strategy: This strategy is different from complimentary strategy discussed previously. In a trademark complimentary strategy, the primary trademark of a company is used in all of its products, with secondary marks used for certain products that are unique. Such a strategy is adopted by Microsoft using the word "MICROSOFT" on all products and secondary marks such as "INTERNET EXPLORER," "WORD," "WINDOWS" for specific products, which perform unique functions in the software industry.[47]

7. Secondary trademarks acting as primary trademarks: In this strategy, the secondary trademarks of an organization act as primary trademarks because the primary trademark of the organization is not used in the branding of the products. Such a strategy is used by FMCG like Proctor & Gamble (P&G). P&G uses name trademarks such as Tide, NyQuil but does not use P&G on its products.[48] Customers who buy P&G products often relate the products with their names rather than the company, which has produced them.

Copyright Strategy

A grant of a copyright on creative works usually gets a long duration of protection. Individuals and organizations can acquire immense financial benefits if they use this long duration of protection intelligently. Here are some of the copyright strategies that companies have adopted over the years and have reaped in huge financial rewards.

1. Complimentary copyright, trademark and design strategies: Though trademark protection plays a very important role, copyright protection is also necessary. Sports companies often

[47] Mark Radcliffe and Peter Astiz, "Best Practices in Managing Innovation and IP for Tech Companies," (December 16, 2011) available at http://www.insidecounsel.com/2011/12/16/technology-best-practices-in-managing-innovation-a.

[48] Ibid.

employ a copyright strategy to gain market dominance and popularity. Misuse of artistic designs, which include the logo design of the franchise, misuse of team jerseys in ambush marketing and surrogate advertising, might undermine the profitability or the integrity of the company's brand. Team jerseys and merchandise are protected under the Copyright Act 1957, since team jerseys include artistic work on which copyright subsists. Care should be taken to protect the merchandise and jerseys under the Design's Act of 1911. By not protecting them under these laws would lead to a lot of fake merchandise being floated in the market, which may not be of good quality. This would eventually undermine the brand name and cause a lot of loss to the franchise in terms of revenue.[49] Indian Premier League franchisees have adopted this complimentary strategy.

2. Copyright derivative strategy: When an individual or an organization acquires a copyright over a manuscript, a song, a playright or a film and so on, he or she also gets additional offerings known as "derivatives." Derivatives are

> **Derivatives are given to ensure adequate incentive to create new work.**

given to ensure adequate incentive to create new work. For example, for the *Harry Potter* novels of J. K. Rowling, by virtue of the copyright of J. K. Rowling on the novels, she also gets additional offerings called derivatives which generate significant downstream revenues. These derivatives are none other than exclusive rights associated with (a) movies, (b) apparels, (c) video games, (d) board games and (e) merchandising.[50] J. K. Rowling through the copyright derivative strategy used the copyright of the book for producing the *Harry Potter* movie

[49] Rodney D. Ryder and Ashwin Madhavan, "'Intellectual Property League': The Importance of IP in the Indian Premier League," *Journal of Intellectual Property Law and Practice IV*, no. 12, 901–903.

[50] Paul Flignor and David Orozco, "Intangible Asset & Intellectual Property Valuation: A Multidisciplinary Perspective" available at http://www.wipo.int/sme/en/documents/ip_valuation.htm.

> J. K. Rowling is the only author in the world to have made US$1 billion from writing the Harry Potter series along with the derivatives.

series along with Warner Bros, which has generated millions of dollars at the box office. J. K. Rowling is the only author in the world to have made US$1 billion from writing the Harry Potter series along with the derivatives. She has created the iconic *Harry Potter* brand, which has a value of more than US$15 billion.[51] All this was possible because of the derivative strategy.

[51] Judith Aquino, "How Harry Potter Became A $15 Billion Brand" (July 13, 2011) available at http://www.businessinsider.com/jk-rowling-business-methods-2011-7#.

3 Intellectual Property—Defending Position

"Enforcement is a part of IP management."
One of the goals of enforcement is for the company to create
a reputation of willingness to litigate, balanced with an awareness
of the rising costs of litigation.[1]

After reading this chapter, you will be able to

- Understand the common issues concerning enforcement
- Know the process involved in IP enforcement
- Understand the meaning of Mareva Injuctions, John Doe Orders, Norwich Pharmacal order, and Anton Piller orders
- Understand the meaning of cease and desist letters
- Know about what kind of litigation strategy an organization needs to adopt to enforce its IP
- Understand mediation and arbitration in relation to IP enforcement
- Understand trademark, copyright, patents, design, plant varieties, and circuit layout infringements

Litigation in almost all jurisdictions of the world' requires time, patience, and to top it all, money. However, if litigation is handled more cautiously and is a part of the organization's business objective, then it is highly recommended.

The average number of litigation cases filed in India as a percentage of the number of rights registered in respect of patents,

[1] Julie L. Davis and Suzanne S. Harrison, *Edison in the Board Room* (New York: John Wiley & Sons, 2001), 40.

trademarks, and designs for the period 1996–2004 was approximately 0.04 percent. A similar figure for the United States in 1988 was approximately 1 percent.[2] One of the reasons for this low percentage could be that infringement of IPRs is not prevalent across businesses, but there are insufficient statistics to determine whether this is so.

It is an accepted fact that due to the reason mentioned above, some IP owners get discouraged from actively enforcing their rights. However, we should not come to the conclusion that all owners behave in the same manner. There is a silent majority of IP owners who enforce their IPRs without having to file a court document or step into the witness box. In many respects, it is these business organizations that are maximizing their IP enforcement strategy.

The importance of enforcement of IP as part of IP management and supporting of IP commercialization cannot be doubted. Not only must an organization be confident that it can enforce its IPRs but it may also wish to be proactive and drive its business objectives by seeking out infringers. As with many other aspects of managing a business, the trick is to find the balance.

COMMON ISSUES CONCERNING ENFORCEMENT

Each of the pieces of legislation in India related to IPRs address in some degree, the aspects of enforcement of those respective IPRs. Here are some common themes.

Unauthorized Exercise of Monopoly Rights

Enforcement of IP is all about maintaining the organization's monopoly position or competitive advantage over its competitors.

---

[2] Kevin G. Rivette and David Kline, *Rembrandts in the Attic, Unlocking the Hidden Value of Patents*, (Boston: Harvard Business Review, 2000), 47.

In this respect, it is exercising the fundamental economic right to ensure that no other person/organization takes advantage of the effort that it took to acquire those rights. On every occasion where there are alleged infringing acts it is a case of studying the alleged infringing act and comparing it against the monopoly rights that are held by the organization. Only after comparing the infringing act should the organization take the next step on how to deal with the infringer. Generally, the best and easiest option is filing a complaint in the court. There are other ways to handle such infringing acts apart from filing a court case. This will be discussed in the coming pages.

Defensive Action

Each and every piece of IP legislation sets out various defenses to infringement actions. This is the second step in analyzing the prospects for the organization enforcing its rights. One important point to note while taking a defensive action is to know the degree of knowledge held by the alleged infringer. For these reasons, the use of disclaimers and notices becomes very important.

Opposing the Grant of Registration

In relation to the forms of IP that involve a formal registration process, there is an opportunity for a competitor to oppose the grant of registration to the organization. This enables a competitor to delay the grant of IPRs to the organization. Of course, there are rules that preclude parties from running frivolous actions. However, IP has become so intricate and complex that it would be rare for a court to conclude that an argument posed by a competitor was frivolous or lacked substance.

For example, if we see this in relation to patents, the information that is presented in opposition proceedings is not guaranteed to be kept confidential. In these circumstances, the organization is left with a dilemma, and here two important questions arise:

(a) Should it bypass the hearing and take the case straight to court because the court will have the power to suppress the release of confidential information? (b) Alternatively, does the organization proceed with the opposition without submitting the relevant information? And thereby suffer the risk that it may lose the opposition proceeding because critical information was not presented.

Challenging the Registration

It is open to the defendant in IP enforcement proceedings to challenge the validity of the IPRs asserted by the organization. In relation to registered forms of IP, this can involve lodging a counterclaim that the registration should be revoked on the basis that the relevant criterion for registration has not in fact been met.

> **The threat of IPRs being lost in the heat of battle adds to the complexity of enforcement of IPRs.**

The threat of IPRs being lost in the heat of battle adds to the complexity of enforcement of IPRs. An organization may find more value in being able to assert the right rather than following through with an actual action or proceeding. This is because, in many cases, letters of demand are sufficient to achieve an acceptable outcome. Often, this depends on the muscle that the organization is able to flex.

International Issues

The true opportunity to catch the "big fish" from commercialization of IP lies in penetrating the international markets. Not only is it often complex and costly to secure IPRs in those markets, it is also complex and costly to enforce those IPRs in those jurisdictions. Each country is entitled to rely upon its own sovereignty and its own laws. If foreign IPRs are being infringed by an overseas competitor, the Indian organization is faced with the dim prospect of litigating in another jurisdiction that is unfamiliar and also the fear that the foreign courts might be hostile toward Indian organizations. One more important aspect that must be kept in mind is that countries such as the United States and countries in Europe are significantly more expensive than India. Finally, international IP enforcement is often undertaken in the context of having to fight against an established competitor. It is relatively rare for Indian IP owners to hold a strong market position in overseas markets. Enforcing those IPRs in those overseas markets will often entail having to litigate against a competitor who already has a competitive advantage and who can enjoy significant advantages by using its financial muscle to delay the litigation and manipulate the court system.

Expertise of Courts

If an organization is going to make a sacrifice to litigate to enforce its IPRs it will want confidence that the judge hearing the matter understands not only IP law but is also able to pick up the technicalities involved in this highly specialized field of law. The Indian legal system does not enjoy a special division devoted to IPRs. Although the National Judicial Academy is seeking to establish specialist areas, the allocation of judges to hear IP matters has not traditionally been undertaken on the basis of expertise. This can be compared with the position in the United States where a particular court was established to deal with IP issues and litigation because the federal government recognized the importance of an IP system for the growing economy.

Precedent Value

To proceed with the enforcement action, the organization must consider determining whether the marketplace in which the organization conducts business takes note of such an action. Or, whether to proceed with an enforcement action is the precedent value that the litigation will bestow? Of course, this is a double-edged sword for the organization. A success in the action may be enough to drive infringers and competitors away from the market. The failure may see the collapse of its business together. For this reason, it is imperative that the organization thoroughly assesses its IP enforcement strategy in the context of its whole business. Where stakes are this high, the IP advisers for the organization will usually recommend the advice of senior barristers. Senior counsels experienced in IP litigation are usually worth their weight in gold (and often there is a fair amount of weight). They bring to bear on the decision process a wealth of experience in arguing the same or similar cases before the courts and in particular, the relevant judges on a regular basis. They will not only be able to add value to determining prospects of success but also, as is the case with most litigation, be able to greatly assist in determining the appropriate time to settle and the terms of such settlement.

Remedies

Each form of IP legislation sets out the remedies that are open to an organization for successfully enforcing its IPRs. Those remedies include a right to be paid damages or an account of profits (to be elected by the plaintiff) as enshrined under Section 111 of the Patents Act, 1970. In addition, the owner of IPRs is able to seek interim and final injunctions.

Damages and Account of Profits

The owner of IPRs who has established infringement of those rights must elect as to whether to be compensated for that infringement by payment of damages or account of profits. There is a doctrinal difference in these forms of compensation. Account of profits is intended to prevent unjust enrichment to the defendant whereas damages are designed to put the plaintiff in the same position, as it would have held if the infringement had not occurred. The difference in the amount of money that might be awarded by the court is hard to define. Usually, the plaintiff will seek to undertake an enquiry as to the profits that may have been earned by the defendant.

Additional Damages

At least in relation to infringement of copyright and EL rights, the owner of the IPR will be able to seek an order that the infringers pay "additional damages" where the court is satisfied that there has been a flagrant infringement of the IPRs.

Innocent Infringement

Some of the IP legislation limits the remedies available where the defendant can establish that the infringement was innocent.

Limitation Periods

Most of the forms of IP legalization specify the periods within which an action for infringement must have commenced (known as the "limitation period"). In all cases, the period is six years from the date when the infringement occurred. A failure to commence an action within that period means the right to enforce the IPRs in respect to the alleged infringing act will be lost. The practical effect of such a significant delay in enforcing IPRs is in most cases unlikely to be significant because the commercial imperative has probably passed by.

PROCESS OF IP ENFORCEMENT

The first step for an organization to find out is whether there is any cause of action involved to enforce the IPRs of the organization. Cause of action can arise because of two reasons; the first is, whether there is any counterfeit activity being carried out on behalf of the infringer and second, whether there is any dispute between two organization with regard to the IPRs. If it is a counterfeit issue, then the strategy to be employed by the organization is very simple. It should directly go in for an injunction in the court of law. Injunctions are of four kinds, namely: (a) Mareva injunction; (b) Anton Piller; (c) John Doe Orders, and (d) Norwich Pharmacal.

If it is not a counterfeit issue and it becomes a legal dispute between two entities on who owns the IPRs, then in that case litigation, arbitration, and mediation strategies can be sought after.

Important

Mareva Injunctions

Mareva injunctions are used to restrain defendants from removing assets from the jurisdiction of the court so that a defendant to an action cannot dissipate his or her assets from beyond the jurisdiction of a court to frustrate a judgment.[3]

The first Mareva Injunction order in India was passed in *Koninklijke Philips Electronics v. Overseas Business Corporation and Ors,*[4] against the defendants Overseas Business Corporation and its associates. Koninklijke Philips Electronics was manufacturing consumer products under the trademark PHILIPS and had registered its mark. Overseas Business Corporation were trying to export a consignment of 855 pieces of 14" black and white televisions bearing the trade mark PHILIBS. These television sets were lying in New Delhi. The issues, which were raised, were whether this amounted to trademark infringement and what measures could the court take to stop such infringement.

---

[3] Mareva Injunction and Anton Piller, "Form the Selected works of Vinayak Burman" (July 2007) available at http://works.bepress.com/cgi/viewcontent.cgi ?article=1000&context=vinayakburman.

[4] Koninklijke Philips Electronics N.V. & Anr. V. Overseas Business Corp.; MANU/DE/2056/2001 available at the Manupatra Legal Database at www.manupatra.com

The court held that there was a similarity between the trademark of Koninklijke Philips Electronics and the mark, which was being used by Overseas Business Corporation. It was likely to cause confusion in the minds of the consumers. An Injunction was granted to Koninklijke Philips Electronics in this case, as there was a deceptive similarity between the goods. Overseas Business Corporation and its associates were restrained from exporting the television sets under the mark PHILIBS and releasing or allowing the said consignment of 855 pieces of 14" black and white televisions under the mark PHILIBS to be taken out of the country. A local commissioner was appointed to inspect the premises of Overseas Business Corporation and others and the commissioner was empowered to seize these goods if it was necessary.

Anton Piller Order

Anton Piller orders can be made by the court in a civil action to allow an applicant/plaintiff to enter the respondent's premises to inspect, search, and seize to preserve evidence and prevent the destruction of evidence. They are particularly effective in cases of alleged trademark, copyright or patent infringement. To obtain such an order, the applicant must prove that

1. it has a cause of action or has suffered damages;
2. the offending party possesses specified documents or objects that constitute vital evidence to substantiate the applicant's claim and
3. there is a well-founded belief that the evidence may be hidden, moved or destroyed before the case comes to trial.

Anton Piller orders are often used together with Mareva injunctions. The genesis of the Anton Piller order can be traced in India in the case of *Anton Piller v. Manufacturing Processes* (1976) RPC 719. A court would generally bestow an Anton Piller order only if the following three conditions are fulfilled:

1. Existence of a strong prima facie case
2. Potential or real damages
3. Presence of clear evidence must exist that the defendants have in their possession incriminating documents or things and that there is a real possibility that they may destroy such material before any proceedings interparties can be made.

John Doe Orders

John Doe orders can be made by the court of law when the applicant who has suffered damage because of IP infringement does not know the infringer and is unable to indentify the infringer. In such a situation, to avoid delays in the process of justice, due to not knowing the infringer, the court names the defendant as John Doe, until the defendant is identified. The orders passed by the court of law in such cases are known as John Doe orders.[5] John Doe orders enable IP owners "to serve the notice and take action at the same time against anyone who is found to be infringing the copyright of the movie. The order does not specify any one defendant in particular. It is meant for anyone who is likely to infringe the copyrights of a product."[6]

In the year 2011, the producers of the movie *Speedy Singhs* moved the Delhi High Court seeking an injunction against copyright infringement. The case was filed against unknown persons and a few cable operators. The Delhi High Court passed a John Doe order restraining individuals from in any way displaying, releasing, showing, uploading, downloading, exhibiting, playing, defraying the movie Speedy Singhs, without a proper license from its producers. The order also restrains those who may wish to release or distribute the film without

---

[5] Gowree Gokhale, Aarushi Jain, and Payel Chatterjee, "John Doe Orders: A boon for IP Protection" available at http://www.legalera.in/Front-Page/john-doe-orders-a-boon-for-ip-protection.html.

[6] Tania Sarcar, "Delhi High Court issues yet another John Doe Order to protect Speedy Singhs" (September 26, 2011) available at http://spicyipindia.blogspot.in/2011/09/guest-post-delhi-hc-issues-yet-another.html.

permission through CD, DVD, Blu-ray, VCD, Cable TV, DTH, Internet, MMS, tapes, conditional access system or other media till December 19, 2011.[7]

Norwich Pharmacal

A Norwich Pharmacal order requires an individual to disclose certain documents or information to the applicant. The individual must be a party involved in a wrongdoing, for example, copyright infringement.

The Delhi High Court in the case *Souza Cruz v. N. K. Jain*[8] gave the first Norwich Pharmacal order in India. Souza Cruz was a corporation incorporated under the laws of Brazil and manufactured cigarettes under the trademark "HOLLYWOOD." An individual named N. K. Jain manufactured and exported cigarettes under the trademark "Hollywood" and in cartons identical to that of Souza Cruz. Two very important issues were raised in this case. The first one was (a) whether there was a case of infringement of trademark or not? The Delhi High Court held that N. K. Jain was not only replicating the plaintiff's carton but was also marketing his cigarettes under the trademark "Hollywood," which was registered as a trademark by Souza Cruz in more than 120 countries including India. This amounted to trademark infringement and that Souza Cruz would suffer losses if N. K. Jain was permitted to pass his cigarettes as that of Souza Cruz. The second and a very pertinent question that was raised was (b) whether the Delhi High Court had competence to entertain the dispute or not? The court held that although Souza Cruz was situated in Brazil and did not have any sale in India and that N. K. Jain was not selling his goods in India, does not in any way mean that the court cannot entertain the dispute. The court could entertain a dispute not only where N. K. Jain resides but also where the infringing activity is taking place, which in the present case was Delhi.

---

[7] Ibid.
[8] *Souza Cruz v. N. K. Jain PTC* (Suppl) (2) 892 (Del).

CEASE AND DESIST LETTERS

If the cause of action is a dispute between two IPRs holders, then the first step to take is to send a cease and desist letter (Notice) to the infringer who claims to have IPRs over the infringed goods or services. Notice is sent when you know your opponent who you claim to have infringed your IP. The organization decides to send a private letter to the infringer, which may accomplish the goal intended by the organization, that is, to put an end to the infringement. If the infringer takes the cease and desist letter seriously and stops the infringement, then this strategy is more effective than spending years and lots of money on litigation. A cease and desist letter usually precedes litigation.

The cease and desist letter should address the following elements:

1. It should specify the form of IP that is being infringed. With respect to registered IP, this includes identifying the registration details, which enables the recipient of the letter to search the relevant register to confirm the IPRs that are being enforced.
2. It should set out a description of the alleged infringing act including the date when the act was considered to have occurred.
3. It should clearly demand that the recipient of the letter cease to act in an infringing manner and that if the recipient fails to do so then the organization may seek an appropriate remedy from the court without further notice.
4. It would usually identify the nature of remedies available. It is also open to the organization to place other demands upon the infringer, which could be otherwise obtained from a court including the following:

   • Delivery up or destroying the infringing articles.
   • Providing documentation of sales or other exploitation of the infringing articles.
   • It is usual to seek a response within a reasonable time frame from one to two weeks although this will vary depending on the circumstances.

The IP adviser for the organization will most often issue a letter. There are two reasons for this: (a) The IP adviser will be able to craft the letter in a manner that should avoid any reasonable prospect of an action for unjustified threats. (b) A letter from a firm of lawyers sends a message to the recipient that the organization is serious about protecting its IPRs and has already taken advice on its legal position.

Before issuing the cease and desist letter, it should be noted that a number of practical steps be taken:

1. Obtaining evidence of the infringing act: This may entail purchasing articles and obtaining a statement from the individual who purchased the infringing article together with any supporting documentation such as receipts. Photographs and videotape are also useful evidence to have in support of the enforcement action in the event that the organization wishes to obtain orders from a court.
2. The accurate details of the infringer should be obtained to the best of the ability of the organization. This includes undertaking company and business name searches.

The cease and desist letter should be sent by registered post to the infringer and by facsimile if a fax number of the infringer is known. Depending on the urgency of the matter, it may also be appropriate to have the letter of demand personally delivered.

The effect of the cease and desist letter is significant. First, it protects the organization against an order for costs where the plaintiff would have otherwise argued that it would have agreed to the demands had it been notified to them prior to any court action. Second, if the infringer repeatedly infringes the IPRs after receiving a letter of demand it would be evidence of a deliberate intention to infringe those IPRs. This may be persuasive for a court in deciding whether to grant an injunction or consider whether there has been a flagrant infringement that would entitle the organization to additional damages. Third, it will also preserve the right of the organization to elect to obtain the order for an account of profits because the infringer has been made aware of the organization's IPRs.

If the reply of the notice is detrimental to the organization, and the infringer continues to infringe then the organization can take one of the three steps mentioned below:

1. Litigation
2. Conciliation/Mediation
3. Arbitration

LITIGATION

Litigation is the most sought after IP enforcement strategy for companies but it is also the most time consuming and expensive one. It is a legal battle in the court of law where the alleged infringer and the affected organization are locked into battle on who will eventually win the case that would ultimately mean gain in IPRs that was in dispute. Sun Tzu famously said that there is no instance of a country having benefitted from a prolonged warfare.[9] In the same way long IP litigation that is the norm in today's world could end up making the organization go bankrupt. The famous Kodak–Polaroid dispute is one such example where the IP enforcement strategy of Kodak went completely wrong and which ultimately resulted in the payment of almost a billion dollar fine to Polaroid. Kodak never recovered after losing the case to Polaroid and finally shut shop in 2011.

> **Litigation is the most sought after IP enforcement strategy for companies but it is also the most time consuming and expensive one.**

Though litigation is a very strong recourse that organizations take to enforce their IP, but it should be

[9] Lionel Giles, "Sun Tzu on the Art of War: The Oldest Military Treatise in the World" (Translated from Chinese) available at http://www.chinapage.com/sunzi-e.html.

the last resort. An organization should always go in for litigation with a plan. Without a plan, the litigation may prove to be detrimental for the financial health of the company.

> **An organization should always go in for litigation with a plan.**

All of these issues should be set out in an appropriate risk management plan that would usually be prepared by its advisers. The organization should seek from its legal advisers a budget for the conduct of the IP enforcement proceedings. The advisers to the organization should also be able to specify the critical "break points" in which an organization may seek to reassess its position and, if thought appropriate, change track. This may entail settling or not continuing with the action.

Apple Enforcement Strategy: A Case Study

IP has been successfully used as a strategic weapon in today's generation of competition. Apple treats all its IP as a business asset, and thereby engages in litigation to protect the illegitimate use of its assets. To enforce its IP, Apple Inc. has filed more than 350 cases with the U.S. Patents and Trademark

> **Apple treats all its IP as a business asset, and thereby engages in litigation to protect the illegitimate use of its assets.**

office over two years from 2008 to 2010. In 2010, Apple filed a suit against HTC alleging infringement of 20 of its patents related to iPhone's user interface, underlying architecture and hardware. In 2012, both companies ended the patent suit by a 10-year agreement for licensing both companies' current and future patents to each other. Samsung was recently directed by a U.S. court to pay US$1.05 billion as damages for the infringement of the latter's design patents. Samsung had infringed Apple's rounded-rectangle and edge-to-edge glass designs. In 2011, Apple filed a law suit against Amazon.com, an e-commerce company, alleging trademark infringement for latter's use of word "App Store" which may be further likely to lessen the goodwill associated with Apple's App Store. The litigation is still going on in courts. The Victoria School of Business and Technology was forced to change its logo by Apple as the former's logo had an outline of an Apple and Apple contended that the school's logo falsely suggested Apple had authorized the school's activities.

McDonalds Protects Its IP Worldwide: A Case Study

McDonald's Corporation, the world's largest of hamburger fast food restaurant, has adopted a robust IP litigation strategy and has been successfully involved in a number of legal cases involving trademark infringement for the prefix "Mc." In 2004, McDonalds sued MacJoy for using a very similar trade name in Philippines. McDonald's forced to change the latter's name to MyJoy even though they started their business five years before McDonald's opened its first outlet in Cebu City. The Philippine Supreme Court upheld the right of McDonald's over its registered and internationally recognized trademarks.[10] In 1994, Elizabeth McCaughey, owner of a coffee store in San Fransisco was forced to change the name of her coffee shop, McCoffee, which had operated under that name for 17 years.[11] In 1988, McDonald's prevailed in preventing a popular hotel brand "Quality Inn International" from opening a new chain of hotels under the name "McSleep" as it could lead to trademark infringement and unfair competition.[12]

---

[10] Market Watch, "Philippine Supreme Court upholds McDonald's trademark rights" available at http://www.marketwatch.com/story/philippine-supreme-court-upholds-mcdonalds-trademark-rights.

[11] Jim Carey, "Big Mac versus the Little People" available at http://www.mcspotlight.org/media/press/littlepeople.html.

[12] *Quality Inns Intl., Inc. v. McDonald's Corp.*, 695 F. Supp 198.

Tips and Techniques

What are some of the important points to consider while developing a litigation strategy in IP enforcement:[13]

1. Before going in for litigation, there has to be plan to be put in place on how the litigation strategy will proceed.
2. It should be closely related to the company's litigation philosophy and ethical value system.
3. What considers a desirable outcome for the organization?

   - The economic parameters or significance of the case.
   - If it is a really important case, then the organization will throw in all of its resources to get a favorable outcome. If it is not an important case, the organization may set strict economic guidelines for counsel and litigation.

4. What kind of damages is likely to be gained from the infringer in the litigation?

MEDIATION/CONCILIATION

Mediation is a form of an alternate dispute resolution, which is completely different from conventional litigation. It is a kind of a facilitated settlement negotiation process. The parties can themselves agree to mediate, either before a dispute arises or after. The parties may employ an ad hoc mediation process or submit the dispute to mediation through a private organization.[14]

---

[13] Harry Payton and David Wotherspoon, "Managing Litigation: Developing Effective Litigation Strategies/ Defining Success in Litigated Matters" available at http://mlrm.net/Shared%20Documents/litigation-strategies.aspx.

[14] Roberta Jacobs-Meadway, "ADR: Arbitration and Mediation of IP Disputes as Alternatives to Litigation" available at http://www.buildingipvalue.com/05_NA/082_084.htm.

This form of alternate dispute resolution is suitable when both parties agree that an acceptable outcome of the dispute would be some form of shared rights; for example:

A licensing agreement or a supply contract, rather than "success" for one party and "defeat" for the other as is traditionally provided by litigation. Such disputes are common in the field of intellectual property where there can be several intellectual property rights in a single entity and each might be owned by a different party as well as separately licensed to other parties. A mediated outcome in such instances also has the advantage of preserving ongoing business relationships, while the confidentiality of the process is advantageous to parties who wish to preserve the confidentiality of certain information related to their intellectual property and perhaps also their business reputations.[15]

Tips and Techniques

Why choose mediation?[16]

1. Greater control of the parties in the mediation proceedings.
2. The outcome of the mediation is known sooner by the parties, whether the matter will be settled or can the differences be narrowed.
3. It is less expensive and fast as long as the result is possible, that is, there is a resolution between the parties.

---

[15] Susan Corbett, "Mediation of Intellectual Property Disputes: A Critical Analysis", *New Zealand Business Law Quarterly* 17[(January 27, 2011) March 2011], 51–67.

[16] Roberta Jacobs-Meadway, "ADR: Arbitration and Mediation of IP Disputes as Alternatives to Litigation" available at http://www.buildingipvalue.com/05_NA/082_084.htm.

There are a number of factors to consider in choosing a mediator:[17]

1. Subject matter expertise
2. Mediation experience
3. Mediation style (evaluative or facilitative) and
4. Legal expertise

The outcome of mediation depends upon on how the parties in dispute behave. If the parties are not ready to compromise, then mediation is unlikely to succeed.

A Hypothetical Case Study

ABC, an India based beverage company, is suddenly faced with competition in India by a foreign company, DEF, based in a country with an economy, which is smaller than India. DEF produces a beverage product that tastes very much like ABC and to top it all, the bottle of the beverage looks very much like ABC's beverage bottle but is less expensive (and, ABC believes, of lesser quality). ABC's beverage bottle prominently bears the ABC trademark and DEF's beverage is sold under a different and distinguishable mark, but ABC has evidence to show that because of the similarity and distinctive appearance of the bottle, potential buyers will be confused about the source. DEF purposely copied the general shape and color scheme of ABC's beverage bottle, the only difference being the color scheme was slightly different and that DEF used its own trademark on the bottles. The overall impression of DEF's bottle design is one of similarity to ABC's bottle. In India, the laws protecting design are very recent and laws regarding trade dress are nonexistent, so the importer of DEF's beverage bottle is surprised to receive a cease and desist letter from ABC's lawyers. DEF hires Indian lawyers of its own, and discovers the difficult and uncertain

---

[17] Roberta Jacobs-Meadway, "ADR: Arbitration and Mediation of IP Disputes as Alternatives to Litigation" available at http://www.buildingipvalue.com/05_NA/082_084.htm.

road on which the company has embarked. On the other hand, ABC's lawyers know that since the trade dress and design laws may prove a hindrance to their case and would cost the company a fortune, the time is ripe for mediation.

> **Mediation is infinitely flexible in comparison to the limits of judicial relief.**

Mediation is infinitely flexible in comparison to the limits of judicial relief. Negotiated agreements eliminate or substantially reduce risk and cost. In the hypothetical example mentioned earlier, ABC has invested substantial resources in the successful design of its product. Now, it is faced with spending large amounts on litigation that may not work to its advantage. On the other hand, its competitor sees an opportunity to break into the Indian market with a less expensive product, but needs a safe design and marketing programme that will not result in continuous litigation. Instead of suing each other, legal counsels from both sides seek out a mediator with technical and trade dress expertise to facilitate an early settlement. To the delight of both sides, the settlement between ABC and DEF takes place.

Here are the elements of their negotiated settlement:

1. DEF agrees to redesign its product and submit that new design to ABC for approval. Time limits for submission and approval are established, and the design submission is directed to one or two specific people at ABC.
2. A method of expedited dispute resolution is established if disapproval is contested. The parties eliminate likelihood of confusion and functionality as issues to be resolved. The only issue to be decided is the overall similarity of appearance between the specific design in which ABC claims protection and DEF's new design.
3. ABC waives any claim for damages or lawyers' fees.
4. Lines of commerce and geographical limits on the agreement are established. DEF can sell only its new design in the India, but is not restricted in other markets.

5. DEF is allowed a defined period within which to sell off or rede-
ploy the existing inventory in stores and its own warehouses.
Orders placed and accepted before the date of settlement may
be completed.
6. Releases for past acts apply to this product but not to unknown
products or activities.
7. The settlement is confidential. Neither party may issue press
releases or otherwise publish any information about the agreement, but each may tell its employees on a need-to-know basis
that the case is settled and that DEF will be selling a different
product in the specified territories.

ARBITRATION

Arbitration is the private, nonjudicial adjudication of a commercial dispute, usually by a panel of one or three private arbitrators
appointed by the parties, which results in a binding outcome.
There are several reasons why arbitration should be preferred
over litigation. It takes less time during arbitration than it takes
in litigation to solve a dispute. Another advantage of arbitration
for dispute resolution is that it is chosen by the parties themselves, rather than forced upon by one party against the other.
Multijurisdictional disputes between parties can be resolved in a
better manner in arbitration rather than in litigation where different rules and procedures may apply in different jurisdictions,
which could cause immense discomfort for the parties involved
in the litigation dispute. Arbitration proceedings are generally
held behind closed doors and not viewed by the public. This
allows the parties to keep the fact and details of the dispute hidden
from the public, as sometimes details and facts of the dispute may
involve confidential information that if leaked to the public may
be detrimental to the parties involved in the arbitral proceedings.
In arbitration, each party has a right to choose an arbitrator on the
tribunal. "The obvious attributes of an arbitrator are that they have
the knowledge of the legal system(s) involved, language abilities,

business experience and outlook, reputation, technical expertise, arbitration and drafting expertise, and neutrality or impartiality. Other considerations are nationality, background, bias, attitude and any politics with a co-arbitrator."[18] Another advantage is that of cost. The cost of arbitration is much less than it is in litigation. In arbitration, the parties are flexible to choose where they would like the arbitration proceeding to take place, the rules followed in the proceedings, and so on.

Tips and Techniques

Why choose Arbitration?

- Cheap
- Flexible
- Confidential
- Less time to solve the dispute
- Freedom to choose the arbitrator

Arbitration is usually preferred over mediation because the binding of the arbitration panel's decision would put an end to the dispute. Other factors may weigh in favor of arbitration:[19]

1. the ability for discovery of documents, not depending on voluntary disclosure; and
2. the ability to secure an evaluation of the merits and value of the case in nonbinding arbitration.

---

[18] Karen Fong, "Arbitration of IP Disputes: Eyes Wide Shut" (December 14, 2009) available at http://www.inhouselawyer.co.uk/index.php/intellectual-property/7673-arbitration-of-ip-disputes-eyes-wide-shut.

[19] Roberta Jacobs-Meadway, "ADR: Arbitration and Mediation of IP Disputes as Alternatives to Litigation" available at http://www.buildingipvalue.com/05_NA/082_084.htm.

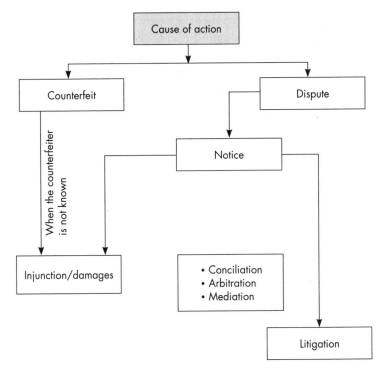

Figure 3.1 Enforcement

Figure 3.1 explains the strategy an organization should adopt to enforce its IP properly and effectively.

A POSITIVE STRATEGY ON IP ENFORCEMENT

If the organization wishes to implement an IP enforcement strategy that is proactive, it will usually seek to achieve the following objectives:

1. to prevent competitors from entering into the market for as long as possible; or
2. to come out with a strategy to generate further licensing revenue.

The proactive IP enforcement strategy has been effectively implemented by Priceline.com,[20] which obtained patents on its business methods, such as the reverse auction air tickets, and took a giant corporation like Microsoft to court by challenging the patents held by Microsoft and eventually settling the dispute in which Expedia (a Microsoft web site) agreed to pay royalties to Priceline.[21]

Proactive IP enforcement strategy must fit with the business objectives of the organization. Common elements include the following:

1. Identifying potential infringement: This entails establishing a process and culture within the organization that facilitates the identification of infringement. This may be as simple as staff noting counterfeit products being sold at the local fete and reporting that to relevant key managers on Monday morning.
2. Establishing an "aura" for the guarding of IP of the organization: Many of the major technology companies have achieved a well-known position in the industry for being voracious in protecting their IP. Sports companies such as Nike and Reebok protect their brands by taking similar stringent efforts. Of course, this needs to be undertaken in a balanced fashion otherwise a strategy can have a negative impact.
3. Searches in the IP registers to ascertain who is using similar technologies or brands: In relation to patents, if the searches of the patents register reveal regular hits of the organization's technology it may give rise to potential infringement actions. If the organization's patent is regularly cited then it is probable that it is a fundamental piece of technology, which cannot be worked around. This presents a reservoir for licensing opportunities.

[20] Troy Wolverton, "Priceline.com Files Suit Against Microsoft" (October 13, 1999) available at http://news.cnet.com/2100-1001-231384.html.

[21] Clare Saliba, "Priceline Expedia End Patent Flap" (January 10, 2001) available at http://www.ecommercetimes.com/story/6605.html.

UNJUSTIFIED THREATS

Most of the IP legislations provide for a counterattack from a party who has received a threat that it will be sued for infringement of IPRs, which is unjustified. Consequently, any organization purporting to enforce its IPRs needs to tread carefully otherwise it may face having to pay damages and be the subject of injunctions. The terminology used in the Trade Marks Act is in respect of "groundless threats" (Section 142, Trademarks Act).

A "threat" is not defined in the IP legislation but it seems that it can be made in any manner, whether oral or in writing. It has been found that it can be made under a "without prejudice letter." Till date there is yet to be a decided case dealing with a threat by way of email, although there is no reason as to why this could not be so.

The infringement action must be undertaken with "due diligence." In other words, the organization cannot wait too long to commence and pursue its action for infringement otherwise there will be a risk of counteraction for the groundless threats.

To avoid an allegation of unjustified threats, the organization should follow these when dealing with cease and desist letters:

1. Only assert actions that can be proved
2. Only refer to multiple forms of IPRs if infringement can be proved of all of those IPRs
3. Only assert infringement where and when there is a will to actually institute proceedings

PATENTS AND INFRINGEMENT

The following activities have been held to be infringement activities over a registered patent. These activities were laid down in the case of *Raj Prakash v. Mangat Ram Chowdary* AIR 1978 Del 1:

1. Making a patented product
2. Using the patented process to make a product

3. Exporting a patented product for commercial purposes
4. Importing when the goods are introduced into the jurisdiction
5. Making, hiring, selling, or otherwise disposing of a product resulting from the use of a patented method

Actions for enforcement of patents invariably involve a challenge on the validity of the patent. Under the Indian patent law, the sale of a patented product without conditions entitles the purchaser to use the product freely, although the patent owner may impose conditions on the sale concerning its use and these conditions will apply to any person who has notice of them. Of course, there are some aspects where the patent system can be used to the advantage of the organization seeking to enforce its patent rights. If the organization is aware of a patent infringement, it can request the patent office to publish a complete application for a standard patent. This puts the infringer on guard and entitles the applicant to the relevant remedies once the patent is granted.[22]

If the organization becomes aware of a competitor's patent application, the organization is open to lodge a notice with the patent office that it is concerned that the competitor's invention is not patentable. This has been provided under Section 55A of the Patent Act. The competitor will then be notified of this notice and the Commissioner of Patents can consider it in the course of examination of the application.

It is also open to an organization to pre-empt any infringement actions by a competitor. The organization can seek a declaration from the court that its exploitation of an invention will not constitute infringement of another person's patent.

Before commencing any such action the organization must request the competitor for a written admission that the proposed exploitation by the organization would not infringe the competitor's patent and give the competitor "full written particulars" of the proposed exploitation and undertake to pay a reasonable sum for the competitor's expenses in obtaining advice about whether the proposed exploitation would infringe the claim.

---

[22] Section 54(1) of the Patents Act (1970).

These preconditions pose some commercial difficulties for the organization. Informing a competitor of its proposed commercialization strategy and taking legal advice will usually not sit well with the management of the organization. Not surprisingly, any decision to seek a noninfringement declaration needs to be weighed against the business objectives of the organization.

The effect of obtaining a noninfringement declaration is that the organization is free to exploit the invention in a manner that was disclosed to the competitor. This raises a difficulty if the commercialization strategy changes, as is often the case once the reality of market conditions is felt by the organization. Nevertheless, this can be a powerful tool for an organization seeking to break into a new market, which is dominated by one or few competitors. The competitor may be able to use its financial muscle to manipulate the court system by extending litigation against the organization to prevent its entry into the market. A declaration for noninfringement will cut through this litigious play.

Bajaj v. TVS (Patent Dispute)

Bajaj Auto holds an Indian patent for the DTSi technology, which stands for digital twin spark ignition, in 2007. Most of the two wheelers of Bajaj including the high-volume Pulsar, Discover, and Avenger are largely based on the DTSi platform. On September 3, 2007, a controversy regarding the DTSi technology arose between India's two-wheeler manufacturing giants Bajaj Auto Ltd. (Bajaj) and TVS Motor Company Ltd. (TVS) when Bajaj accused TVS of using its patented twin spark technology. Bajaj contended that the CC-VTi (controlled combustion variable intelligent) technology used in TVS new 125 cc motorbike "Flame" infringed on its DTSi patent. However, in 2009 the Supreme Court upheld the order of the Madras High Court and ruled in favor of TVS motors allowing it to launch its motorcycle "Flame."[23]

---

[23] Chanchal Pal Chauhan, "TVS Motor Files for Engine Patent", (September 6, 2007) available at http://articles.economictimes.indiatimes.com/2007-09-06/news/28406773_1_patent-tvs-motor-twin-spark-plug-technology.

COPYRIGHT AND INFRINGEMENT

Infringement of copyright must relate to a protected work. There must be some connection between the original work and the alleged infringement work. In relation to literary, dramatic, musical or artistic works an infringement will be established if there is a substantial part of the copyright work reproduced and considering comparing the alleged infringing work against the copyright work. What also needs to be addressed is the issue of quality rather than quantity. If a person authorizes another person to perform an infringing activity then that first person will be also liable for infringement.[24]

If the infringement is shown to be innocent then the copyright owner cannot seek damages although it may be entitled to an order for account of profits. On the other hand, if an organization can establish a flagrant infringement of its copyright then it may be able to obtain an order for "additional damages." For these reasons, the use of appropriate copyright notice and letters of demand are an important step in enforcing copyright.

Defenses (Fair Dealing)

It is worth noting that not all copying of a substantial part of a copyright work will be unlawful. The Copyright Act, 1957 sets out a range of defenses to an action for infringement of copyright including research and study or criticism or review. With respect of computer programs, the copyright will not be infringed if a person

1. makes back-up copies of the software;
2. develops inter-operable products by exercising one of the copyrights;
3. copies to correct errors that prevent the original software from operating; or

[24] W. R. Cornish and David Llewelyn, *Intellectual Property: Patents, Copyrights, Trademarks and Allied Rights* (New York: Sweet & Maxwell, 2003).

4. exercises those copyrights in the course of security testing computer systems of which the original software is a part: see s. 43(1) (ab) of the Indian Copyright Act, 1957.

Section 52 of the Copyright Act enumerates other defenses that are not limited to the following:[25]

1. A fair dealing with a literary, dramatic, musical, or artistic work for the purposes of

   - research or private study;
   - criticism or review, whether of that work or of any other work.

2. A fair dealing with a literary, dramatic, musical, or artistic work for the purpose of reporting current events

   - in a newspaper, magazine or similar periodical, or
   - by radio-diffusion or in a cinematograph film or by means of photographs.

3. The reproduction of a literary, dramatic, musical, or artistic work for the purpose of a judicial proceeding or for the purpose of a report of a judicial proceeding.
4. The reproduction or publication of a literary, dramatic, musical, or artistic work in any work prepared by the secretariat of a legislature or, where the legislature consists of two houses, by the secretariat of either house of the legislature, exclusively for the use of the members of that legislature.
5. The reproduction of any literary, dramatic, or musical work in a certified copy made or supplied in accordance with any law for the time being in force.

[25] See Section 52, Copyright Act for all the defenses available under Fair Dealing.

Limitation Period (Section 88, Limitation Act, 1963)

The Copyright Act provides that the limitation period is three years from the date on which the infringement took place. This means that the organization whose copyright has been infringed can approach the courts within the three-year limitation from the time the infringement took place.

Groundless Threats (Section 60, Copyright Act, 1957)

A person who has received a groundless threat of infringement of copyright can obtain a declaration suit, wherein he or she has the right to obtain an injunction from the court against the continuance of such threats and can also recover damages that the person might have sustained by reason of such groundless threats. This remedy would not be available to the person, when the person making such threats has made them after taking due diligence that there is an infringement of copyright. This remedy is only available when there is no proof available of the infringement of copyright.[26]

Customs Seizures (Sections 55 and 58, Copyright Act, 1957)

It is open to the organization to request Customs to seize any articles, which may constitute infringement of the organization's copyright. The customs has the power to seize and destroy infringing articles.

TRADEMARKS AND INFRINGEMENT

Trademarks form the most common ingredient in any IP litigation in Indian courts. This is probably due to there being less risk of

[26] Section 60, Copyright Act 1957.

a trademark removed from the register than say a patent because the criterion for registration is less problematic. It is easier for the human mind to determine whether something is distinguishable than whether an invention is novel. An action for trademark infringement will also be coupled with claims that the "infringer" has committed the tort of passing off and/or breached provisions of the Competition Act.

Infringement will occur if a person uses, as a trademark, a sign that is substantially identical with or deceptively similar to, the registered trademark in relation to the designated goods or services. Infringement will also occur if the use is substantially identical with or deceptively similar to a trademark that is used in respect of goods or services that are closely related to, or are of the same description as, the designated goods and services unless the defendant can establish that such use is not likely to deceive or cause confusion. Ancillary infringing acts include applying a trademark to damaged goods or altering or obliterating a mark that has been applied to designated good. The essential feature of a claim for infringement is that a comparison must be made of the marks. This is both visual and oral. The courts take account of what a reasonable person in the relevant market would think.

A person will not be infringing a registered trademark if, amongst other things,

1. it uses the person's name in good faith;
2. the use of a sign is in good faith and for the purpose of indicating quality, quantity, purpose, value, or geographic region of the goods or services;
3. the use is for comparative advertising, although there are obvious risks in undertaking a comparative advertising campaign particularly with respect to liability under the Competition Act;
4. parallel importation (where the trademark has been applied with the authorization of the owner of the registered trademark).

The use by another person of the mark must be "as a trademark." If the mark does not inherently distinguish the designated goods or services then there is a risk that the infringer may claim that its use is not "as a trademark" and that it is merely describing the goods or services for which the mark is applied. This is perhaps one of the most common forms of rebuttal in any action to enforce a registered trademark.

When to Commence an Action

An action can be commenced while the application is on hold but it is not possible to obtain an order from a court until registration is granted. For this reason, it is common for a party to seek to expedite the examination of a trademark where there is a suspected infringing activity.

Groundless Threats (Section 142, Trademarks Act, 1999)

A person who has received a groundless threat of trademark infringement can obtain a declaration suit, wherein he or she has the right to obtain an injunction from the court against the continuance of such threats and can also recover damages that the person might have sustained by reason of such groundless threats. This remedy would not be available to the person, when the person making such threats has made them after taking due diligence that there is a trademark infringement. This remedy is only available when there is no proof available of trademark infringement.[27]

Limitation Period

The Trade Marks Act does not set out an express provision dealing with limitation periods for commencement of infringement actions.

---

[27] Section 142, Trademarks Act 1999.

Trademark Infringement: A Case Study (Coca-Cola)

In 1993, Golden Agro Products assigned rights to a number of products (Limca, Thums up) to Coca-Cola. The agreement contained a clause that allowed Coca-Cola to use the trademark "Maaza" only on products sold in India, and nowhere else. Golden Agro later amalgamated with Bisleri International. In 2007, Coca-Cola came to know that Bisleri is marketing products under the trademark "Maaza" in Turkey. Coca-Cola promptly sent a legal notice to Bisleri, who replied that in addition to using the mark internationally Bisleri also intended to use the mark in India. In 2009, Coca-Cola moved the Delhi High Court to stop Bisleri from selling Maaza in India. Finally, in February 2013, the Delhi High Court ruled stating that Bisleri could not market Maaza in India, though it can use the brand in overseas markets.

Bisleri Dispute: A Case Study

In 2011, Tata group's Mount Everest lost a trademark dispute against Bisleri. The dispute began when Mount Everest filed a trademark infringement suit against Bisleri before the Delhi High Court in 2008. The suit was filed for using the words "from the Himalayas" on bottles of its packaged natural mineral water brand Bisleri. Subsequently, Bisleri had moved the Intellectual Property Appellate Board (IPAB) to remove the registration of the trademark "Himalaya." Bisleri argued that Himalaya was a word with geographical origin and cannot be registered as a trademark under Sec. 9 of the Trade Marks Act. Deciding over the matter, the IPAB held that the registration of the word "Himalayan" does not give exclusive rights to any company to use the term as a trademark for its products (see Table 3.1).

CONFIDENTIAL INFORMATION AND INFRINGEMENT

An organization can restrain a third person who received the information from the initial recipient if it can be shown that the

Table 3.1 Timeline

Date	Event
September 18, 1993	By a Master Agreement dated September 18, 1993, Golden Agro Products Ltd. sold the trademarks, formulation rights, know-how, IPRs and goodwill etc. of their products Thums Up, Limca, Gold Spot, Citra, and Maaza to the Coca-Cola Company. Though Aqua Minerals (now Bisleri) was the proprietor of its trademark, the secret beverage base for manufacturing Maaza was with an affiliate company of the Bisleri known as Golden Agro Products Ltd.
November 12, 1993	The Coca-Cola Company and Bisleri entered into a deed of assignment by way of which the trademarks, formulation rights, know-how, IPRs, and goodwill as regards the brand Maaza were conveyed to The Coca-Cola Company.
October, 1994	The License Agreement for Maaza between the Coca-Cola Company and Golden Agro Products Pvt. Ltd. was entered into and executed.
March, 2008	Bisleri became aware of the fact that the Coca-Cola Company had filed for registration of Maaza Trademark in Turkey.
September 7, 2008	Bisleri sent the Coca-Cola Company a legal notice repudiating the licensing agreement thereby stopping Coca-Cola from manufacturing Maaza and using its trademarks etc. directly or indirectly, by itself or through its affiliates.
October 15, 2008	The Delhi High Court passed an order restraining Bisleri, its officers, employees, agents, and sister concerns from using the mark Maaza or any other deceptively similar trademark in relation to mineral, aerated water, nonalcoholic drinks and syrup, and other preparation for making such beverages. Bisleri and its officers etc. were also restrained from using and/or disclosing to any person the know-how, formulations, and other IP used in the preparation of beverage bases and beverages sold under the trademark Maaza.
October 20, 2009	A single judge bench of the Delhi High Court passed an order, which permitted the Coca-Cola Company to continue using the trademark Maaza and market its products in India.
Later in 2009[28]	Bisleri approached the Division Judge Bench of the Delhi High Court, which passed an order clarifying the use of the trademark Maaza by Coca-Cola. The order does not prevent Bisleri from manufacturing the goods (Maaza) in India for export purposes.

[28] Ratna Bhushan, "Bisleri Barred From Selling Maaza Mango Drink Locally" (February 1, 2013) available at http://articles.economictimes.indiatimes.com/2013-02-01/news/36684704_1_maaza-trademark-coca-cola-bisleri-international-chairman.

third party was aware that the information was of a confidential nature. Once the information is released, the damage is almost irreparable. In many circumstances, damages will not be adequate to compensate the organization for the loss of competitive advantage that the confidential information would otherwise give. India does not have a law that protects confidential information or trade secrets. The only provision that provides for some kind of remedy is Section 27 of the Indian Contracts Act that bars any person from disclosing any information, which he or she acquires as a result of a contract and Section 66C and Section 43A of the Information Technology (IT) Act (discussed further). Till now there has not been any case law regarding confidential information in India.

How to Bring an Action for Confidential Information?

A right of action will lie for breach or infringement of confidential information wherein an organization can prove that the other party has used confidential information, directly or indirectly obtained from it and without its consent. Although there have not been any case laws in India that have dealt with confidential information, but the amendments to the Indian Information Technology Act in the year 2008 include a provision that deals with individuals/companies stealing confidential information. In the absence of blanket legislation on the protection of data and confidential information, IT Act provides for data protection and acts as a guiding rulebook. It is better to err on the side of caution to deal with data, especially third-party data, in a more secure manner.

Under Section 43A of the IT Act, there is some relief provided to companies whose personal data and privacy have been violated. A person who is involved in stealing confidential information shall be punished with imprisonment of either description for a term that may extend to three years and shall also be liable to fine with may extend to ₹1 lakh.[29]

---

[29] Section 66C Information Technology Act 2000 (Amended in 2008).

To avoid bringing action for confidential information, organizations must follow the following safeguards:

1. "Privacy Policy" for handling of or dealing in the information
2. Collection of information

   - Consent from provider of information while collecting information
   - Disclosure of purpose and intended recipients
   - Duty to keep the information secure

3. Disclosure of Information

   - Disclosure to third parties with prior consent; third parties should not disclose it further
   - Disclosure to certain government agencies mandated under law without prior permission
   - Body corporate should not otherwise publish the data/information

4. Transfer of Information

   - Prior consent of provider of information
   - Allowed only if it is an obligation under a contract
   - Same level of data protection should be ensured

5. Reasonable security practices and procedures while dealing with data/information

   - Comprehensive documented information security program and information security policies
   - International Standard IS/ISO/IEC 27001 on "Information Technology/Security Techniques/Information Security Management System" approved as compliant
   - Audit of mechanisms, practices, and procedure

Compliance with the IT Act can be attained through an established internal policy framework. The policies that are required to e-secure organizations are listed below:

1. Information and Communication Technology (ICT) Policy—a policy to govern the ICT structure of a company by providing the acceptable standards of IT usage or related services.
2. Privacy Policy—a policy to govern the collection, usage, handling, processing, and disclosure of personal information/data of a customer. The policy reconciles privacy expectations with privacy rights.
3. Cyber Law Policy—a policy to seek compliance with the cyber laws for the time being in force in the Union of India such as the IT Act, various "rules," and clarifications.
4. E-Security Policy—a policy to ensure that the basic computer security (e-security) perimeters are well in place. Perimeters such as firewalls with secure passwords, correct maintenance of routers, encryption, and so on.
5. Software Usage Policy—a policy to counter soft-lifting, counterfeiting, renting, original equipment manufacturer (EM) unbundling, uploading and downloading, hard disk loading, so on and so forth, with respect to software.
6. Internet Usage Policy—a policy to keep employees in line while they are online by banning inappropriate sites, prohibit the wasting of computer resources, enforce language guidelines, keep web copy clean, and using various other measures to secure Internet usage.

4 Intellectual Asset Management

"Increasingly, companies that are good at managing IP will win. The ones that aren't will lose."[1]

After reading this chapter, you will be able to

- Understand the importance of IP management
- Understand the core elements of IP management that include (a) IP development, (b) IP policy, (c) IP licensing, (d) market watch, and (e) organization structure
- The forms of IP management structure in a company; whether it should be centralized management or decentralized
- Case studies of companies on how they manage their IP assets
- The importance of an IP holding company

INTRODUCTION

Let us begin this chapter with a short story about Xerox. We all are aware of the Xerox photocopying machine that has pioneered photocopying in the world. We are also aware that Xerox pioneered many of the key breakthroughs in the computer industry, but then why does not anyone talk about Xerox as a pioneer in the computer industry. This is because of a single and most important factor that it was not able to capitalize on the technology it developed. Xerox could not become a leader in the computer industry

---

[1] Rob McInnes and Sylvie Tso, "Developing an IP Strategy for Your Company", available at http://www.sprusons.com.au/pdf/newsletters/Issue%202/IP_strategy.pdf.

because it managed its IP poorly, which also included the GUI. Instead of managing such a vital invention appropriately, Xerox ignored the potential of the GUI and lost out to Apple Inc., which developed its own GUI and patented its version of the GUI for its computers. Steve Jobs, the former CEO of Apple, proclaimed in 1996 that "Xerox could have owned the entire computer industry today,"[2] had it protected and managed its vital IP assets properly.

> In the year 2008 alone companies in the U.S., United Kingdom, Germany, Japan, China, India, Brazil, and Dubai lost almost US\$4.6 billion worth of IP assets.

It has been found that in the year 2008 alone companies in the U.S., United Kingdom, Germany, Japan, China, India, Brazil, and Dubai lost almost US\$4.6 billion worth of IP assets. This research was conducted by Purdue University's Center for Education and Research in Information Assurance and Security.[3] To avoid such a loss, organizations should have a good structured IP management system (IPMS) in place.

An example of poor IP management would be General Electric (GE), which was taken to court by a small company called Fonar Corp for infringing the latter's patented magnetic resonance imaging (MRI) technology. To GE's horror, it was forced to pay Fonar Corp US\$128.7 million that was equal to 10 times the annual revenue of Fonar. For Fonar, it was blessing in disguise and it made full use of the 128 million dollars by distributing the same to its shareholders as patent infringement dividends.[4]

---

[2] Chunka Nui, "The Lesson That Market Leaders are Failing to Learn from Xerox PARC", available at http://www.forbes.com/sites/chunkamui/2012/08/01/the-lesson-that-market-leaders-are-failing-to-learn-from-xerox-parc.

[3] "Vital Information More Vulnerable in Current Economic Climate", (January 30, 2009) available at http://www.efytimes.com/efytimes/fullnews.asp?edid=31950.

[4] Kevin G. Rivette and David Kline, *Rembrandts in the Attic* (Boston: HBS, 2000), 98–99.

In the words of Michael C. Volker, an entrepreneur active in the development of new high-technology ventures,

> Intellectual Property Management is all about maximizing profitability. For a high tech venture, intellectual property is the lifeblood of the enterprise. Managers should develop a corporate culture, which understands the importance of this. Engineering managers should be looking at licensing out that IP which is not commercially critical to the organization, thereby generating additional profits for the company from "old" technology. And, they should also be looking at licensing in technology which might tie in to their own.[5]

This book goes on for some length in canvassing the breadth of the phrase "Intellectual Asset Management." For the purposes of this book the phrase "Intellectual Asset Management" takes on the following elements:

1. Addressing a well-coordinated regime for identifying IP
2. Managing the functions that relate to acquiring IP, including R&D, licensing-in, and acquisition of IP
3. Analyzing the IP of competitors and other players in the market
4. Analysis and evaluation of IP held by the organization in the context of business objectives
5. Selection of IP for protection, licensing, and commercialization
6. Strategies for protection of IP
7. Strategies for enforcing IP.

In an era where intellectual capital[6] has gained importance, IP management is fast becoming an issue that is concerning not just technology transfer officers but also the governing boards of organizations. The next few pages will highlight the five important elements that form the foundation of IP management within

---

[5] Mike Volker, "Business Basics for Engineers", available at Intellectual Property Management http://www.sfu.ca/~mvolker/biz/ipm.htm.

[6] All the knowledge that the organization possesses which has a potential for value generation.

an organization. They are (a) IP development, (b) IP licensing, (c) market watch, (d) IP policy, and (e) organization structure.[7] Without these elements, managing IP would be difficult and result in fewer benefits for the organization.

IP Development

The development of IP in various forms such as products, services, business models, training methods, and so on is very crucial for organizations. It is essential for firms to have a method in place to transform these essential forms of IP into physical forms for commercial utilization. IP development is not an easy task and it requires a high degree of cooperation from the entire management of the organization. For an effective IP development strategy, an organization should have the following:[8]

1. A motivated staff
2. Separate departments for idea generation, proposal scrutiny, commercial viability, and so on
3. A state-of-the-art infrastructure in terms of technology to create new inventions
4. An excellent management team
5. Alliance agreements with other organization that can promote its innovation (e.g., Infosys and its Innovation 3.0 strategy)
6. An excellent enforcement strategy of its IP policies

IP Licensing

A number of companies around the world have large IP portfolios, which they themselves do not fully use. Such unused IP can be licensed out to other organizations in return for royalty.

---

[7] Vinod V. Sople, *Managing Intellectual Property—The Strategic Imperative* (New Delhi: Prentice Hall of India, 2006), 24.

[8] Ibid.

> **Companies such as IBM and HP have made billions of dollars from IP licensing.**

Companies such as IBM and HP have made billions of dollars from IP licensing. Today, organizations are worried about managing and protecting their IP on a global scale, because the expense of handling IP is increasing every year, while at the same time, they are realizing the immense benefits of IP licensing. We deal with IP licensing in Chapter 7 "Intellectual Property Licensing," where several case studies of foreign companies and Indian companies are dealt in detail.

Market Watch

Every organization, which has an IP portfolio, must have a market watch policy to find out newer opportunities to develop newer products for the market. Market watch helps the organization in the following ways:

1. A better understanding of the market
2. To find out about the available technologies in the market and improve upon them
3. To keep a close watch on infringers
4. To find prospective IP licensees (who would be willing to license in the organization's technology for their own product development)

IP Policy

It is important to remember that it is not necessary to have an IP policy for the sake of having a policy. It should be noted that the organization must satisfy itself that there is a need to set out a statement of principles concerning the management of IP. This will be appropriate for an organization at different stages of its development. An IP policy should specifically

1. Emphasize the importance that the organization places on IP management and commercialization
2. Give management an understanding of the strategic importance and role of IP assets in the scheme of all other assets of the business
3. If structured carefully and drafted appropriately, fit with other policies and governance tools put in place by the board or governing body
4. Give guidance to employees, consultants and strategic partners about the processes involved in utilizing and enhancing IP

Important

What should an IP policy address?

The content of an IP policy is driven by the business objectives and strategies of the organization. Broadly, an IP policy should address the following:

1. Support for researchers to identify and protect IP: This would extend to ensuring appropriate training of staff in IP principles and application of those principles
2. Policies outlining the duties and responsibilities of persons within an organization regarding IP such as disclosure of technology, record keeping, and re-wards structures for staff
3. Policy on ownership of IP by staff, consultants, and students
4. Procedures to assist employees to identify IP controlled by other persons to avoid infringement actions
5. Procedures concerning various approaches to protecting IP and commercialization
6. Policies concerning the sharing of benefits arising from commercialization
7. Regular reporting to shareholders
8. Policies and procedures for dealing with conflicts
9. Mechanisms to assist employees to learn about successful IP commercialization

---

An organization that establishes and implements procedures and policies to address these issues will be in a much better position to make the most of its IP and facilitate an efficient and effective commercialization strategy. It is equally important for an organization to involve its staff while addressing IP policy issues.

Organization/Management Structure

Efficient and effective use of IP assets cannot be engineered without an appropriate management structure within the organization. There is no one easy answer to this. The factors that influence the decision include the objectives of the organization and the role of IP in achieving those objectives, the size, and structure of the organization, the complexity of the organization, the industry in which the organization operates (including whether the IP is important to competitors or whether it is export focused) and the expertise within the organization in dealing with the IP.

A range of options exists so far as a management structure is concerned. It may entail establishing a separate business unit that is given responsibility not only in management of the IP but also in context of financial responsibility. This may involve treating the IP portfolio as a company-wide asset and ensuring that the relevant business unit has the same stature and the persons within it the same seniority, as other important aspects of the business such as finance, marketing and business development. It would entail leaders of that business unit attending executive meetings and reporting to corporate governance structures.

Commercialization committees may be set up to help analyze and consider the strategic aspects of use of the IP. These committees, usually subsets of the board of the organization, can recommend further work be done on the strategies or send the strategies to the board for executive decisions. Commercialization advisory boards may be useful where the participants comprise people outside of the organization who seek to bring skill and experience not otherwise within the organization itself. They may touch on issues of structuring, royalty expectations, and analysis of competitors and clients. Most organizations that are focused on their IP will have an IP assessment committee who will look at whether IP protection should be obtained.

While it might be true that companies require managers who understand the nuances of IP, the mere ability to create strategies to manage IPRs is not sufficient. To have effective IP management strategies, effective organization structures and implementation tools must accompany them.[9] Organizational structures governing the management of IP are of two types: (a) centralized structure and (b) decentralized structure.

In a centralized structure, the decisions are taken by a few individuals who are usually at the top management level and a few supporting individuals who are below them. The decision to manage the IP is taken at the top level and then the task on how to manage them is delegated to departments below within the organization.[10] One example of a centralized structure is that of IBM,

> **IBM with its large patent portfolio has pioneered in the field of IP licensing because of its centralized structure.**

which is centralized at the corporate level. IBM with its large patent portfolio has pioneered in the field of IP licensing because of its centralized structure. The top-level management at IBM is divided into two separate arms, that is, the operational arm and the licensing arm. The operational arm does the day-to-day management functions of IBM where as the licensing arm, that is the IP Group manages and licenses its IP to various other companies. The IP Group at IBM is split into (a) technology, (b) legal, and (c) business. This IP Group comprises of lawyers, inventors, salespersons, licensing executives, and other business-related people. Figure 4.1 shows the centralized IBM structure.

---

[9] Lanning G. Bryer, Scott J. Lebson, and Matthew D. Asbell, *Intellectual Property Strategies for the 21st Century Corporation—A Shift in Strategic and Financial Management* (New Jersey: John Wiley & Sons), 4.

[10] Ibid.

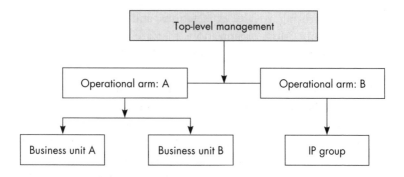

Figure 4.1   Centralized IP Management Structure

Nestle has a huge IP portfolio that includes trademarks as well as patents. To manage its vast IP portfolio, it follows a decentralized structure.

In a decentralized structure, there are multiple, potentially competing decision makers where any department or individual may decide to undertake the new project. In this structure, the decision making is localized at specific levels.[11] A decentralized structure is useful for an organization where the IP issues encountered by the various business divisions of the organization are not complex and where there is no need to leverage know-how across business divisions. For example, Nestle S.A. (Nestle) headquartered in Switzerland has 52 operating entities in different countries across the world including U.S. and India. Nestle has a huge IP portfolio that includes trademarks as well as patents. To manage its vast IP portfolio, it follows a decentralized structure. Its IP assets are managed by subsidiaries called Societe des Produits Nestle S.A. (Societe) and Nestec, S.A. (Nestec). Societe and Nestec own many of Nestle's trademarks (such as Kit Kat) and patents and the technical know-how, which they license to the operating entities

---

[11] Lanning G. Bryer, Scott J. Lebson, and Matthew D. Asbell, *Intellectual Property Strategies for the 21st Century Corporation—A Shift in Strategic and Financial Management* (New Jersey: John Wiley & Sons), 4.

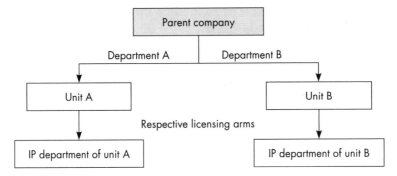

Figure 4.2 Decentralized IP Management Structure

across the world. In return, the operating entities remit periodic royalty payments to Societe or Nestle as the case may be. This decentralized structure at Nestle is further subdivided by two other entities—(a) strategic business units and (b) strategic generating demand units. While the former concentrates on product development and trademark fidelity for Nestle's most important and strategic trademarks, the latter develops the marketing strategies and determines the geographical market where the product is launched or going to be launched. Figure 4.2 shows the decentralized Nestle structure.

BUILDING AN EFFECTIVE INTELLECTUAL PROPERTY PORTFOLIO

As Michael Volker puts it: IP commercialization is one form of creating wealth. Any wealth, creation strategy will contain steps to spread the risk of: the investor. Likewise, an organization seeking to commercialize its IP is better placed if it is applying a strategy that relies on more than one IP asset.

Building a suite of IP or in simpler terms getting hold of a lot of IP will not only protect the asset base of the organization but also assist in attracting new investors. Of course, the value of additional IP assets is directly linked to the desire and ability of the organization to utilize those assets. Merely creating IP assets for the sake of it is unlikely to protect its position or attract appreciation from persons outside the organization.

DUE DILIGENCE PHASE/IP AUDITING

An audit of the IP assets of an organization should be carried out in a manner that is robust and supportable by documentation held by the organization and interviews with key managers. An IP audit is another form of due diligence. The standards and principles applied in due diligence investigations for investments projects or mergers and acquisitions are equally applicable.

IP Auditing

The gathering of information for the IP audit should involve discussions with key managers of the organization to enable the auditor to understand the nature of the business, the core IP that drives revenue. This period of initial investigation is critical in establishing rapport with the management of the company and to get feedback on likely pitfalls that may be relevant to the company in commercializing its IP. This will often be sufficient to identify key forms of IP and the major risks faced by the company moving forward toward full commercialization of its IP portfolio.

Stage 1: Identifying the Intellectual Property

The identification of IP in an existing business is not a quick, cheap or simple exercise. Hence, it is important for an organization to carefully consider the importance of IP to its operations before embarking on what may be a fruitless and costly journey. However, if performed well, the result of an IP audit for the organization is a system that will

1. be a clear understanding of its IP asset base;

2. readily and contemporaneously identify and record new IP assets;

3. identify the material risks that apply to its existing IP asset base;

4. increase the awareness among its staff and contractors of IP principles and enable them to be applied in accordance with the IP principles of the organization;

5. be a sound basis for proceeding with commercialization of elements of that IP asset base.

A review and audit of IP held by an organization will also enable the organization to manage its IP portfolio efficiently and assist in persuading potential investors and its shareholders of the potential for growth in the company. Without being tangled by definitions, it is worth understanding the difference between an IP audit and an IP review. An IP audit should be a process of capturing information about the IP that an organization holds. An IP review goes beyond that. The review of IP looks not only at the IP held by an organization but also at how the organization is using its IP.

The IP review can confirm the soundness and fitness for the intended purpose of the IP, be the source of generating additional licensing revenue, provide grounds for implementing strategies to overcome competitors and provide recognition to staff for valuable efforts in research and development. These issues are of fundamental importance. Any IP review needs to have a context. What is the purpose of the review? The identification of these actual or potential objectives will have a direct influence on the manner in which the IP is conducted and the tangible outcomes of the audit including reports and assets identified.

Stage 2: Assessing Control of the Intellectual Property

The second stage of the due diligence process is to identify the degree of control, if any, that the organization has over the IP identified. This involves

1. Ascertaining the ownership of the IP. How was it developed? Who developed it? When was it developed? What assistance did the organization have in developing or acquiring it?
2. Reviewing the license arrangements (if any) and other contractual restrictions that apply to that IP and all documentation related to the development and acquisition of that IP.
3. Proof of the information obtained from the above due diligence such as certificates of registration, correspondence, laboratory books, contracts, and NDAs.

Most forms of IP legislation expressly state any IP created by an employee in the course of his or her employment will vest in the employer. The distinction between an employer and an employee becomes critical. Much will depend upon the level of independence held by the creator of the IP and the complexity of the task undertaken by the creator. To illustrate this, a common issue is whether the IP was developed with the assistance of students of a research organization. Students are not employees of a research or academic institution so any IP they may create, as a general rule, will be owned by them unless they have transferred their rights to another person by a contract or other form of writing.

SPECIFIC ISSUES FOR TYPES OF INTELLECTUAL PROPERTY

Performing due diligence on the IP of an organization will be influenced by the types of IP that the organization is likely to own. In the IP audit, the IP auditor would be expected check that those criteria have been established or comment upon the likelihood of that criteria being established. This step can be difficult and time consuming. Often it will not be possible to obtain the necessary facts to form a view of whether IP exists. Alternatively, such opinions may be required from specialists in the relevant IP field. For these reasons, those steps may not be undertaken until the organization can assess the importance of that IP to its business.

Patent Issues

One of the challenges about patent registration is that a competitor can seek to overturn the patent registration by filing an opposition proceeding under Section 25 of the Patents Amendment Act of 2005.

Patent search is usually carried out by highly qualified practitioners in the patent office, which is mostly imperfect. It requires an understanding of the fields that are new and expanding. It requires a skill of searching databases and general publications not just in India but internationally.

An investor or purchaser of the organization may not be satisfied to know that the organization has protected its patent portfolio by registering its patents under the Patents Act. He or she may want to get as comfortable as possible about the fact that the patent portfolio position is solid and well protected before committing to the transaction.

The value of a patent rests with the scope of the claims made. If too broad, the risk of invalidity rises. If too narrow, a competitor can produce competing technology without fear of infringement. A proper due diligence task will involve a patent agent reviewing the claims of a patent as provided under Section 127 of the Patents Act to determine its scope and determine whether the claims are fairly based on the disclosure contained in a specification. To do this the IP auditor will review the patent application, specification and claims.

To decide whether the innovation was obvious at the time of the application, the IP auditor needs to discuss the nature of the innovation with the experts within the organization and other persons skilled in the relevant field as per Section 12 of the Patents Act 1970. That information can then be compared with the results received from searches undertaken to test whether there was any prior art in existence before the priority date.

To conduct international searches, the IP auditor as per Section 13 of the Patents Act 1970 may need to conduct the same as to find out whether there was prior art existing before the date of the patent. If so, the patent could be open to challenge even though that information may have been available at the time the application was accepted. The IP auditor as per Section 14 of the Patents Act 1970 should also review the files of the organization to check that it has disclosed to the patent office all it knew about prior art at the time of the application of the patent.

If the organization discloses the innovation that is the subject of the patent before the priority date of the patent and without the protection of an NDA, then the patent could be open to challenge. The purpose of the disclosure (even if a NDA was signed) may jeopardize the validity of the patent. The IP auditor will therefore wish to review the files of the organization to check whether such risks exist. The economic monopoly derived from a patent is confined to the jurisdiction in which the patent is registered. Patent registration in India does not, by itself, give the patent owner monopoly rights (Section 46, Patents Act 1970) as it is in the U.S. The IP auditor will therefore need to ascertain the jurisdictions in which patents are held. An investor may want the IP auditor to perform broader searches for key markets to ascertain the risks of infringement and competitor activity in those countries.

One important thing that should be kept in mind is that an organization should file for patent protection in only those countries where it makes economic sense to do so. This strategy is excellently implemented by DuPont, which files and protects patent where it is doing business as this helps in reducing costs for managing its IP.

Trademark Issues

An organization may own a wide range of names, phrases, and logos as part of its business. The mark may be valuable IP even though it is not the subject of trademark registration. The task for the IP auditor is to find out which marks are used to build the goodwill of the organization.

Consequently, the best place to start enquiries about the trademarks of an organization will be with those persons who are responsible for marketing the organization, its products, and services. At worst, the inconsistent use of the trademarks of the organization can place the protection of the marks in jeopardy.

The IP auditor should find out all the names, phrases, and logos used by the organization and the context in which they are used. The questions that he needs to ask are the following: (a) Are they used consistently? (b) Are they used in a manner that enables the marks to be protected? If logos have been used, then copyright might also subsist in the mark.

The IP auditor should also conduct searches of business names registers in each jurisdiction and other markets where the organization or purchaser may intend to trade. Therefore, there is always a chance that a business has registered a name that is similar to the marks of the organization—this may result in a potential claim for infringement by or against the organization, depending on the status of trademark registrations and the history of the use of those competing marks. The Internet domain name registries also offer an alternative source of competing marks. Searches of them may present the same issues as with a search of the business name registers.

Finally, the manner of use of the trademark symbols of ™ and ® should be checked to ensure that such use is consistent with the Trade Marks Act 1999.

Pfizer: How Does the Largest Pharmaceutical Company Manage Its Trademark Portfolio?

Pfizer Inc. is the world's largest research-based pharmaceuticals company with revenues of US$51.3 billion. Pfizer's best-known products include the prescription medicines Lipitor, Viagra, and Celebrex. The company's over-the-counter brands include Listerine, Benadryl, and Sudafed. Pfizer has three business

> **With some 40,000 live trademarks, protecting its valuable brands is critical for Pfizer.**

segments: health care, animal health, and consumer health care. Its products are available in more than 150 countries.

Recently, Pfizer has been engaged in an organization-wide effort to operate more efficiently and reduce costs. Centralizing and streamlining its trademark management processes is one such initiative that helps the company protect its valuable brands and yields a variety of important benefits.

With some 40,000 live trademarks, protecting its valuable brands is critical for Pfizer. The company implemented a global initiative to combat counterfeiting, giving its trademark rights management continuous, professional attention. Pfizer also recently launched an effort to centralize and streamline its trademark payment processes. The goal is to deliver greater efficiencies while reducing risk and error. In 2004, Pfizer began to consolidate its trademark management processes, which had been dispersed among several departments and external legal counsel. The Intellectual Property Global Services (IPGS) group was created with overall responsibility for trademark research, filings, renewals, and database management. This department now has offices in New York; Morris Plains, New Jersey; and Karlsruhe, Germany. Following the establishment of the IPGS group, Pfizer transferred responsibility for a portion of its trademark renewals to Thomson IP Management Services.[12]

By joining hands with Thomson IP Management, Pfizer has benefitted immensely; for example, an acquisition took place and Pfizer discovered that the acquired company had lost a number of renewals because they were not entered into the system or were entered incorrectly. But since Pfizer had a good IP management system in place, it was able to ensure that nothing was lost.

---

[12] "Pfizer a Case Study", available at http://thomsonipmanagement.com/docs/CM10158-07_PfizerCaseStudy.pdf.

It is clear from this example that to maintain your IP stock, you need to have a strong IP management system in place and there are organizations which provide services, to organizations to handle their IP portfolio in an organized manner like Thomson.

Copyright Issues

In India, there is not a formal or mandatory registration system for copyright. This presents difficulties for an IP auditor who is seeking to identify the risks of the copyright being challenged or invalidated. The essential elements of copyright in India are that the work is

* original,
* created by an Indian citizen, and
* published or communicated.

The auditor would have to ask questions while dealing with copyright issues; for example, (a) who created the work? This is a particular trap where the copyright work was created as part of a joint venture or partnership. (b) How the work created will be important? (c) Did it involve the use of other copyright works? If so, (d) did the organization or the author have licenses to use that copyright work and does that license extend to exploiting it as part of the derived work? This can be a trap for software because many software products rely upon other applications to enable them to function. (e) Was it hard to create the work? If not, there may be an argument that copyright does not subsist in the technology because insufficient skill and expertise has been applied to create the technology (and therefore the work is not original).

If the copyright works are used or likely to be used in international transactions the Copyright Act under Chapter IX provides that, the IP auditor should check whether the copyright works are marked with the © symbol and appropriate copyright notices to determine whether protection for international markets is maintained or not.

Know-How and Confidentiality

It is the know-how secret that is intrinsically valuable to the trade, that often gives the organization its competitive advantage. As discussed in Chapter 3, the legal protection and foundation for commercialization of know-how rests with being able to retain a degree of confidentiality about that know-how.

For the purposes of an IP audit, it may not be necessary for the organization to disclose the substance of the know-how to the IP auditor. From a due diligence perspective, the IP auditor will need to understand the processes that the organization has in place to safeguard the methodologies and information that make up the know-how. Provided those processes are in place the IP auditor can proceed on the assumption that the know-how itself meets the legal criteria for confidentiality protection. If this approach is taken then the organization and investors should recognize and accept that the due diligence report will contain a qualification that the IP auditor has not considered the nature of the know-how and does not comment on whether the claim for legal protection can be substantiated. This may be a material qualification for an investor. It may, for example, include copyright in the documentation that sets out the know-how methodologies, or any software embedded in the use of the know-how or other know-how arising from the way the software is applied.

The IP auditor will usually study and analyze

1. the formal written records, if any, that set out the methodologies within the know-how;
2. the mechanisms to keep those written records secret and ensure that use is qualified;
3. the process for requiring persons within and outside the organization to sign NDAs;
4. the tracking and documentation of the NDAs;
5. the robustness of the NDAs including the description of the know-how that may be included in the NDA.

It may be appropriate to conduct a search of the industry to test whether the know-how is truly confidential. Obviously, this must be done with great care and close consultation with the organization so that at all times the organization is comfortable with the process that the IP auditor will apply to this task. Both the IP auditor and organization must carefully consider the scope of information that the IP auditor will release in making those enquiries. This search may encompass a review of literature in the relevant industry, interviews with key players in the market such as other entrepreneurs and researchers and a review of trade publications and patent registers. Ultimately, the scope of these searches will depend on the importance that the know-how plays in the generation of revenue for the organization.

The IP auditor should obtain from key managers within the organization, including staff in the sales and marketing areas, written confirmation that those person are not aware of anything that could cause them to believe that the know now has been disclosed to unauthorized persons without the completion of an NDA and compliance with any other procedures put in place by the organization to ensure confidentiality is maintained. If this certification cannot be obtained, then the IP auditor would be entitled to qualify its report to this effect.

Usual Documents for an Audit[13]

An IP auditor will ask, as a minimum, to inspect and review the following documentation:

1. All applications and certificates of registration for registrable IP
2. All files relating to the protection, maintenance and enforcement of IP—this will give the auditor an indication of

---

[13] This concept has been summarized in Paul McGinness, *Intellectual Property Commercialisation: A Business Manager's Companion* (Australia: Lexis Nexis Butterworths, 2003).

competitors (who may have filed oppositions to the applications for registration or potential infringers)

3. License and assignment agreements (both by and to the organization)

4. Laboratory notebooks and other research records for all IP—to enable the IP auditor to determine the inventors and reconcile with any patent applications or registrations

5. NDAs—these will provide a summary of the know-how and trade secrets that the organization considers to be valuable

6. Manuals that set out processes or methodologies applied by the organization

7. All litigation files affecting the IP (including files that may relate to contractual disputes where the technology may be involved)

8. Agreements that supported the funding of the research and development of the IP—this will enable the IP auditor to ascertain whether other parties have a claim to the IP

9. All publications by researchers employed or contracted by the organization that relate to IP held by the organization

10. All marketing material used by the organization to promote the technology in which the IP subsists—this will enable the IP auditor to confirm whether all trademarks reflect the terms, phrases, and logos used in the course of the business of the organization

11. All documentation relating to the engagement of persons who may have been involved in the development of the IP (such as consultancy agreements, scholarship agreements, workplace agreements, executive contracts

12. IP policies and manuals.

OPPORTUNITIES TO BUILD THE BUSINESS

An organization should focus on areas that can materially improve its profitability by leveraging off its IP base. This is principally focusing on existing or new fields in which to establish a competitive advantage. This may entail

1. undertaking new research and development;
2. fast-tracking existing research and development (which may have funding implications for the organization);
3. revisiting the organization's existing IP portfolio. This may entail filing new applications to register IP, extending the scope of existing applications for registration or expediting examinations. It may also entail taking a "patent blitzkrieg."
4. attacking competitors by establishing an IP enforcement strategy, increased monitoring of applications to register IP by competitors and lodging oppositions to such applications;
5. establishing alliances and terms with competitors and others in the industry by cross-licensing, licensing-in IP, co-branding services or products or acquiring other organizations.

An organization should always look at its IP portfolio with regard to business under three different heads:

1. The IP that is helping the organization in its business and that can be licensed and defended
2. The IP that is having the potential to be included in the business
3. The IP has no business or commercial interest. This particular form of IP is available for licensing, or be allowed to expire or be abandoned.

The Dow Chemical Company employed this strategy. The case study of this company would be discussed in detail in the later pages of this chapter.

ONGOING DISCLOSURE OF INTELLECTUAL PROPERTY

An important part of achieving a sound IP portfolio is to ensure that any IP audit is supported by an ongoing commitment to internal disclosure of IP by the organization and staff and contributors of the organization. With respect to the staff of the organization this can be done through a carrot and stick approach. Incentives and recognition can be offered that fosters disclosure of the IP and a team approach to its development. The contractual arrangements for staff and contractors should also set out clearly the expectations of the organization so far as the disclosure of any IP is concerned.

Keeping employees informed of the progress of the protection and commercialization of IP in which they have been involved can reinforce these simple steps. Staff should be given an easy-to-use system for the notification of new ideas. For IP that has been rejected by the organization, it is often worth considering giving the employee an opportunity to commercialize it.

An often-overlooked aspect is conducting exit interviews with staff and contractors to find out as much information as possible about the creation of any undisclosed IP and how those people think the organization could better deal with the management of IP.

Intellectual Property Registers and Databases

The wealth of information that can be collected from an organization through an IP audit should be captured in a form that enables constant use and maintenance. There are two forms through which this may occur. The first is a register that seeks to capture the core information relating to the IP held by the organization.

The second alternative is to establish a database that helps the organization undertake the strategic analysis of the IP audit results. This necessarily involves an IP register but its functionality involves more than that. The following functions have been noted to be important in the developing of any IP database.[14]

---

[14] K. Hale, "Creating the Portfolio Database", in *Profiting from Intellectual Capital,* ed. Patrick Sullivan, (New York: John Wiley and Sons, 1998), 132–133.

Intellectual Property Database Functions

1. Identify IP that has value, but not used
2. Restricted access for different information
3. Identify nonperforming assets
4. Strengths and weaknesses of the IP
5. Reflect the strategic direction of the organization
6. Identify the costs concerning the maintenance of the portfolio
7. Group patents together in accordance with specific parameters such as product/service/business industry
8. Identify potential or actual competitors
9. Easy to amend and add new information by relevant people—neither time consuming nor technically difficult

The database should be developed on a software platform that enables fields to be selected and for an iterative use. The organization must apply significant thinking to the nature of the reports that it will want to drive out of this database. Ideally, the database should be set up through the organization's intranet.

MAINTENANCE OF INTELLECTUAL PROPERTY

Having taken the time, effort, and money to create the IP, the organization deploying an IP management strategy will implement a system to maintain that IP. This should be more than just paying the registration fees, although the importance of that function should not be treated lightly. Maintenance of IP also entails enforcing the monopoly rights held by the organization against "infringers," using appropriate markings to designate ownership of the IP and judiciously challenging the IPRs of others (especially competitors) when the result might trigger a counterattack against the validity of the IPRs of the organization.

Most importantly, IP management should involve regular reviews of the importance of the IP to the organization. These reviews will confirm for management that the costs incurred in maintaining the IP are justified having regard to the income and strategic benefits of retaining that IP. Of course, this analysis cannot be done by any one person or unit. It is not the job of the in-house counsel. It is not the job of the marketing team. It is not the job of the inventor. It involves all of them and others who are given the role of securing the strategic direction of the organization. In some instances, this review process will involve assessment of the trends and opportunities associated with particular markets and geographic regions. This cost–benefit analysis encompasses a focus on where costs can be trimmed. Looking at where the expenses are incurred in a manner consistent with good financial management will maximize the value of the "good" IP. Is the organization using too many IP advisers? Can the organization use fewer advisers who have systems to provide the organization with consistent quality information about its IP assets and usage? Can the registration systems be synchronized across geographic regions to achieve economies of scale?

SELECTING INTELLECTUAL PROPERTY TO COMMERCIALIZE

It is not unusual to find an organization that has an IP portfolio but without a strategy to maximize the utility of that IP portfolio. This is more likely to be the case where the organization has followed a "research push" approach to creation of its IP. In these circumstances, the organization is faced with a dilemma of identifying which IP will be commercialized. If the organization has undertaken a market pull approach then it may nevertheless be necessary to reconfirm the commercialization strategy and give priority to other forms of IP that have been developed through the course of the research program.

The organization should assess the various forms of IP like any other assets used in its business. Which of them will enable it to achieve its objectives? These questions may include the following:

1. Will the commercialization of the IP enable the organization to achieve and maintain a competitive advantage? Will the IP enable the organization to distinguish itself from its competitors?
2. Will it enable the organization to acquire market share?
3. Will the IP enable the organization to position itself for further strategic moves?
4. Does it have the best cost/risk/benefit analysis?
5. Will it enable it to achieve a broader public policy objective such as being for the benefit of India?

Indeed, in some circumstances, it may not be better to commercialize the IP at all but to squirrel it away until other technology is developed that may present new opportunities. Alternatively, keeping quiet about IP may help the organization maintain a competitive position if it believes its competitors would be able to quickly catch up in the technology race once they become aware of the new development engineered by the organization.

The selection of IP assets for commercialization must be undertaken against clearly defined criteria. That criterion may vary over time as the strategic direction of the organization evolves. It may vary according to the nature of the IP. It may depend on the success or failure of previous commercialization activities or on the budgetary restraints of the organization.

If the objectives of commercialization are broader than merely generating revenue then the above criteria may need to be revisited. In particular, public sector organizations will have other influences to consider because their roles are designed to deliver outcomes for the "public good." For such agencies, the following criteria may be relevant:

1. Applying the technology for the benefit of the community
2. Application of the technology by industry or the community
3. Facilitation of alliances with other organizations.

The criteria most often posing difficulty will be assessing the market potential for the technology. This investigation ordinarily involves understanding the factors that will influence the demand for the technology, including and understanding the factors that may influence the supply of the technology. Obtaining the information to assess these factors can be difficult; for most businesses, access to accurate information is the Holy Grail. Accordingly, the organization will need to use its business networks and may need to engage consultants to investigate the relevant markets, particularly overseas markets.

It may be appropriate to apply weightings to the IP evaluation criteria to enable a ranking of the IP assets for commercialization objectives. The criteria should then be assessed against an estimate of the costs that may be involved in achieving the commercialization objectives including further development, consultancy, legal, and accounting services, protection of IP or dealing with IP litigation. Finally, the organization should assess the risks of commercialization of the IP asset, which may include threat of competitive actions such as litigation, failure to retain key staff, failure to secure the IPRs in the technology or the opportunity being lost due to delay.

How America Online (AOL) Managed Its Unutilized IP: A Case Study

In February 2012, Starboard Value LP, a major shareholder of AOL, wrote a letter to the board of AOL highlighting the fact that AOL had a robust portfolio of 800 extremely valuable and foundational patents, which was unrecognized and underutilized. The 800 odd patent portfolio covered Internet technologies that focused in areas such as secure data transit, e-commerce, travel navigation, search-related online advertising, and so on. The letter further stated that private companies specializing in monetization and valuation of IP advised Starboard that AOL's patents might be infringed by various leading IT companies. The letter was taken due note of by the AOL board and within a matter of few months, the AOL board announced that it had sold its 800 patents to Microsoft for US$1 billion along with the right to license a further 300 patents. Microsoft in turn sold 650 of these patents to Facebook for US$550 million.[15]

This example shows how a company of the size of AOL managed its underutilized IP portfolio and gained financially.

Microsoft's Kinect Entertainment System: A Case Study

Microsoft's development of its Kinect Entertainment System presents a very interesting example. Kinect allows individuals to interact with the company's gaming console Xbox 360 without a game controller, using only gestures and spoken commands. Microsoft sold around 8 million units in the first 60 days following Kinect's launch, making it one of the fastest-selling consumer electronics devices. Throughout the development of Kinect, IP specialists worked closely with technology leaders and business executives to position the device in the marketplace. The team started out by producing a map that showed potential points of differentiation for the new product. In evaluating each of these points, the company considered both the benefits created for consumers as well as the IP implications. By the time the product was launched, Microsoft had filed 600 patents to protect Kinect related innovations. Most important of all, the company was able to avoid areas with an abundance of existing patents, reducing the likelihood of future legal disputes.

> **Microsoft had filed 600 patents to protect Kinect related innovations.**

> **Microsoft's trademark, copyright and trade secrets group worked closely with the marketing team to develop the new brand.**

[15] Joff Wild, "A slowly turning tide" 2013 IP Value (11th Edition, Intellectual Asset Management) at 8.

Similar to its integration of IP and R&D activities, Microsoft's trademark, copyright and trade secrets group worked closely with the marketing team to develop the new brand. The company had initially considered 90 names, testing them with consumers and conducting worldwide trademark searches at the same time. In the end, only eight names were shortlisted, Microsoft completed an international trademark clearance process, seeking around 100 independent legal opinions from multiple jurisdictions. The company eventually filed trademark applications for four names. Marketing research indicated that "Kinect" would receive the best response.

This example depicts that tight integration of IP management with R&D and marketing is critical for companies that develop significant technologies in-house.

Intellectual Property Management Tools

There is a range of simple things that an organization can implement to assist with the management of its IP in addition to an IP database:

1. IP awareness training gives all relevant persons within the organization an understanding of IP principles and an opportunity to transfer the respective views and knowledge.
2. Personnel and other resources are very important to maintain the databases. IP databases can become redundant very quickly.

Leadership from senior management and ultimately the chief executive is paramount to the success of any IP management strategy. Unless it has the full backing of leaders in the organization, an IP management strategy is doomed to fail. Information sharing forums help to maximize the options available to the organization in dealing with its IP assets. This entails communication between the managers, researchers, and lawyers.

The financial reporting systems also facilitate proper IP management. A standard line item in regular management reports indicating the costs of maintaining IP assets will assist the CEO and the board to weigh up whether the IP management exercise is bearing fruit for the organization.

Dow Chemicals: A Case Study

Herbert H. Dow incorporated the Dow Chemical Company in the year 1897. The first commercial production of bleach was started by this company way back in 1898. Today, Dow is a leading science and technology company that provides innovative chemical, plastic and agricultural products. As of today its annuals sales are a whopping US$30 billion. The company serves in more than 150 countries and has a wide range of market ranging from health and medicine, food, transportation, personal home care, construction and so on.

From the beginning, Dow managed its patent portfolio. As the company grew, the management of the company's jewel—that is the patent portfolio was handled by various departments of the company for example the Dow Patent Department, Inventions Department and so on.

Soon it was realized by the management of the company that the vast IP portfolio that Dow owned could be used as corporate assets. As we all know, IP means codified knowledge of an organization with legal ownership. The Dow Company defined its intangibles as *IP*, *intellectual assets*, and *intellectual capital*. IP meant the same as has been stated earlier. Intellectual asset was defined as codified knowledge providing value to the company and intellectual capital was defined as all knowledge with a potential for value.[16]

---

[16] C. W. Holsapple, *Handbook on Knowledge Management: Knowledge Directions* (New York: Springer, 2003), 493.

The moment Dow realized the potential of its intellectual assets and IP, it immediately set up Intellectual Asset Management Teams (IAMTs). These teams are generally cross-functional teams sponsored by the business leadership and representing a key technology area and value center of the business.

The job of the IAMTS is to handle the Intellectual Assets of the company and leverage the IP assets. Dow has generated immense revenue from the IAMTS and an opportunity was identified to significantly grow its licensing income through this system. By the year 2000, the licensing income had increased from US$25 million in 1994 to US$60 million.

In the 21st century, the strategy of Dow has changed. It now leverages from its intellectual capital; therefore, it has set up the Intellectual Capital Management (ICM) Program. In the year 2000, the first ICM program was initiated for a product named Polyruethane. In its ICM model, DOW has three components working side by side:[17]

1. Organizational capital, which includes business models, hardware, software, databases, patents, trademarks, copyrights, and other codified knowledge.
2. Human capital, which includes knowledge, experience, innovativeness and problem solving abilities of each individual in the organization.
3. External capital has all the characteristics of an open innovation approach. In this component, the company ties up with strategic partners, investors, communities, suppliers and so on.

ICM represents all value adding knowledge embodied in its work force, processed including IP, and so on, whereas IAM represent the value creating and extracting component. ICM is the

[17] Julie L. Davis and Suzanne S. Harrison, *Edison in the Boardroom—How Leading Companies Realize Value From Their Intellectual Assets* (London: John Wiley, 2001), 154–155.

next logical step in managing intangibles beyond IAM for Dow Chemicals.[18]

By adopting an IAM program and an ICM program, Dow has benefitted immensely. Managing intangibles with the help of the IAM and ICM has had a measurable impact on the company's income and growth.[19]

Sharon Oriel, director of the IAM Center, puts it correctly that the organization is beginning to see itself not as a chemical company but as a knowledge company.[20] This is how a company of the size of Dow manages its intangible assets.

As discussed in the preceding chapters as well as in this chapter, the value chain of IP that begins from innovation and ends in commercialization is very much vital for organizations in today corporate day and age. Companies across the world have adopted different types of IP strategies as discussed, in order to reap in huge financial benefits as well as market monopoly. Companies have become more vigilant vis-à-vis their IP, by adopting strategies that shape their organizations' next moves. This chapter would be incomplete if we did not discuss one of the recent trends prevailing in the corporate world on dealing with an organization's IP portfolio. The next section discusses the emerging approach of managing an IP portfolio of a company by establishing a separate IP holding company.

IP HOLDING COMPANY

An IP holding company (IPHC) is a separate set up of a parent company wherein the parent company transfers all its IP Assets to the IPHC to reduce the burden of taxation and for the purposes of corporate restructuring. In today's dynamic environment of

---

[18] Ibid., 155.

[19] Ibid., 157.

[20] Julie L. Davis and Suzanne S. Harrison, *Edison in the Boardroom—How Leading Companies Realize Value From Their Intellectual Assets* (London: John Wiley, 2001), 158.

business, IP is the most precious asset of any company without which it has no existence or future.

IPHCs are also set up in tax havens. This serves the following purposes:

1. Centralized management of R&D activities, thereby ensuring efficiency in management of IP
2. Corporate restructuring
3. Easier licensing permissions
4. Helps in expansion of market share and exploration of new markets
5. Unification of legal costs
6. Administrative synergies
7. Tax savings

Example: In 2009, fast food giant McDonalds Corp. shifted its European head office from the United Kingdom to Switzerland to benefit from favorable taxation slabs present there for IP.

Modus Operandi

1. A parent corporation creates a separate holding company/ offshore company to hold IP and other assets for the benefit of other subsidiary operating companies of a group or third parties.
2. By doing so, the IP is essentially cordoned off from legal claims filed by the clients and business partners of the operating companies, which exploit the IP. Thus, it is the group member and not the IPHC that has entered into contractual relationship with the third parties regarding the sale of product or a service, which are sold under the terms of the license agreement with the IPHC.
3. Also, since the IPHC is a nontrading concern, it does not have any contractual relationship with any of the third parties directly; it becomes next to impossible for any third party or user to bring a claim against the IPHC.

4. Also, by bundling all the IP in a centralized set-up no subsidiary-operating company can deprive another subsidiary-operating company of the same parent to have access to the IP vested in them, thereby ensuring efficiency, timely decisions, and no management tussles.

CONCLUSION

Whether an IPHC is right for your company will depend on a number of factors, including your company's management structure and the states and/or the foreign jurisdictions where your company sells its products. Many companies have found that setting up and operating an IPHC has resulted in substantial tax savings, increased efficiency in managing IP assets, and separation of those assets from other company liabilities. In many situations—especially if an offshore company will own the IP assets—it is most beneficial to establish the IPHC before the IP assets are legally created.

5 Brand Protection and Management

A brand is not a product. It is the sum total of everything a company does—the good, the bad and even the off strategy—that creates a large context or an identity in the consumer's mind.[1]
—*Scott Bedburry, Formerly with Nike and Starbucks.*

After reading this chapter, you will be able to

- The importance of a brand to an organization
- The purpose of having brands
- The various elements of branding strategy
- The characteristics involved while selecting a brand
- The importance of protecting the brand
- The meaning of brand positioning and communicating the brand
- The importance of brand audits and brand licensing

"Brand" has become a motif that captures whole series of concepts. A brand is a trademark. A brand at its narrowest refers to the mark used by an organization to distinguish its goods and services from its competitors. This chapter concentrates on the marks or logos that an organization uses to distinguish its goods or services from those of its competitors.

The value of brands can be many times more than all the physical assets owned by the organization and Coca-Cola is perhaps the

---

[1] "Great Quotes on Branding", available at http://www.thinkmktg.com/index. php/weblog/comments/great_quotes_on_branding.

most prominent example. According to Interbrand, Coca-Cola's brand value in 2013 was US$79.2 billion.[2] The technology on which Coca-Cola's business was founded is nothing more than a recipe. The company has a brilliant process for nurturing and safe guarding secrets and building upon the competitive edge that flows from the recipe and the brand magic associated with the product.

Another example of a company that has a brand value worth billions is Apple Inc. It is the needless to mention that the brand value of Apple has been boosted because of the recent success of the Apple iPhone 4 and iPhone 5 as well as the iPad 2. The brand value of Apple Inc. in May 2011 was at an all time high of US$153.3 billion beating Google Inc., which had a brand value of US$111.5 billion.[3]

In recent years, there has been an increasing focus on whether organizations are recognizing the value of their brands, as with other forms of IP. In the United Kingdom, for example, a survey showed that one-third of respondents identified their corporate trademarks as the most important type of IP.[4]

PURPOSE OF BRANDS

Brands[5] can be used to promote the business as a whole or specific products or services. A brand may be used to promote a particular form of technology, which is not necessarily related to a product or service. The primary aim is to provide recognition

---

[2] Best Global Brands 2013 available at http://www.interbrand.com/en/best-global-brands/2013/Best-Global-Brands-2013.aspx.

[3] "Apple Brand Value at $153 Billion Overtakes Google for Top Spot" available at http://www.bloomberg.com/news/2011-05-09/apple-brand-value-at-153-billion-overtakes-google-for-top-spot.html.

[4] Pricewaterhousecoopers and Landwell, "UK Intellectual Property Survey 2002" available at http://www.landwellglobal.com/images/uk/eng/custom/uk_downloads/ip%20survey.pdf.

[5] J. Thomas McCarthy, *MC.Carthy on Trademarks and Unfair Competition*, 4th Edition. Vol I. (n.p.: Thomson Reuters, 2001) Para 4.18.

to the organization and its products or services, and to create a positive impact on the mind of its customers. This in turn will induce (directly or indirectly and consciously or subconsciously) the client to select the organization's products or services ahead of a competitor. This generates revenue and profits that satisfies the interests of shareholders, investors, and other stakeholders

Having brands is a means to differentiate a company's products and services from those of its competitors. Evidence shows that customers will pay a substantial price premium for a good brand and remain loyal to that brand.[6]

A well-known brand can give to the organization an opportunity to set premium prices for its products or services, attract a greater degree of "repeat business," attract new clients or introduce new products or services. Brands can present licensing opportunities for the purposes of driving additional revenue from associated or even unrelated products or services. In fact, the licensing of a brand may be a defensive measure.

So an organization that has established a well-known brand can be better placed to drive revenue for its business. Leveraging those brands becomes another form of commercialization of the organization's IP.

Elements of Branding

The selection and building of a brand comprises many elements. At the outset (a) the management of brands should be understood in the light of the business of the organization as a whole and (b) the strategy to be applied for the communication of brands will vary according to the fluctuations encountered by the organization over time. Not only must (c) the organization understand what the client desires or demands; it must also form a view as to whether the organization wants to be positioned to fulfill that desire or demand. This inherently involves an understanding of

---

[6] "Introduction to Brands" available at http://tutor2u.net/business/marketing/brands_introduction.asp.

Figure 5.1 Elements of Brand Strategy

whether other organizations are already fulfilling those desires or demands and deciding whether those competitors are doing it better than the organization itself. (d) The objective of the brand and the brand strategy should be designed to assist the organization to distinguish, in the mind of the client, the organization, its products or services from its competitors (Figure 5.1).

HP introduced the "Invent" slogan as part of its brand to emphasize that it was a "smart" company, not just a seller of IT hardware. The brand value of HP in 2011 was US$35.4 billion.[7] Semiconductor chip giant Intel introduced the "Intel inside" slogan to achieve greater recognition from all of those consumers who touched a product that relied on Intel's semiconductor chips. It left the consumer with the impression that if the PC did not have the slogan then the PC must be lacking something. The brand value of Intel in 2011 was US$13.9 billion.[8]

> HP introduced the "Invent" slogan as part of its brand to emphasize that it was a "smart" company, not just a seller of IT hardware.

[7] Supra Note 1.
[8] Ibid.

Jack Trout, in his book *Big Brands Big Trouble*, writes[9] whether any brand strategy is successful depends on the objective of the strategy. The strategies would become more varied and multi-layered as an organization grows. The ultimate corporate strategy of delivering profit for shareholders depends on a wide range of factors. The management team bears the responsibility of assessing the importance of those factors at different times in the life of the organization. The importance of the brand in those phases will vary.

The importance of brands needs to be kept in perspective. The success of any brand is intricately linked with the success of the business itself and the reputation of those who are responsible for managing the organization. There is not much point in ploughing thousands of dollars into a brand development unless the business has the fundamentals to succeed.

What Is to Be Branded?

The form of brands that can be protected as registered trademarks is very broad. Is the brand to be applied to the organization as a whole, a product or service or a combination of all of them? Is there good reason to distinguish between them? These questions will reoccur as the organization grows, expands its client base and identifies new opportunities that are related to its core business.

Using an existing well-known brand for a new product or service can give a springboard into the new activity. There may be efficiencies gained from being able to market multiple activities under one campaign. It obviously avoids the time and expense of creating new brands. There are of course risks to such "brand extension". If the new activity is not successful, the value or goodwill of the brand may be damaged. If the new activity is in a field different to the traditional activities of the organization, there may be confusion in the marketplace about the message that is

[9] Jack Trout, Big *Brands Big Trouble—Lessons Learned the Hard Way* (n.p.: John Wiley & Sons, 2002), 182–185.

associated with the brand. From a commercialization perspective, sticking with the existing brand also means that the organization is not building its portfolio of IP, which in turn may result in lost opportunities to achieve other leveraging opportunities such as through licensing or assignments of the IP.

Selection of the Brand

The following five characteristics are critical to a successful brand:

1. **Memorable.** It should be short; easy to say and write; easily pronounceable. This may entail the selection of a catchy name but also the use of logos, mascots slogans, packaging, or personalities. The essence of a trademark is that it is some distinctive thing that points out that the goods are the goods of a particular organization. This was a decided in a very famous English case way back in 1891.[10]
2. **Available and protectable.** A brand should be available in the market, which means that it is not in use by any other organization. Moreover, that brand should be easily protectable.
3. **Transferable.** Portable across product, geographic and cultural boundaries so that the organization can implement consistent strategies and marketing campaigns to meet a range of market opportunities.
4. **Adaptable for new trends.** Names and logos that may capture the "cult" of a certain period of time may forever be linked to that period and instead take on an "old fashioned" feel.
5. **Meaningful.** In the sense that it is credible, having regard to the nature of the organization's business without being too descriptive to jeopardize the protection afforded to the brand. Choosing the name of an animal for a brand name, such as "Puma," will presumably conjure in a person's mind the positive characteristic that is associated with the animal.

---

[10] *Richard v. Butcher*, (1891) 2 Ch. 522.

Sony: The Brand Was Born: A Case Study

The selection of "Sony" by the Japanese technology giant illustrates some of the above principles. Until 1958, the company's name was Tokyo Tsushin Kogyo or was known by its English equivalent of "Tokyo Telecommunications Engineering Company." The name was recognized by its leaders to be difficult to pronounce and was unknown at that time outside of Japan. Management recognized that the U.S. was its key future market. It considered "TTK" but most of its international competitors used abbreviations such as IBM, RCA, and AT&T. One of the founders of the company, Akio Morita, took the Latin word for sound, *sonnus,* and combined it with an English expression he had heard, "sonny-boy", that to him conveyed attributes of youthful energy and irreverence that was consistent with his visions for the company. Morita's pronunciation of the "o" was short rather than the longer "o" pronounced by speakers of English. Thus, the name Sony and the brand was born.[11]

Dell: A Case Study

Dell has made a mark in branding and advertising. It has always been a smart branding company. Since its inception, its advertising and branding has been easily identifiable and focused on the key purchase factors. Dell is very sophisticated in its brand strategy and market research. On its web site, note the short phrases that cover the top purchase factors for each product. These phrases communicate to the product and the brand as a whole to the customers.[12] Dell is using one of the elements of branding strategies (Figure 5.1) to communicate to the customers about the various products available.

---

[11] J. Nathan, *Sony: The Private Life* (New York: Houghton Mifflin Harcourt, 1999), 52–53.
[12] www.dell.com

"Dell is positioning the retail channel as stressful, expensive, limited in selection, compared to its direct selling model."[13] The Dell tagline remains *"Easy as Dell."*

Protecting the Brand

A foundation plank in any branding strategy is to ensure that the brand is protected. As a general rule, laid down under the Trade Marks Act,[14] the organization should avoid names that are descriptive of the goods and services in which it trades while selecting a brand. As laid down under Section 9(1)(b), the brands should avoid geographic names that indicate the origins of the product or service because any person can use a geographic name in that manner. If geographical names are used then the trademarks registry has the authority to refuse the registration under Section 9(1)(b) itself.

There are many examples of organizations that use initials in their brands. In fact, it is hard to successfully obtain trademark registration for personal names. The practice of the registry in this regard has been to require evidence of distinctiveness before acceptance of the application for registration.[15] In the Bombay High court decision,[16] it was held that the word "Sulekha," according to its ordinary significance is a female's personal name and was properly registered on evidence of distinctiveness. The objection of the hearing officer that the "Sulekha" in respect of fountain pens was distinctive was overruled.

More often than not organizations have to show an already established reputation to succeed in obtaining trademark registration for

---

[13] Todd Wasserman, "New Ads a 'Go' for Dell", *Brand Week Magazine*, November 24, 2003, available at http://www.allbusiness.com/marketing-advertising/branding-brand-development/4680540-1.html.

[14] Section 9, Trade Marks Act 1999.

[15] K. C. Kailasam and Ramu Vedaraman, *Law of Trade Marks & Geographical Indications, Law, Practice and Procedure*, 2nd edition (Nagpur: Wadhwa and Company, 2005), 108.

[16] In *Mehta v. Registrar of Trade Marks*, AIR 1962 Bom. 82.

initials. From a trademark protection perspective, this is not ideal for an organization that is still in its infancy. To maximize the chances of securing a registered trademark, organizations should think of common names not associated with products or services or invent new names. At the end of the day, the mark should be distinctive.

Avoiding Similarities

The selection of an appropriate brand must address the legal pitfalls. A brand should not be similar to any existing brand or else the organization may be at risk of violating the Trade Marks Act, or the tort of Passing Off.

This can become an expensive exercise where the organization that spent money on graphic designers, other consultants in developing the brand, stationery, and media and advertising costs only to find that another person/organization can obtain an injunction. In a worst case, it may have to pay extra money for damages because of the unauthorized use of another person's brand.

These pitfalls emphasize the need to undertake thorough searches before adopting a brand. An organization should search the following information resources and seek advice on the results of those searches:

1. Trademarks register; laid down under Section 6 of the Trade Marks Act of 1999
2. Domain names register
3. General Internet search
4. Trade and telephone directories
5. Brand compilation publications
6. Companies register; Section 147 and 148 of the Companies Act
7. Business names registers

A brand encompasses a copyright work and the organization should seek consent from the author for the use of the brand because, without that consent, such use may otherwise infringe the author's moral rights.

Some Names Cannot Be Used As Brands

The Trade Marks Act provides for grounds for refusal of registration of trademark/brand in the course of business. Certain names are unacceptable for registration under Sections 9 and 11 of the Trade Marks Act. This will limit the names that can be selected for the brand of the organization.

Securing Ownership

The ownership of IP in any drawing and logos, to the extent copyright exists, will be owned by the author. The law is laid down under Section 17 of the Copyright Act 1957. Any organization engaging a graphic designer to assist with the development of a brand must ensure that the contract transfers ownership of any copyright or other IPRs to the organization together with the relevant warranties and indemnities.

Who Is the Target Audience for a Branding Strategy?

The most important aspect in brand strategy is the target. The first question that every organization should ask itself is who is the target audience Once the target audience is found, the brand should be selected and the product marketed. The entrepreneur should have a clear view about its intended market for the technology, goods or services. This will directly impact on the selection of the brand, the message that the organization intends to associate with the brand, and how that message is communicated. It should also be noted that there should be a common or core thread attached to the brand that applies to any audience otherwise there is a risk of fragmentation of the goodwill in the brand which reduces the effect and value of the brand.

Important

The two key brand management principles with regard to target audience are

1. Positioning determining what you want your brand to be
2. Communication creating an expectation in the customer's mind of what the brand is all about

---

Within each category of audience, the strategy may be different. Customers located in different countries may react in different ways to a brand or the method of communication because of cultural differences. Entry into foreign markets presents its own idiosyncratic challenges. Should the domestic brand be used? Should a new brand name be formed?

The audience may be segmented within a class dictated by price or quality. An organization may wish to be present in all or many segments of the market. In these circumstances, the organization may establish a hierarchy of brands that enables the organization to leverage off the goodwill associated with an established brand as well as differentiate within the field of goods or services.

The strategy to improve brand awareness by staff of the organization may be driven by the need to avoid inconsistent use of the brand from within the organization that may impact on how the customers hear or see the use of the brand at a day-to-day level. Alternatively, the brand strategy may be designed to encourage the morale and values of the staff. When IBM sought to reestablish itself in the personal computer field it published 8,000 copies of *The Spirit and Letter of IBM Brand Identity* for internal distribution. It set out the principles of the IBM identity. A key strategic benefit was to overcome the inconsistent use of the IBM mark that had developed over many years.[17]

---

[17] Alex Simonson and Bernd H. Schmitt, *Marketing Aesthetics: The Strategic Management of Brands, Identity and Image* (New York: Free Press, 1997), 55–57.

BRAND POSITIONING

What is the message that the organization wants to send to its audience associated with the brand? What "feel" does the organization want the client to associate with the brand? This may be related to the margins that the organization wishes to achieve. Big Bazaar Stores (Future Group) aims at the low-priced, high-volume retail assorted goods market. Mercedes Benz aims at the high-price, low-volume car consumer. Both are recognized as premier in their respective markets. An organization that seeks to expand into new markets must assess whether its existing brand can "carry" it to the position it wants to establish in the new market. Where the brand has established an association centered on quality in a field it is unlikely to use the same brand in a similar field but for a different level of quality good or service. If the field is totally different then there may be strategic benefits in extending the brand.

Lenovo/IBM and Brand Positioning: A Case Study

Lenovo, which has acquired the PC division of IBM, is benefitting from the brand position that IBM had while it manufactured PCs. With the addition of the IBM brand to its portfolio, Lenovo has been provided the luxury of being able to differentiate in its service and industry leadership without incurring the costs of establishing the high-value, skilled-labor operation of IBM. Lenovo purchased the PC division of IBM by paying almost US$1.2 billion dollars. Much of this value clearly stems out from the IBM brand rather than its tangible assets. The IBM brand is a blessing for Lenovo as it removes the barrier to Lenovo's products outside the People's Republic of China. It now seems a more reliable and trustworthy technology company, even to customers who are fully aware of the fact that the PC division is now with Lenovo and not with IBM. Merely a stamp of approval from such a highly respected company like IBM means a lot to the customers in any market in the world.[18]

[18] Chris Grannell, "IBM Reboots", February 7, 2005, available at http://www.brandchannel.com/features_profile.asp?pr_id=217.

Nike and Its Brand Positioning: A Case Study

As advertising consultant Scott Bedburry writes in his book *A New Brand World*, Nike reinvented its marketing and products to a great extent. The Nike brand became a category protagonist for competitive sports and fitness. Nike advertising took thousands of approaches for its core brand positioning during the time of Bedburry's tenure in Nike. The company's advertising department was constantly on the move by refreshing the marketing and brand positioning. Nike's design became one of the world's premier product design. It introduced newer products in the markets at regular intervals and at such frequency that the average product life cycle fell from one year to just three months.[19] By this move Nike made sure that its brand was quite well positioned in the market.

COMMUNICATING THE BRAND

Internet Implications

The advent of the Internet may be seen by many as introducing a new era for branding and that it should entail a different strategy with new names and new legal challenges. Does the Internet medium require a different profile than would be required in an offline environment? As brands are dictated by the objectives of the organization, the answer will largely be determined by the role of the Internet in the business model of the organization. For some products that embody IP, such as books and software, the Internet presents a new distribution method. For organizations that generate revenue by relying on the provision of services that exploit the know-how of individuals, the Internet may only present a new channel for communication.

The number of domain sites now available adds greater complexity to branding through the Internet. It raises challenges for protecting the brand from cyber squatting as greater number of

---

[19] Scott Bedburry, *A New Brand World* (New York: Penguin, 2003), 4.

domains can be used to register a domain name that uses existing brands. It has been estimated that a major organization will need to register at least 300 name variants to protect its core brands. Of course, the breadth of choice may give organizations with a portfolio of brands an opportunity to spread its brand recognition. Historically, an organization has had to make a choice as to which of its brands it wants to use for an online environment.

McDonalds initially chose to use "McD.com" as its domain name and was caught out when a journalist from *Wired* magazine registered "McDonalds." This resulted in a settlement that saw McDonalds fund PCs for a New York school to retrieve the McDonalds' domain name.[20]

The use of metatags enables web sites to be found by users of the Internet. This has opened the door for competitors to attract customers and improve the level of awareness of brands. It also has potential legal risks. If the metatag is in fact another person's trademark or brand there is a risk that the true trademark owner may sue for trademark infringement or deceptive conduct. In the U.S, courts have however, held that unauthorized use of trademarks in metatags is contrary to U.S. trademark law.[21] Under Indian law, there is some doubt as to whether such conduct would give rise to liability. It is important to note that there is no case law on metatags that has been decided by any courts in India.

In the age of the Internet, it is quite common to use hyperlinks between web sites. The growth of the Internet has led to a numerous brands establishing their foothold in the virtual sphere. Companies use hyperlinks that have their brand names included, so as to make people click on the various web sites to generate traffic and sell products. So far, Indian courts have not come across any case that involves the hyperlinks of companies, which constitute trademark infringement. Again, the test will be whether there is a likelihood of confusion. If the link has the effect of directing

[20] J. Quittner, (1994). "Billions Registered, Wired," available at http://www.wired.com/wired/archive/2.10/mcdonarlds.html.

[21] *Brookfield Communications, Inc v. West Coat Entertainment Corp.*, 174 F 3d 1036 (9th Cir April 22, 1999).

the user to another person's site then there is unlikely to be confusion or even use "as a trademark." If, however, the link causes the user to be directed to a competitor then there may be greater scope to argue that a user could be misled. Much will depend on the presentation of the competitor's web site.

Managing the Brand

Having established a brand for the organization or its products or services, the onus remains on management of the organization to maintain the support for the brand. Generally, this involves three principles:

Important

1. Consistent use of the brand—not changing the structure of the core elements of the brand unless such change is dictated by a change to the parameters for the business of the organization
2. Consistent use of the message, values or attributes that are associated with the brand
3. Ensuring that the marketing and business activities and the message that staff issue to the market reinforce the "brand position." The form that this reinforcement takes depends in large part on the nature of the business, how competitors also seek to respond to the organization's marketing and business successes or failures and external impacts on the business of the organization.

Management of the brand involves all persons who take part in the business of the organization. Poor performance by people or the products will adversely affect the brand.

We all know that Coca-Cola is one of most popular brands on the face of the planet. However, in spite of having a strong brand, the Coca-Cola management has felt that change is necessary. The Coca-Cola Company has followed the three principles mentioned above on how to manage brands. The corporate culture involving a super-brand like Coke can result in managers becoming over-confident in the product as well as the processes and procedures that have built up throughout the company over time. The danger is that the public will simply get bored with the brand.[22]

Therefore, the Coca-Cola Company has undergone radical changes over the years. When Chief Executive Robert Goizueta was at the helm of affairs, he demonstrated that the company was earning less than its cost of capital. Therefore, he led Coca-Cola through a great change in management structure. By adjusting the way the businesses and managers were assessed and by radically reforming key relationships with Coca-Cola bottlers, Goizueta oversaw a spectacular improvement in performance.[23]

Responsibility for Management of Brands

The importance of the brand to the organization will have a necessary impact on who has responsibility for its management and key decisions on how the brand is used. It is more likely that senior executives and the CEO will be intimately involved in the development of the strategy for use of the brand where the brand has a direct and significant impact on the revenue of the organization. Companies such as Coca-Cola that has intangible assets representing 92 percent of its market capitalization are more likely to involve a CEO or other senior managers in strategies for its use.[24]

---

[22] Edward De Bono and Robert Heller, "Thinking Managers, Coca Cola Management", available at http://www.thinkingmanagers.com/companies/coca-cola.php.

[23] Ibid.

[24] Ibid. Also see "The Coca-Cola Company (KO), Balance Sheet of the Year 2008", available at http://finance.yahoo.com/q/bs?s=KO&annual.

6 Intellectual Property Risk Management

To identify and then manage threats that could severely impact or bring down the organization is known as Risk Management.

After reading this chapter, you will be able to

- Understand the concept of risk management
- Understand what does risk management do to an organization
- Understand specific risks relating to IP such as commercialization, and so on
- Understand the meaning and types of IP insurance

An organization should never be in an illusion that it is shielded from any risk. The concept of managing risk has been in practice for quite some time. An organization commercializing its IP has to see whether its IP is well protected from any risk.

The management of risk emphasizes on placing priorities on the objectives, projects, and actions in a manner that achieves the desired outcomes and hopefully minimizes the chances of failure. In the context of commercialization of IP, this can relate to entering into a joint venture arrangement, a licensing or assignment deal, undertaking an initial public offer (IPO) or obtaining venture capital investment. In these scenarios, the organization and the parties it will deal with will each go through a risk management exercise, either consciously or unconsciously. The focus of risk management as a separate distinct consideration assists the organization to make balanced judgments and limits the chances of not considering fatal risks.

According to Professor Mark S. Beasley, professor of accounting and director of the Enterprise Risk Management Initiative at North Carolina State University, "Financial executives and businesses are beginning to embrace the concepts of organization risk management, but implementation and effectiveness are still in their infancy."[1]

According a recent survey[2] by the Liberty International Underwriters (LIU) and Marsh, it is surprising to note "that three-quarters of risk management and insurance professionals did not know a rough percentage contribution of intangible assets to the business," which is serious cause for concern and needs to be addressed within the four walls of the organization.

> **Three-quarters of risk management and insurance professionals did not know a rough percentage contribution of intangible assets to the business.**

ORGANIZATION RISK MANAGEMENT: WHAT DOES IT DO?[3]

Let us first understand what risk management within an organization does?

1. It makes the manager of every department of the organization responsible for evaluating financial controls and handling documents that are in his or her department. By managing data like this would improve accuracy and completeness.
2. It identifies departments that have inadequate controlling measures so that plans can be initiated to resolve problems.

[1] Stephen Taub, "Risk Management: More Talk Than Action," June 23, 2006, available at http://www.cfo.com/article.cfm/7104872?f=search.

[2] The 2011 Intellectual Property Survey Report produced by LIU and Marsh available at http://uk.marsh.com/NewsInsights/FeaturedContent/The2011IntellectualPropertySurveyReport.aspx.

[3] John Verity, "Risk Management," November 17, 2003, available at http://www.cfo.com/article.cfm/3010975?f=search.

3. It tracks the progress of outstanding action plans and also describes who is responsible for those actions and sets the expected time for resolution. This helps in motivating the staff.
4. It ensures systematic data management that ensure multiple reviews and verification.

For an adequate risk management plan to be developed and be successful, the persons who carry out the actions need to be given some ownership in the development process of the risk management. If it involves technical expertise, be it scientific, legal or financial, then persons with that particular background should be involved. The decision makers, who will take ultimate responsibility for the success or failure of the plan, must understand and approve the risk management plan. This seems to mean that a great number of people must be involved in activities but this is not necessary in some instances. Often the number of people involved in the development of a risk management plan can be distilled down to a handful of individuals.

For the purposes of the commercialization of IP, the process can be confined to a simple methodology that picks up the fundamental elements of the Indian standard.

A risk management process can be limited to the following five tasks:

1. Set or recognize objectives for the IP project.
2. List the potential risks arising from that project. These may be technical, financial, legal, commercial, political or administrative.
3. Plot the risk on a qualitative risk chart applying the measures of the risk set out in the Indian standard. The Indian standard identifies five qualitative measures each for consequence or impact for risk and the measures of likelihood of risk. If the purpose of the risk management analysis is to identify the critical and significant risks arising from an IP commercialization project then there is no reason why these measures cannot be reduced for ease of analysis.

4. Identify the options for treating those risks.
5. Identity the responsibilities for implementing those actions, who will perform them and the time frames for the performance of those actions.

This process gives the organization a risk management or project plan together with a risk register. It provides a guide to the lawyers who are tasked with the responsibility of preparing legal documentation to address risks. It forms the foundation for briefing of the board, and can be used to address queries from audit committees, auditors, stakeholders, and external queries, for example, parliamentary committees for public sector bodies.

SPECIFIC RISKS RELATING TO INTELLECTUAL PROPERTY

Legal Issues

There are some obvious legal risks arising from commercialization of IP:

1. The organization does not in fact own or adequately control of IP that is to be commercialized. This may not only prevent the commercialization project from proceeding but also may result in it being terminated.
2. Failing to apply for, or properly monitor or manage, the registration of IP.
3. Risk of another party claiming rights in the IP and taking infringement action against the organization. This has consequences not only for the completion of a deal but may also result in paying damages and tainting the reputation of the organization. In a worse case, it can spell doom for the whole of the business, and may cause investors to withdraw from the organization even though the claim for IP infringement may not be successful against the organization.

> **The total cost to Kodak for its ill-managed risk strategy was more than US$1 billion**

An example of another party claiming rights in IP can be the historic patent dispute between Kodak and Polaroid over the instant photography business. Kodak ignored the patent wall that Polaroid, a much smaller competitor, had built around its growing instant camera business. As discussed earlier in the book, Kodak, ignoring the patents of its much smaller rival, launched a line of instant cameras and films in 1975, which bore identical resemblance to Polaroid's cameras and films. Polaroid sued Kodak and after a 15-year legal battle, won the case against Kodak. The total cost to Kodak for its ill-managed risk strategy was more than US$1 billion, which also included legal fees of over US$100 million and led to a loss of a decade's worth of R&D. All this would not have taken place had Kodak employed a robust risk management strategy and keeping a close watch on its competitors in the market, loss of IPRs such as the failure to renew trademark registration, properly monitor applications or retain sufficient evidence of creation of the technology.

There have been many cases decided by the Indian courts that have dealt with IP damages, which is a genuine risk when dealing with IP. The risk of IP damages can run into lakhs of rupees if the IP has been infringed upon or has not been duly protected. As seen in the case of *Microsoft Corporation vs Ms. K. Mayuri and Ors*,[4] where Microsoft was involved in litigation with one Ms. Mayuri. The dispute was regarding unauthorized hard disk loading of Microsoft's software on the hardware assembled and sold by Ms. Mayuri. When this was brought to the notice of Microsoft, it filed a copyright infringement case against Ms. Mayuri and the court awarded compensatory damages to the tune of ₹10 lakhs because of the sale of spurious and pirated software.

In another case that came up before the Delhi High Court,[5] Adobe Systems filed a copyright infringement case against Thinking

---

[4] 2007 (35) PTC 415 Del.
[5] CS(OS) 946/2004.

Machine Private Limited on the ground that Thinking Machine was engaged in the business of hard disk loading, that is, pre-loading various pirated and unlicensed software of Adobe free of costs on to the computers that were being assembled and sold by Thinking Machine, as an incentive to the customers to purchase the machines from them. The Delhi High Court ordered damages to the tune of ₹9.78 lakhs along with a 10 percent annual interest if the damages were not paid within 90 days of the demand by Adobe. Apart from these damages, Adobe was also entitled for the costs of the case along with the lawyers' fees of ₹50,000.

Commercial Issues

The failure or inability of staff to notify the organization of their bright ideas, innovations or creative works presents IP-centric risks for the organization. Consequences for the organization include an inability to attract investors because it does not have an adequate IP portfolio, dilution of the competitive advantage of the organization and theft or improper disclosure of IP (especially confidential information). It was reported in May 2001 that Lucent Technologies discovered that two of its staff had disclosed trade secrets related to its technologies to a competitive company based in China. The staff were arrested and it became apparent that the objective of the staff was to set up a major telecommunications company on the back of this "stolen" technology.[6] In another incident involving trade secret, three of Coca-Cola's employees stole trade secrets of Coca-Cola, including details of a new product with a liquid sample. Eventually the three employees were caught and Coca-Cola reviewed and revamped its security procedures in relation to trade secrets. In this case, world-famous Coca-Cola's

---

[6] Simon Romero, "TECHNOLOGY; F.B.I. Says 3 Stole Secrets From Lucent," May 4, 2001, available at http://www.nytimes.com/2001/05/04/business/technology-fbi-says-3-stole-secrets-from-lucent.html.

main drink secret formula was not compromised but it definitely raised issues in the corporate circles of the company.[7]

Although commercialization of IP raises issues that are not peculiar to a commercial transaction or business, it does present some issues that are idiosyncratic due to the nature of IP. Consequently, there are some risks that would be seen to arise only where IP is in issue. Now, if we look at the Internet age, exposures involving IP, privacy, and first-party risks from computer fraud, business disruption, and denial of service pose significant financial risks to companies doing business on the Internet.

Regulatory Restrictions

Commercialization of IP may be jeopardized by the existence or introduction of legislative restrictions. A topical example is the debate surrounding the use of stem cells in genetic biotechnology research. Alternatively, there may be restrictions on the online gambling industry that may impact on development and exploitation of software.

INTELLECTUAL PROPERTY INSURANCE

In the context of commercialization of IP, perhaps the most relevant form of insurance is the recently developed market for offensive and defensive IP insurance. Figures 6.1 and 6.2 explain the defensive and offensive types of insurances.

Defensive IP Insurance

In basic terms, defensive IP insurance covers an organization in the event that it is sued for unauthorized use of another person's IP.

---

[7] "Coca-Cola Trade Secrets 'Stolen'," July 6, 2006 available at http://news.bbc.co.uk/2/hi/5152740.stm.

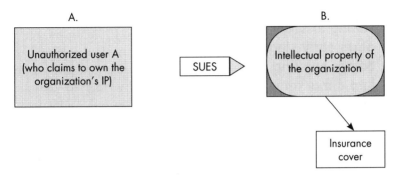

Figure 6.1 Defensive Insurance

Offensive IP Insurance

Offensive IP insurance provides a funding mechanism for the organization to take legal action against persons who use the organization's IP without authorization. The market for IP insurance is typically offered by only a handful of insurers, usually in Europe and U.S. There are some brokers in India who handle it although the use of such products is not high.

As with other forms of insurance acquiring IP insurance involves collecting and providing to the insurer, through a broker, a range of information that will enable the insurer to assess the level of risk of the cover being triggered and of course this will impact on the premium payable by the insured organization. The scope of that information gathering exercise would be expected to include

1. IP portfolio, IP valuation, and confidentiality policies
2. Procedures for identifying infringements
3. Description of business activities
4. Financial information, R&D activities, and documentation
5. Assignments and licenses
6. IP identification procedures and registration documentation
7. Description of the market

The process for obtaining IP insurance, particularly in India, is not easy. At the end of the day, the decision to take out such

> **Taking insurance at an early stage before entering into a market is often cheaper.**

expensive insurance involves a cost-benefit risk analysis. If the organization is entering into a new market where the incumbent players are known to be aggressive and willing to use the court process to keep out competitors, then IP insurance becomes an important factor. Clearly, the timing of the commercial operations and the taking out of insurance is critical. The advantages of taking out IP insurance at an early date are significant. Taking insurance at an early stage before entering into a market is often cheaper because there may be no immediate or serious prospect of litigation which would otherwise affect the premium that the insurer may charge.

Loss of Value Insurance

This form of insurance is relatively recent. It covers loss of IP value such as for losses arising from interruption of business, loss of trade secret advantage, loss of income (such as royalties or license fees) and loss of benefit of R&D expenses. These losses may be triggered by a court order restraining the use of IP by the organization even though the organization was not a party to the litigation.

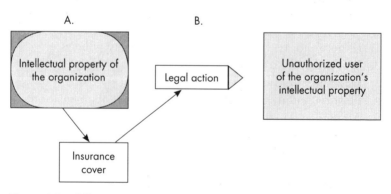

Figure 6.2 Offensive Insurance

Professional Indemnity (PI) Insurance

This is a common form of insurance covering the risks of providing advice in a professional capacity. Such insurance will often cover certain forms of IP. It is important for organizations engaging in clinical research to ensure that staff who are giving advice in relation to clinical trials are adequately insured. Where the commercialization of IP involves the transfer of expertise and the use of know-how or the developments of source code, there PI insurance will be a relevant form of insurance.

Product Liability Insurance

This covers risks arising from damages to persons or property as a consequence of goods that have been manufactured, repaired or altered. This form of insurance is relevant where a product is the end result of the R&D process. Manufacturers and distributors rather than licensors generally take out such insurance.

Directors and Officers Insurance

This covers directors and officers of a company for potential liability (such as breach of director's duties) arising under judgments or settlements and covers investigation costs, defense costs, and costs of appearing at inquiries. The organization may take out a "reimbursement policy," which covers the organization for any indemnity that it has given to directors and officers.

CONTRACTUAL ALLOCATION OF RISK

When entering into a commercial transaction the parties will consider the risks that each of them should bear with respect to the subject matter of that transaction. There are ranges of standard contractual issues that are negotiated at this point to effectively allocate those risks between the parties.

The fundamental principle applied in these negotiations should be to ask the question, "Which of the parties is in the best position to minimize or manage the specific risk?" The risk analysis undertaken will help identify the answer to this question, both in terms of the specific risk and who should be in a best position to minimize it. Once these answers are known, it is then possible to negotiate contractual terms that will reflect these principles. Of course, contractual negotiations are fundamentally an exercise of bargaining strengths. If one party refuses to bargain notwithstanding that it may be the best party to minimize a risk, then the other party may have no alternative to either accept it bears this risk under the contract or to walk away from the deal altogether.

In the IP commercialization context, some examples of situations in which risk management is required are

1. If the organization has developed a technology then it is more likely to be in the best position to minimize the risk of potential IP infringements. This will in part depend on the role of the other contracting parties. If the IP has been developed in a collaborative manner then the allocation of risk may be through mutual indemnities and releases or no indemnities at all.

2. The provision of background IP by an organization will usually result in that organization conceding warranties and indemnities concerning any risk of IP infringement actions arising from the use of that background IP. The organization in those situations is in the best position, amongst the parties, to have minimized the risk of unauthorized use in either the acquisition or development of that background IP.

3. Support and maintenance for the technology will usually result in the risk being allocated to the provider of that support or service. The risk may be in the form of loss or liability arising from the negligence of that provider.

4. The provision of genetic material normally results in risk being allocated to the provider of that material.

5. The distribution of technology will usually result in risk being allocated to the distributor arising from misuse of the product

once it takes control of the technology or the making of misrepresentations and misleading statements to consumers.

The determination of allocation of risks requires a clear understanding from the key managers involved in the negotiation of potential downstream effects and of the technical aspects relating to the technology including the circumstances surrounding its development or acquisition.

Disclaimer/Exclusion Clauses

A party to a transaction will often seek to restrict the amount of risk that it carries by disclaiming any liability for any consequences arising from its actions or otherwise excluding liability. An important factor in negotiating such a clause will be the degree of due diligence that the other party has been able to undertake with respect to the technology and the applicable IP. If the organization has enabled other parties to inspect relevant documents, such as laboratory books, then the other party may be willing to agree to the disclaimer. This is because the other party has been given an opportunity to assess its own risk and withdraw from the transaction or modify its price (if it is a purchaser or licensee) in response to what it finds from undertaking the due diligence exercise. This is quite common in the acquisition of businesses that involve transfer of technology and the assignment of IP.

A constricting factor in these circumstances is that in enabling access to the supporting documentation the commercialization of IP may entail disclosing trade secrets or at least the risk of doing so. The organization must balance the benefit to be gained from completing the transaction where the contractual terms do not include a disclaimer or risk losing its competitive advantage because it discloses to the other parties, through a due diligence process, its trade secrets or other valuable information.

Indemnities

Indemnities are perhaps one of the most contentious contractual conditions in any commercial transaction including those transactions dealing with the commercialization of IP. They are an express form all allocation of risk liability that may be owed to a third party. A reason for the often sensitive approach to indemnities by commercial parties is the breadth of the indemnity clauses. It is often easy to lose sight, and many lawyers often do, of the fact that if a party commits an unlawful act or omission then (in the absence of any other clause) it will be liable to the other contracting party to the extent that act or omission caused loss or damage. So when negotiating an indemnity clause it may be useful to go through the following analysis:

1. What is the risk that the indemnity is seeking to address? Is it clearly identified?
2. Is that risk likely to arise because of a wrongful act of the party who is being asked to give the indemnity (the "indemnifier")? This may be the negligence of the indemnifier, the breach of contractual term by the indemnifier or the indemnifier acting contrary to legislative requirements.
3. Is the risk confined to the acts or omissions of the indemnifier or its agents? If so, then the legal risk is no different than at law in the absence of the indemnity because the indemnifier would have to compensate the other party for the wrongful acts of itself and its agents in any event. If the indemnity purports to make the indemnifier liable for the acts of its subcontractors then there may be cause for concern. This in part will depend upon the contractual arrangements that the indemnifier has with its subcontractors. If those arrangements are "back-to-back" then again there may be no material consequence for the indemnifier.
4. What categories of loss or damage must the indemnifier pay? If it is confined to payment of damages and payment of legal costs on a "party–party" basis then that too is nothing more

than what would be required to be paid in the absence of the indemnity. If it goes beyond these categories to include payment of legal costs of the other party on a "solicitor–client" basis or even on an "indemnity" basis (where all the legal costs incurred by the other party are covered) then the indemnifier must consider how great a risk that presents. This in turn will depend on the nature of the action. For example, in patent litigation these costs could be very significant. If the costs extend to payment of criminal penalties such as fines this would also be beyond the remedy that a defendant would normally pay under Indian common law.

5. Does the indemnity seek to impose liability on the indemnifier for acts that are beyond the scope of the transaction? If so then the indemnifier is almost certainly extending its risks beyond a reasonable limit and the indemnifier would reasonably object to the indemnity having such a scope.

As indemnities can potentially extend the risk for an organization to an unreasonable level many organizations, particularly those in the public sector, have strict protocols for dealing with them. This potential risk posed by indemnities may be addressed through the delegations that an organization issues to its relevant officers and requiring caps on liability to be imposed if a liability under indemnities extends beyond the liability that would arise if no contractual protections were in place.

Limitation of Liability

If an organization cannot exclude liability arising from the particular risk then the next best alternative may be to limit the extent of that liability. The form of this limitation is really a matter of negotiation. Most commonly, it will involve a cap on the amount that must be paid if the organization were to be found liable either by the specification of a dollar amount or the application of a formula.

One of the most common forms of limitation of liability is to exclude "indirect" or "consequential" losses. This is an issue, which can confuse the parties if a clear understanding of legal right to damages is not well understood. Under Indian law, an innocent party is entitled to be paid damages if the organization has acted negligently or breached contractual obligations and those acts or omissions have caused loss to the innocent party. Damages for breach of contract are an amount that would put the injured party in a position as if the contract had been performed. In either case, the loss must have been caused by the wrongful act and the loss must not be too remote. In other words, the loss incurred by the innocent party must have been "foreseeable."

So a party that agrees to the exclusion of "consequential losses" is effectively giving up a right to damages that would normally be expected under common law. Although this is clearly a matter for commercial negotiation, it is often misunderstood that consequential losses are some form of loss beyond what a court would reasonably give if applying standard legal principles. For these reasons, it is useful for the parties to clearly understand each other as to the categories of loss that they would consider to be "consequential loss" or "indirect loss." If this can be identified then those examples may be included as part of the clause so that a court, if it were ever asked to consider the issue, can understand the intended scope of that limitation of liability.

The courts have indicated that "consequential loss" would include damages for wasted expenditure, loss of profits if the IP had generated profits, loss of use of the IP if the organization was prevented from using the IP and the costs of acquiring substitute IP or technology.[8]

Liquidated Damages/Penalties

Liquidated damages are a quantification of the loss a party will be paid if another party to the contract breaches that contract. The amount of damages or the method for calculating the damages is an amount as agreed by the parties in the contract. A reasonable

[8] Halsbury's Laws of India, Para (135–1095).

fundamental benefit is that liquidated damages clauses avoid later argument about the amount of money that an organization must pay to the innocent party for its wrongful conduct. The risk is that the amount determined for liquidated damages is not a genuine estimate of damage that would be suffered by the innocent party and therefore is construed as a penalty. This in turn means the clause would not be enforceable. This leaves the parties in a position of having to renegotiate how much that loss is to be quantified or requiring a third party, such as a court, to determine it.

Guarantees

If the significant risk identified by an organization is the prospect of another party failing to perform its contractual obligations or making payment then one means of treatment of that risk is to require the party to involve a guarantor for the performance of those obligations. It may well be appropriate to obtain a guarantee from the holding company if the organization engages a subsidiary company to distribute technology into new markets. The holding company may have the financial resources to support the subsidiary but also the personnel to actually perform the obligations if the subsidiary were to be "short of the mark." If the main risk is the prospect of not being paid then guarantees from financial institutions may be sufficient. The financial substance of the other contracting parties and the nature of the transaction will influence these alternatives.

Escrow

Risk of a licensor becoming insolvent or ceasing to trade is often addressed in the field of information technology by requiring the licensor to place its source code with an escrow agent. Source code arrangements usually impose an obligation on the licensor to keep the source code up-to-date and authorize the third party to release the source code upon the occurrence of specific events.

Tips and Techniques

How to allocate risk in a commercial transaction involving IP between two companies?

1. Have disclaimer/exclusion clauses in the contract
2. To have indemnity clauses enshrined in the contract
3. Inclusion of warranties is a good way to assign risks
4. Inclusion of a limitation of liability clause in the contract
5. Addition of liquidation of damages clause, guarantee clause in the contract
6. Inclusion of an escrow clause necessary in case of technology contracts

7 Intellectual Property Licensing

*Companies all over the world rake in millions of dollars
as revenue by licensing their technology to others.*

After reading this chapter, you will be able to

- Understand the meaning of IP licensing
- Understand why licensing of IP is important for companies having huge patent portfolios
- Understand the meaning of exclusive, sole, and nonexclusive licenses
- Know more about types of licenses
- Understand how IP licensing is practiced in large firms such as Microsoft, IBM, and McDonalds
- Understand the advantages and disadvantages of licensing IP

Businesses across the globe are always paying attention to exciting new and innovative ideas that can be used to generate revenue. IP licensing is a mode of generating additional income for an owner of IP. He may either commercialize it himself or may obtain additional income by licensing the IP to someone else to commercialize it in a different field. It is only through licensing that the owner of IP may commercialize it in territories that he cannot cover. But in the 21st century, a new distinctive concept has crept into the market that is causing a revolution in the way companies are looking at their IP assets. Instead of incorporating the new ideas and concepts into products and services, today's innovations are being licensed or sold in the idea stage to other companies for significant sums of money.[1]

Let us understand the concept of licensing through the pages of history. When the East India Company established its business in India, it came to the court of the Mughals and asked for establishing a tax regime on the entire stretch of the Grand Trunk road (the term used in those days was—*rahdari*), through which the East India Company traded several goods. The Mughals gave permission to the East India Company to charge tax to anyone and everyone who passed through the Grand Trunk road, thereby establishing total control of the company on one of India's economic lifeline. This eventually led to the East India Company gaining control on the whole of India and it sowed the seeds of the British rule. Now taking this corollary, we can understand the concept of IP licensing, which is licensing a company's IP assets to someone else for some money in return.

> **Licensing is a fundamental mechanism in exploiting IPRs.**

Licensing is a fundamental mechanism in exploiting IPRs. Although with some forms of IP, certain formalities apply, generally licensing of IP can fall into the "too easy" category. Any layman would ask this question: What is licensing? Is it just a case of giving someone permission, a right to use your own invention? This is true to a degree. The transfer of IP rights is accomplished through a legal transaction between the owner of the IP and the person or entity of these IP rights. Such transfer creates a legal relationship, which is contractual in nature and signifies the consents of the transferor and transferee of the technology to transfer and acquire the IP rights. Such transfer may take place in the form of license or assignment of these rights.

---

[1] Julie L. Davis and Suzanne S. Harrison, *Edison in the Boardroom—How Leading Companies Realize Value From Their Intellectual Assets* (New York?: John Wiley & Sons, 2001), Front Jacket.

This chapter is designed to give the reader an understanding of the principal elements of licensing of IP and the nature of issues that are common to most licensing agreements. It also includes a few case studies of how companies of the world and India are benefitting from licensing.

DEFINING "CONTROL" IN AN IP LICENSE

The simple meaning of "license" is to grant permission or authority to another person to do or acquire something. One question arises that is who controls the licensed IP. Of course, it is the "licensor" who controls the IP. Control is traditionally manifested by the licensor owning the IP or having an appropriate scope of license rights from another person to enable the licensor to control the rights relating to the technology.

It is common to consider licensing in a commercialization context as granting a right in the IPRs to another person. This is commonly referred to as "licensing out." It should be kept in mind that many successful commercialization projects also involve acquiring IPRs in technologies that may form part of the end product or process that is to be commercialized. This "acquisition" of a permission to use IPRs is commonly referred to as "licensing in."

Important

The reasons for IP licensing are as follows:

1. To establish a new business or product
2. To improve competitiveness of licensee's existing operations or product
3. As part of acquitting a business
4. To obtain efficiency in licensee's research and development activities

5. Save time
6. To reduce the risks of further research and development

The decision to acquire a license involves undertaking a due diligence exercise of the desired technology, the costs involved, the legal chain of ownership and control, the relationship that can be established with the licensor, and the resulting competitive position of the licensee. Whether this is conducted in a formal manner or not will largely depend on the significance of the acquisition of the license in terms of risk, cost, and time.

SCOPE OF THE LICENSE

Licenses need to define a number of elements, especially the following:

- The element of property to be licensed (for example, the right to use the trademark, Orange)
- The entity to whom the property is being licensed (for example, the local education center now entitled to term itself an NIIT franchisee)
- The geographic extent of the license (for example, only in India, or a particular state, states or region)
- The commercial extent of the license (for example, only for the manufacture and distribution of a particular product or class of product)
- The duration (for example, for a period of five years from the date of the license)

The terms of a license for IP may vary widely with regard to the bargaining power of the parties and the technology involved. Nevertheless, many licenses for technology would be expected to address the following parameters.

Exclusivity

The licensor (who owns the IP) can grant to the licensee (who uses the IP of the licensor under a license) a license of varying scope. A license may be exclusive, sole or nonexclusive:[2]

Exclusive license: This kind of a license is the broadest of all licenses. In an exclusive license, only the licensee has the right to use the technology that has been licensed. All other parties including the licensor are excluded from the use of the technology/IP except the licensee. An exclusive license is more or less similar to assignment of IP. The licensor retains the ownership of the technology/IP in question but licenses away everything else.

Sole license: In a sole license agreement, the license once granted prevents the licensor from licensing the technology/IP to any other company or individual. The licensee alone has the right to reap the benefits of the IP apart from the licensor who also retains the right to use the IP.

Nonexclusive license: A nonexclusive license agreement is completely opposite of an exclusive license. The licensor in a nonexclusive license can license the technology/IP to as many licensees as desired by the licensor. The commercial software licenses of today are licenses on nonexclusive licenses.

Transferability

It is common for clauses that grant a license to specify that the license is "nontransferable." The plain meaning of this phrase is that the licensee is not authorized to permit another person to have access to the technology. It is intended to clearly put the licensee on notice that the license is personal to the licensee. The rights vested by the IP legislation are personal property. Personal

---

[2] Donald M. Cameron and Rowena Borenstein, "Key Aspect of IP License Agreements", available at http://www.jurisdiction.com/lic101.pdf.

property cannot be transferred to another person without the permission of the licensor. However, the license contract is like any other contract. Indian law, built upon the foundation of English cases, provides that the rights of a party under a contact may be assigned to a third party without the consent of the other parties to the contract. In this case, the liabilities remain with the transferor; and also that the liabilities of a party under a contract cannot be transferred to a third party without the consent of the other parties to the contract.

So if a license in IPRs was not described as being "nontransferable" then, in the absence of any other contractual provision, the licensee may be able to transfer the rights (such as reproducing copyright material or exploiting the patented invention) to a third party but the licensee would remain liable for any obligation under the license contract such as payment of royalties, although the licensee may well pass those liabilities on to the transferee in a separate contract. If the licensor wishes to prevent this from occurring, which it usually does, it is prudent to state that the license is "non-transferable."

Defining Intellectual Property License

The transfer of IP rights is accomplished through a legal transaction between the owner of the IP and the person or entity of these IP rights. Such transfer creates a legal relationship, which is contractual in nature and signifies the consents of the transferor and transferee of the technology to transfer and acquire the IP rights, respectively. Such transfer may take place in the form of license or assignment of these rights.

An IP license is a permission to do something, which if done without the license, would be an infringement of IP. "It is the formal granting of permission by someone who owns rights to someone else to use them." This permission is granted through an agreement known as license agreement. Such permission is granted by the licensor, who holds the IPR.

The person who acquires the licence is called the licensee. However, there may be more than one licensor or more than one licensee to a license agreement.

Territory

The statutory-based IP legislation grants rights to the owner of the relevant IP with respect to India. That legislation does not, by itself, give the owner of the IP any monopoly rights in any other jurisdiction; although there are certain treaties to which India is a party that give the owner jurisdiction. There are also certain treaties to which India is a party that give the owner of the IP the same or similar rights in other countries that have also agreed to that treaty provided that particular formalities are fulfilled. Examples of international mutual recognition include copyright in Berne Convention countries (Berne Convention for the protection of Literary and Artistic Works 1886); the Universal Copyright Convention 1952 and Agreement on Trade Related Aspect of Intellectual Property Rights 1995.

The licensor of statutory-based IP has control of the relevant rights where those rights are to be exercised in India. The license may be for all or any part of India and, as noted above, that license may be exclusive for one part of India and nonexclusive for another part.

If the licensor's IPRs are not international then a license entitling the licensee to deal with the technology in other jurisdictions, such as through the granting on a "worldwide license":

1. May be of little value to the licensee if the market for the licensed technology is small.
2. May create a risk that the licensee believed that the licensor represented that the licensor had the relevant IPRs in jurisdictions outside of India. This may be the source of a dispute.
3. May constitute a restraint of trade if the license contract restricts the licensee form competing with the licensor or trading in particular international territories.

The above risks may be addressed by

1. limiting the license to a particular jurisdiction;
2. including a clear statement in the license contract that the license does not extend to any territory outside of India.

The license should clearly specify the countries that are within the terms of the license and whether the license is exclusive or not with respect to each of those countries. If the licensor envisages that it will eventually obtain IPRs for additional territories then the scope of the license should be framed to pick up this eventuality.

Important

Factors that are usually considered in determining which countries should fall within the scope of the license include the following:

1. Has the licensor obtained or is in the process of securing IP registration or other protection in that country? ‾
2. What are the prospects of an application for registration of IP succeeding in that country?
3. What is likely to be the response of competitors in the relevant country if the licensor were to make the technology available in that country? Is it likely to cause a competitor to enter into, or increase the level of, competition in the licensor's established markets?
4. Does the country have an adequate and cost-effective regime for securing and protecting the IP in the country?

The licensor should consider reserving the right to terminate the license contract if

1. the government of the licensed territory prevents the importation of the technology or the payment of royalties or the revenue from the licensed territory;

> 2. the licensee imports into the licensed territory the technology that has been created by another licensee (whether or not the licensor approved the creation of the technology).

Payment

This is of fundamental importance and should be addressed in any license whether or not any remuneration is to be paid. Setting minimum performance obligations to be achieved by the licensee protects the licensor. The licensee may wish to secure the license to remove a competitive technology rather than as a service of revenue. Circumstances can result in changing the licensee's attribute that originally attracted the licensor. Those obligations may relate to revenue earned, units of promotion expenditure or achievement of regulatory or IP registration hurdles.

Term/Termination

A license is a contract. Theoretically, a license may be for any period of time agreed by the licensor and the licensee. However, the validity of a license, in both legal and commercial terms, depends in large part on

1. the nature of the IP that subsists in the technology; and
2. the field of use of the license.

The duration and termination clause lays down the reasons, circumstances, obligations of the parties, and duration of the Agreement. It may also lay down the scope of renewal, if any. It determines issues as to:

• The circumstances for termination of the Agreement (whether a change of control or a failure to meet sales targets or breach of conditions or insolvency or overdue payments). An agreement may also be terminated by serving notice to the other party.

- The duration of the grant (whether the license has been granted for a definite term or for a limited time).

Some forms of IP, such as confidential information and trademarks that can be renewed or maintained indefinitely will have no limits on the term that a license may apply for. However, the monopoly rights that attach to that IP will only continue to be of value to the licensor and the licensee if the IP continues to be protected.

Field of Use: Application of the Technology

The scope of the monopoly rights attached to IP varies according to the type of IP. It is open to the parties to agree to limit the license to any one or more of those monopoly rights. The parties may agree to limit the license in any other manner subject to the principles of contract law and anticompetitive legal principles. Common examples include

1. using the technology for a particular purpose;
2. dealing with the technology for or within a particular industry.

It is good practice to test the description of field of use with persons who have not been involved in the preparation of the license and have the relevant knowledge of the industry and application of the technology. This will assist the avoidance of ambiguities in the wording used in the description of the field of use.

A danger for any licensor is that an exclusive license is given in relation to a field of use that is broader than anticipated by the licensor. In relation to biotechnology, for example, all of the functional applications of an invention may not be known for some time (such as the cloning of a gene and the biological function of the related protein). Ultimately, this is a function of the drafting of the license contract and that task will be greatly aided by persons skilled in the technical field working hand in hand with the author of the license contract.

Sublicensing

As licenses are generally personal to the licensee it would not be usual for a license to entitle the licensee to permit others to have the same rights as granted to it by the licensor. A licensee should therefore seek an express permission in the license contract to sublicense the IPRs to third parties within the overall scope of the head license obtained from the licensor. Sublicensing tends to attract greater importance for exclusive licenses where no other licenses can be granted for the technology within the scope of the license.

The licensor's strategic advantages in permitting sublicensing may include the following:

1. The licensee may be able to improve on the licensed technology and so expand the opportunities for the licensor to earn income streams.
2. The licensee may have the appropriate manufacturing, distribution or marketing network through which commercial use of the licensed technology may be maximized even though the licensee itself may not use the technology for those purposes.

The licensor will often want some degree of satisfaction that the sublicense rights are being exercised and managed in a manner that is in accordance with the terms of the head license and that there are not any issues that could impact on sister licensing arrangements that the licensor may have in place. To this end, the licensor may require the licensee to

1. use an approved form of sublicense;
2. seek the licensor's prior approval before sublicensing rights relating to certain territories, fields of use or purposes of use;
3. provide copies of any sublicensing agreements;
4. notify the licensor of the end of any sublicense and the reasons for it ending;
5. notify the licensor of any dispute between the licensee and its sublicensee;

6. indemnify the licensor for actions of the sublicensee that cause loss to the licensor.

Important

The important parameters for a licensing agreement are

1. Exclusivity
2. Transferability
3. Revocability
4. Territory
5. Payment
6. Term
7. Field of Use
8. Sublicensing

TYPES OF LICENSES

A licensing agreement is nothing but a partnership between an IPRs owner who is generally known as a licensor and a person who is authorized to use such rights in exchange for some agreed payment, which is known as royalty. There are a few types of licensing agreements that are broadly categorized as given in Figure 7.1.

Technology License

In a technology license, the organization's methods, materials, skills, designs, inventions, formulations, drawings, specifications,

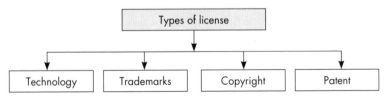

Figure 7.1 Types of License

algorithms—anything that can be used to produce or improve products or services is licensed to the licensee.[3] It is where the licensor authorizes the licensee to use the technology under certain agreed terms and conditions. It is a contract freely entered into between two parties and contains terms and conditions agreed upon. In the technology industry, copyrights are required to protect the software. However, like other copyright licenses, a technology copyright software license, would also need to be defined by the intended scope of the license. For example, if the intended purpose were to permit a specific use of a technology, then the licensing agreement would be an End Use Licensing Agreement.[4] However, this agreement would be insufficient if the purpose of the agreement was to further develop the technology that is being licensed.

In the technology industry, licensing is generally undertaken by various methods, including in-licensing, out-licensing, and cross-licensing. In-licensing agreement is adopted when a company is taking a license from another company either for a technology or for product development or for marketing with an upfront fee. It is done to quickly fill new product pipelines. Out-licensing is adopted when an organization provides a license to other companies for a fee. This is adopted to minimize the risk of manufacturing and distribution.[5] Cross-licensing involves two or more organizations who enter into an agreement where there is a mutual exchange of patent rights. Such agreements are entered into so as to take advantage of each other's technology without the

---

[3] James R. Young, "Technology or Patent License: What's Right for you?" available at http://www.patentlegal.com/articles/tech_patent.pdf.

[4] "End-User License Agreement, the type of license used for most software. An EULA is a legal contract between the manufacturer and/or the author and the end user of an application. The EULA details how the software can and cannot be used and any restrictions that the manufacturer imposes (e.g., most EULA??s of proprietary software prohibit the user from sharing the software with anyone else)." http://www.webopedia.com/TERM/E/EULA.html.

[5] "Exploiting Intellectual Property in a Complex World" available at http://www.pwc.com/en_GX/gx/technology/pdf/exploiting-intellectual-property.pdf at 28.

> **Qualcomm (QCOM) collects almost all its revenue of US\$10.4 billion from selling licenses for and making the chips containing its patented 3G mobile phone technology, known as CDMA.**

threat of litigation from the other. A cross-license agreement can be best explained with an example from the technology industry. In September 2011, Samsung Electronics Co. and Microsoft reached a cross-licensing agreement. Under the agreement, Microsoft will receive royalties for Samsung's android-based smart phones and tablets. Samsung also will work with Microsoft to develop smart phones and tablets based on Microsoft's Windows software.[6]

Qualcomm (QCOM) collects almost all its revenue of US\$10.4 billion from selling licenses for and making the chips containing its patented 3G mobile phone technology, known as CDMA.[7]

Case Study

IBM Licensing

IBM has a long history of patenting since it was founded in 1911. It began its patent licensing drive in 1956 when it started cross licensing all of its patents with other companies including competitors. With the coming up and the growth of PCs in the early 1980s becoming quite lucrative for companies, the decision makers at IBM thought about what should be done because it had already lost the race in the PC manufacturing business even though it had many patents dealing with the PC.[8]

---

[6] Evan Ramstad, "Microsoft—Samsung Deal Strikes a Blow at Google" available at http://online.wsj.com/article/SB1000142405297020422620457659 8661866214854.html.

[7] Steve Levine, "IBM, May Not Be Patent King After All", (January 13, 2010) available at http://www.businessweek.com/magazine/content/10_04/ b4164051608050.htm.

[8] Supra note 1 at 80.

The IBM management discussed two prominent questions that would change the course of the technology industry. The first was whether to practice IBM's monopoly by controlling the patents it had on the PC? And second was whether to license all technology to other firms to grow the technology industry?

IBM chose to answer the second question and in 1987 began a licensing program to license technology to companies such as Compaq and Dell for a royalty. The royalty revenue that came in from the licenses went back into R&D to further the R&D in the many divisions of IBM. This helped IBM to lower costs of doing business and expand R&D.

This mode of licensing was taken to the next level in the 1990s when IBM decided to further its R&D by bringing in new technology and licensing it for royalties. By the 1990s as licensees of IBM became more knowledgeable and sophisticated, IBM came to the conclusion that it needed to adopt a licensing strategy from being a "win–lose" (collecting royalties from those companies that used its patents) to "win–win" (providing value to the license rather than simply licensing its patents). By adopting this strategy, the most talented engineers at IBM went about teaching engineers of the licensees on how to adopt the IBM technology, thereby enabling the licensees to enter the market with much more improved products and to add to that less money spent on R&D by the licensee. In this strategy, IBM benefitted immensely because it got a higher royalty for providing the technical know-how along with the patent and this helped complete the transactions in less time compared to when only patents were being licensed.[9]

We must also note that the IP management structure at IBM is centralized at the corporate level and it has built its licensing program on the centralized model of IP management (as discussed in Chapter 4, "Intellectual Asset Management"). IBM's IP group is split into technology, legal, and business that include a combination of lawyers, inventors, sales persons, licensing executives,

[9] Dan McCurdy, "Out of Alignment—Getting IP and Business Strategies Back in Sync" in *From Assets to Profits – Competing for IP Value & Return*, ed. Bruce Berman, (New York?: Wiley, 2009), 9.

and other business people.[10] This centralized structure has made it easier for IBM to bring in the IP group together with the operational arm of the company. This has helped IBM to look at IP and in particular IP licensing from a much broader perspective.

IBM earns more than a billion dollars from selling and licensing its technology including patents to other companies across the globe. Here are the indicators on how much revenue IBM generates from licensing:[11]

1. From sales, cross-licensing arrangement of patents and other transfers of IP, IBM generates revenues worth US$138 million. This includes value of IP that was sold to other companies or the IP that was spun off to form new companies.
2. From royalty-based fees, IBM generates revenue worth US$514 million per year, which includes patent licensing revenue that accords for 40 percent of the earnings. The remaining 60 percent is from technology licensing which includes technical know-how, transfer of trade secrets, training, and so on (as discussed earlier).
3. From custom development income that includes consultancy services for IBM developers who provide customized software solutions to clients that run proprietary IBM software, it earns US$514 million a year.

IBM annually invests almost US$6 billion in R&D. It works with the clients and enables them to enhance their business through the use of IBM-created IP. IBM has also established centralized IP management functions and executes the necessary steps to identify, protect, and maximize the financial and strategic benefits of IP.[12] Until 2010, IBM had a worldwide portfolio of

[10] John Bringardner, "A New kind of Blue", (October 6, 2006) available at http://www.law.com/jsp/article.jsp?id=1202430463695&slreturn=1.

[11] http://triplehelixinnovation.com/what-universities-can-learn-from-ibms-ip-licensing-strategies/1998.

[12] Saif Aziz, "IBM Innovation and Intellectual Property, IP Trends and Strategy", (December 12, 2012) available at http://bipasiaforum.com/sources/ppt/SaifAziz.pdf.

over 40,000 patents. About half were lodged in the United State
and the remainder split between Europe and Asia.

Some elements of IBM's IP licensing strategy are

1. IBM IP-related revenue includes payments from licensing
   know-how, consulting fees, and other intangibles, not just
   patents.
2. Selected IBM patents are cross-licensed to other companies.
3. Potentially patentable IBM technologies are sometimes placed
   into the public domain.
4. Selected IBM patents are donated to open source projects.
5. IBM engineers search for potential patent infringements.

Within each business unit, teams of engineers and lawyers meet
regularly to review invention disclosure forms filed by unit engineers. About half of the reviewed inventions end up getting filed
as patent applications, earning its inventor a US$1,000 bonus. If
an invention gets a patent, the inventor receives a second bonus.
Each year, the company CEO identifies three or four inventors
who have made a special contribution. Their rewards can reach as
high as US$100,000 (see Figure 7.2).

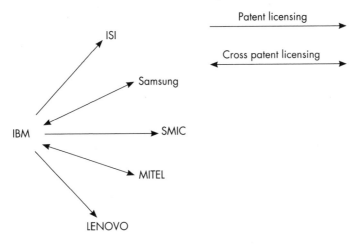

Figure 7.2   IBM Patent Licensing

Patent License

Technology licensing and patent licensing mean the same, but for a better understanding, we have explained them under two different headings. Patent licensing is a kind of license, where the organization is licensing an invention that has been granted a patent to a licensee. This kind of an agreement is relevant for industries that have invested billions into innovation and technology. Patent licensing like any other licensing, creates opportunities for organizations to create revenue from their patents by licensing them to other organizations as well as create newer and better inventions through joint collaborations. Companies in India have also started licensing their patents to companies abroad and have raked in millions of dollars. Let us first look at how Microsoft licenses its patents and also have a look at how two new startup companies in India license their IP assets.

Microsoft Patent Licensing

Microsoft began its IP licensing drive in a big way when in 2003; it decided to have collaborations with other companies by sharing its patents with them commonly known as cross-licensing. Microsoft was of the view that creation and utilization of IP was part of a virtuous circle wherein R&D leads to the creation of more IP, which further leads to the licensing of that IP for valuable consideration, whether in the form of licensing revenue, and so on. This view made Microsoft sign cross-patenting deals with companies such as Nortel and SAP, which enable it to conduct broader-based product level collaboration that in turn led to more R&D.[13]

This new licensing program emerged because of a revamped IP strategy under the able leadership of Marshall Phelps, vice president of Legal & Corporate Affairs Intellectual Property Group, who helped IBM build a US$1 billion annual revenue from its IP licensing program. Microsoft also created a venture known

---

[13] Marshal Phelps and David Kline, *Burning the Ships: Intellectual Property and the Transformation of Microsoft* (New York: John Wiley & Sons, 2009), 45–46.

as IP Ventures to earn more money from its vast IP portfolio. IP Ventures enabled startup companies to license technology from Microsoft that charged licensing fees for some widely used technologies on which it had patents. Such patents included File Allocation Table file system (FAT) used by manufacturers of mobile storage devices and also entered into agreements with technology companies such as Siemens and Citrix.

The IP Ventures program made it possible for entrepreneurs and venture capital–backed startups to license patents from Microsoft at affordable royalty rates. The IP Ventures program has a portfolio of patents that are too specialized for Microsoft or are no longer fit for the company's priorities, but could potentially be a basis for new business.[14] This is "win–win–win" model adopted by Microsoft as it gets revenue from patent licensing, the licensees get affordable readymade patents to use for the development of their products and it has been observed that these patents could eventually find their way in Microsoft's own products. For example, Digital Media Fingerprinting, which embeds traceable data in digital media files, could be used to strengthen Microsoft's digital rights management offerings, and Conference XP, which enables real-time multipoint audio- and videoconferencing, seems like an obvious candidate for inclusion in future Microsoft collaboration products, such as Live Meeting or Live Communications Server. Therefore, startup companies that license some of these technologies today might find themselves in competition with Microsoft in the future.[15] As of today, Microsoft has over 1,100 IP licensing agreements.[16]

[14] "IP Licensing Expanded to Research", (May 9, 2005) available at http://www.directionsonmicrosoft.com/sample/DOMIS/update/2005/06jun/0605iletr.htm.

[15] Ibid.

[16] John Ribeiro, "Microsoft Signs Two New Patent Licensing Deals Covering Android, Chrom", (July 10, 2012) available at http://www.infoworld.com/d/mobile-technology/microsoft-signs-two-new-patent-licensing-deals-covering-android-chrome-197353.

Android and Patent Licensing—Microsoft

> **Microsoft has one of the largest patent portfolios in the world and it also owns several patents relating to Android technology.**

Microsoft in the recent past has had several licensing agreements with big mobile manufacturers. The reason is Android![17] Android is one of the most popular smart phone platform in the world with over 500,000 device activations every day.[18] Since Microsoft has one of the largest patent portfolios in the world and it also owns several patents relating to Android technology and so Android's success is quickly becoming a blessing for Microsoft, which has established licensing agreements with several Android manufacturers to settle patent infringement claims. After landing several key licensing agreements and with a big Samsung agreement reportedly in the works, Android is well on its way to becoming one of Microsoft's fastest growing money makers.[19]

More than 700 licensing agreements have been signed between Microsoft and other companies since this licensing initiative was launched in 2003, with at least five of the licensing agreements with Android vendors such as Velocity Micro, General Dynamics and Onkyo Corp. It has also signed a patent licensing agreement with HTC, which has become quite successful in the Android smart phone market on the strengths of its Android phones the EVO and Thunderbolt.

With 500,000 devices a day, this implies around US$1 billion of licensing revenue if it receives a US$5 fee for each Android

---

[17] Trefis Team, "Android Could be a Billion Dollar Business. For Microsoft", (July 11, 2011) available at http://www.forbes.com/sites/greatspeculations/2011/07/11/android-could-be-a-billion-dollar-business-for-microsoft.

[18] Charlie Sorrel, "Andy Rubin: 500,000 Android Activations Daily", June 28, 2011 available at http://www.wired.com/gadgetlab/2011/06/andy-rubin-500000-android-activations-daily.

[19] Supra note 17.

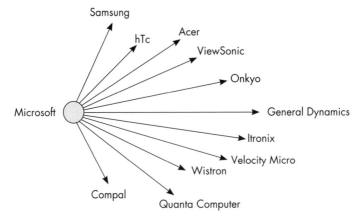

Figure 7.3 Microsoft Patent Android Licensing

device.[20] Microsoft has also signed a deal with Samsung settling a bitter dispute between the two technology giants. Under the agreement, Samsung will pay Microsoft US$10 each for every Android smart phone or tablet computer it sells. The most recent figures suggest that Samsung sold more than 10 million S2 model smart phones for which it would have to pay US$100 million to Microsoft.[21] Android could turn out to be its next billion-dollar business and one of the largest IP licensing revenue generators for any company in history (see Figure 7.3).

Ittiam Technologies and Cosmic Circuit: Case Studies

Two small Indian companies based out of Bangalore have also begun licensing IP to other companies for a royalty fees. Ittiam Systems' annual revenue touched US$20 million for the financial year 2012, driven by IP developed out of India. With a portfolio of more than 30 patents, it has taken the route of IP licensing to generate more revenue by licensing its patents to other companies.

---

[20] Supra note 17.

[21] John Halliday, "Samsung and Microsoft Settle Android Licensing Dispute", (September 28, 2011) available at http://www.guardian.co.uk/technology/2011/sep/28/samsung-microsoft-android-licensing-dispute.

Founded in 2001, Ittiam has been a supplier of media processing and communication technologies for a range of applications including smart phones, tablets, video communication and networking systems, media broadcast systems and Wi-Fi communication. The company is one of the very few in India to have successfully deployed the IP licensing model, something which Wipro had sought to do by starting an IP based company in the U.S. in the 1990s, but which did not really take off.[22]

The second company that has benefitted from IP licensing is Cosmic Circuits, which was founded in 2005 in Bangalore by a group of former Texas Instruments employees. It offers IP licensing and also builds products in the analog and mixed signal technology space, designing semiconductor chips that go into a variety of consumer electronic products. As of now, it has 50 customers that license its technologies. IP licensing has paid off handsomely and Cosmic Circuits is now counted in the top 100 small companies in India.[23]

Trademark License

Organizations use trademark licensing to maintain global presence and also to create a secondary stream of revenue. This kind of an agreement is also known as a franchise agreement. Organizations adopt trademark licensing through various relationships: (a) letting another organization use the trademark for the business in which the licensor is operating; (b) through a jointly owned subsidiary of multiple parent companies in a mutual trademark holding company (MTHC), with the goal of sharing trademarks while finding safer avenues toward at least some of the benefits of the wholly

---

[22] K. C. Krishnadas, "Ittiam Revenues Cross $20 Million", (March 22, 2012) available at http://www.techonlineindia.com/article/12-03-22/Ittiam_revenues_cross_20_million.aspx.

[23] "Building IP Licensing", (October 4, 2010) available at http://articles.timesofindia.indiatimes.com/2010-10-04/infrastructure/28250264_1_licensing-indian-market-domain.

owned model, corporations may consider the formation of jointly owned MTHCs.[24]

While a lot of importance is given to patent licensing, not much attention has been placed of trademark licensing, despite the fact that licensing a trademark has a lower risk to significantly improve IP related cash flow.[25]

It must be noted that for companies, one of the most important intangible asset is their brand/trademark. A lot of care is given to the brand to make it popular among the masses and significantly increase the revenue by selling the brand through various products and services.

Copyright licensing agreement is done for literary work and artistic works of individuals. The agreement is generally for manufacturing, distribution, and marketing of their work. Licensing of the copyright is generally done by transferring a limited number of rights in a work such as right to make movies, merchandising, screenplays, and so on. Such kind of an agreement is usually signed between authors of famous books and publishers for the publishing of books and between authors and the entertainment industry for adapting the story of the books in the form of plays, movies, and so on. This is also known as Copyright Derivative Strategy, which was discussed in Chapter 2 of this book.

SELECTING THE LICENSEE

Choosing a licensee can be similar to choosing a business partner, particularly where exclusive licenses are being granted. In determining whether to grant a license in technology, the licensor must carefully consider the persons who wish to obtain a license for the technology. This decision is just as critical as any other issue

---

[24] Lanning Bryer and Matthew Asbell, "Combined Trademarks in a Jointly Owned IP Holding Company" May–June 2008 of the Trademark Reporter, available at http://www.inta.org/TMR/Documents/Volume%2098/vol98_no3_a4.pdf.

[25] Steve Hoffmann and W. Drew Kastner, "Cash in Your Unused Brands", *Managing IP*, March 2009, 31.

related to the granting of a license in technology and has greater importance where the license relates to the establishment and penetration of technology into new markets, such as manufacturing, distribution, and marketing agreements. This aspect should form part of the licensor's due diligence when deciding to commercialize the IP in the technology.

PREPARING FOR LICENSING

Licensing is just one form of generating revenue from technology and the IP that subsists in that technology. In determining whether licensing is the most appropriate form of commercialization strategy, the licensor should prepare a business plan that analyzes the strengths, weaknesses, opportunities, and threats arising from licensing the technology. This should result in the licensor clearly understanding the objectives and material risks in pursuing a licensing strategy. Flowing from that high-level plan the licensor is able to begin the process of selecting licensees that will be consistent with the licensor's business strategy.

An early challenge for a licensor is to attract potential licensees. Where the technology has clear market opportunities, this may not be difficult. The R&D phase of the technology may itself have created sufficient interest in relevant sectors to result in approaches from potential licensees. Often the circle of organizations that have an interest in the science or application of technology will be a natural medium for seeking licensees. In other circumstances, the licensor may have no connection to the industry or sector that is the logical fit for the new technology. The licensor has the task of not only convincing others that the technology is sound and has a competitive edge but also of establishing confidence in the licensor with whom potential licenses are prepared to engage.

Following the conclusion of negotiations for a licensing arrangement, the parties commonly record their understanding in a document in simple terms rather than seeking to reflect the arrangement in a formal contract. In addition, the parties are likely to wish to undertake or continue with due diligence enquiries of the other party and the technology concerned. The document is usually reflected in a "deal memo" or ore formally in a letter or MoU.

Any such document is likely to have within it a number of unresolved issues. The parties will not consider some of those issues important enough to record as they are not "deal breakers" or they may be "unseen" and only come to light once the process of preparing the formal contract is undertaken. The latter consequence is usually a function of the time that the parties have to complete the commercial deal or inadequate advice.

It is critical that the parties clearly understand the role and legal effect of the deal memo. Even though the parties may contemplate at the time of agreeing to the terms of the MoU that a formal contract is still to be concluded, it is still possible that the deal memo is itself a legally enforceable contract. Accordingly, the parties should clearly state in the deal memo whether or not the deal memo or any part of it is intended to be legally binding upon them before they execute a formal contract.

Important

The licensing deal memoranda should also specify

1. for major projects, a timeline for various milestones to be achieved;
2. all commercial terms related to the licensing arrangement such as royalties, timing, and methods of payment, performance criteria;
3. the essential elements of the scope of the license;
4. an outline of the timing disclosure of confidential information (not previously disclosed) required by the recipient to satisfy its requirements such as evaluation of the project and any third party approval required to be obtained;
5. the date for completion of the formal contract and the consequences of a failure to do so;
6. a description of any improvements that the licensee intends to undertake in relation to the technology and the

arrangements for those improvements to be granted back to the licensor;

7. any policy or administrative issues that are non-negotiable for a party ;
8. who should maintain and protect the IP in the technology and arrangements for action including the sharing of costs;
9. the effect of the license ending;
10. the governing law.

COMMON CLAUSES FOR LICENSING TECHNOLOGY

The most distinguishing feature of licensing is that it allows flexibility to the parties, which means, the parties are free to incorporate any clause that they deem fit for the licensing agreement. There are a number of clauses that are commonly found and are peculiar to licensing agreement. To add to the general clauses found in the agreement, there are the usual "boilerplate" clauses that can be found in any contract of substance such as:

1. Governing law
2. Waiver
3. Entire agreement
4. Notices
5. Variation
6. Dispute resolution

In addition to the boilerplate clauses, some other clauses that are generally inserted or are specific to the licensing agreements, which the licensor or the licensee might expect to be raise are as follows:

Framework of a License Agreement

It is always preferred that the terms of the Agreement is laid down in writing. The terms of an agreement forms the framework of the Agreement. This framework serves as its skeleton. Generally, following terms are included in the Agreement:

Identification of the parties. An agreement is made between the party who has the right to grant the license and the party who wishes to exercise that license. Additional details, including the addresses of the parties, the jurisdiction of incorporation (for corporate entities), and the effective date of the Agreement, may also be included in the identification section of the Agreement.

Recitals. The recitals narrate the relationship between the parties up to the time of agreement. The recitals are very useful tools in explaining the context and background of the license to a reader, and it also assists in the interpretation of the Agreement.

Definitions. It serves as the dictionary to the Agreement. For illustration, the parties can include the definition of terms like "licensed patents," "use," and "royalty" to make crystal clear the rights and obligations of the parties.

License grant. It lays down the scope and extent of the rights granted to the licensee, as well as any limitations on those rights. It deals with the subject matter of the license, its limitation as to the application in a particular territory, its field of use, and the extent of its exclusivity.

Technical assistance. Depending on the kind of technology, there may be provision in the Agreement to provide the licensee with technical assistance in the form of documentation, data, and expertise.

Consideration. This provision of an agreement lays down the consideration that the licensee is required to pay to the licensor. The mode of payment is also laid down in this provision.

Obligations of the parties. It lays down the obligations of each of the parties during the term of the Agreement. It depends upon the type and complexity of the Agreement. It may be both positive as well as negative. The positive obligations may include the duty to report infringement, whereas negative obligations may include a duty not to compete with the licensor. Also, it is essential that the obligations of the parties are clear and unambiguous.

Duration and Termination. Like a commercial agreement, a license agreement defines both a defined term of the agreement and also lays down provisions outlining when a party may terminate the agreement, and reason for termination. Also, it deals with the effect of termination in advance, so as to give the parties enough chance to plan the exit strategy in the light of full knowledge of the consequences of termination of the Agreement. This clause may also include the provision as to renewal of the Agreement after expiry.

Technological improvements. This provision is meant to clear the situation, in case conflict arises as to rights on improvements of the technology. The license contains the provision of a grant back of the improvements to the licensor.

Conflict resolution. Since the disputes regarding the licensing agreement may incur huge costs, the parties seek to abate these costs in the Agreement. Therefore, the provision conflict resolution in the Agreement deals with regulation of the manner in which disputes between the parties may be resolved, so that the costs involved in dispute resolution may be contained. The process of settlement may also include arbitration clause in the Agreement.

Other clauses. This part of the agreement may include the remainder of provisions like representations and warranties, provision as to sublicense, confidentiality and secrecy.

Challenges by the Licensee

Generally, a licensee will not be able to successfully challenge the validity of a patent that is the subject of the licensed technology unless the licensee can prove that

1. it relied upon a misrepresentation by the licensor concerning the validity of the patent or the infringement proceedings are against the licensee; or
2. the licensee claims the patent has expired; or
3. the licensed technology does not fall within the terms of the patent.

IP Infringement

If the licensor were indemnifying the licensee against third-party IP claims, the license contract would also normally reserve to the licensor the right to manage the proceedings. This approach accords with the principle that the licensor is the "insurer" for the claim and so should be able to manage the consequent risk.

INDEMNITY CLAUSES SPECIFIC TO LICENSE CONTRACTS

The licensee would seek an indemnity from the licensor for any claims made by a third party or infringement of IPRs during the term of the licensing agreement. Here are some of the ingredients of the indemnity clause that may be included in a licensing agreement:

1. Required regulatory approvals not obtained by the licensor for the exploitation and use of the licensed technology
2. Inaccurate information provided to the licensee by the licensor in the course of due diligence undertaken by the licensee. There are instances when incomplete information is provided due to lack of understanding or miscommunication.

Keeping these two points in mind it is important on the part of the licensor to take all necessary steps before licensing out the technology and it is also the responsibility of the licensee to double check everything whatever the licensor does with regard to the licensed technology. This must be done to avoid legal hassles in the future.

Survival—After the End of the License Contract

The rights following from a termination of a license contract should be clearly spelt out. It has been suggested that the following questions arising from termination of know-how license agreements are the source of most know-how license contract litigation:[26]

1. Must the licensee stop using the technology?
2. May the licensee stop paying the licensor for any ongoing use or disclosure or the information?
3. Is the license entitled to complete all contract already entered into prior to the termination?
4. Must the licensee stop disclosing the know-how information to his or her own lawful sublicensees?
5. Is the licensee entitled to acquire ownership of the IPRs if certain events cause the termination? Examples may include insolvency and subsequent deregistration of the licensor (being the owner of the IPRs).

The license contract should contain a clause that the licensee has to return or destroy any information relating to the technology (especially confidential information). This is usually at the licensor's option. The licensee should cease using or in any way referring to the licensor's trademarks.

Clauses relating to indemnities, ownership of IP, confidentiality, and limitations on liability should continue after the end of the license contract.

---

[26] Arnold, White and Durkee (eds), *1988 Licensing Law Handbook,* (New York: Clark Boardman Company Ltd, 1988), 48.

Computer Software Licenses

Computers and computer software have revolutionized the way people to business in the 21st century. Software companies are reaping in huge profits by licensing the software that they develop. The licensing of software is now quite common and certain conventions and principles have been established in the course of its commercialization. The form of IP relevant to software is copyright, and in some circumstances, patents.

This short case study would look as to how Microsoft began its IP licensing journey with an agreement with Sun Microsystems, another leading IT based company based in the U.S.

Microsoft and IP Licensing

Microsoft began its tryst with IP licensing in the year 2003. In December 2003, Microsoft announced it was expanding its IP policy to provide the IT industry with increased access to the company's growing IP portfolio, signaling to the public that the company is "open for business"[27] (a concept similar to open innovation that has been discussed in Chapter 2) when it comes to IP licensing. The first IP licensing agreement of Microsoft was with Sun Microsystems. The two companies entered into a broad technology collaboration agreement to enable their products to work better together. The significant elements of the agreement were

1. The agreement provided both companies with access to aspects of each other's server-based technology and enable them to use this information to develop new server software products that would work better together. The cooperation initially centered on Windows Server and Windows Client, but later on included other important areas, including email and database software.
2. Microsoft communications protocol program: Sun agreed to sign a license for the Windows desktop operating system

---

[27] Supra note 13 at 53.

communications protocols under Microsoft's Communications Protocol Program.

3. Microsoft's support for Java: The companies agreed that Microsoft would continue to provide product support for the Microsoft Java Virtual Machine that customers have deployed in Microsoft's products.

4. Windows certification for Sun server: Sun and Microsoft announced the Windows certification for Sun's Xeon servers.

5. Both companies agreed to pay royalties for use of each other's technology, with Microsoft making an upfront payment of US$350 million. Sun agreed to make payments when the technology is incorporated into its server products and has done so.

Microsoft has expanded the concepts of open innovation beyond licensing and cross-licensing to using IP as venture capital through its global program called IP Ventures, which demonstrates the true potential of IP by creating opportunities for both startup and existing firms, with the help of combining world-class computer science research with entrepreneurial spirit.

Case Studies Involving IP Ventures

1. Microsoft IP Ventures was recently seeking to license imaging technology called Interactive Image Cutout. SoftEdge, a company specializing in e-enablement and multimedia document generation entered into a partnership with Microsoft. The new company was offered a "field of use" exclusive license of the Microsoft technology in exchange for an upfront payment and a royalty based on a percentage of the net sales of their product. Apart from this, SoftEdge also provided for the free quality assurance testing for the new version of Microsoft Word.

2. Microsoft IP Ventures established a wholly new corporation called "Wallop" that was formed to take social networking to the next generation. Wallop's site offered an online experience by invitation only, customizability and multimedia content management and Flash Player movies to add to their site. Microsoft developed all these technologies. Microsoft acquired

an equity stake in the company while Wallop received the code, the patents and access to the researcher who developed the technology.

3. IP ventures results has created a sustainable and cyclical corporate entrepreneurship effort with innovation at the forefront. It has invested over US$60 million invested into IP venture companies and successfully is spinning out two companies a year.

The main objective of IP ventures is to spin off the IP that falls outside the scope of Microsoft's operation. And surprisingly, it has fueled the imagination of several entrepreneurs by making profit itself.

It should be noted that the business model of Microsoft IP licensing is not for revenue generation. Microsoft started IP licensing since it was not able to handle the large IP portfolio (patent portfolio). IBM as mentioned earlier rakes in more than a billion dollar in revenue from IP licensing. The purpose of taking Microsoft as an example is to show, how a company that was known to be a monopolist and involved in several antitrust disputes with the government changed its strategy completely by adopting an open approach to deal with IP, which has really helped Microsoft to manage its vast patent portfolio.

Phillips and IP Licensing

Philips Electronics spends nearly US$2.1 billion on R&D annually, which helps develop new technology and other IP. To safeguard a proper return on these investments, Philips Intellectual Property & Standards organization (IP&S) protects the fruits of Philips R&D through IPRs. IP&S actively seeks opportunities to license Philips' technologies to third parties. In the year 2005, Philips acquired several LED lighting business worth US$5.2 billion after buying out Agilent, a leading LED manufacturing company. The company claimed the broadest IP portfolio in the LED lightening industry. Now, over 300 companies have access (license)

> **Philips and Sony have collected more than US$2 billion in royalty revenues related to licensing of CD related patents.**

to Philips' comprehensive portfolio of patented LED system technologies and solutions.

Philips and Sony have collected more than US$2 billion in royalty revenues related to licensing of CD related patents. Philips and Sony jointly licensed their CD, laser technology portfolio to all players at reasonable prices at an early stage. This prevented competitors from trying to developing alternative technologies, and also the acceptability of the CD was faster and more universal.

HP and IP Licensing

HP is consistently recognized as one of the world's most innovative companies. The company has recently invested UN$3.3 billion apart from earlier investments, which has led to thousands of patent grants. HP owns one of the world's largest patent portfolios–comprised of more than 37,000 worldwide patents.

> **HP owns one of the world's largest patent portfolios–comprised of more than 37,000 worldwide patents. Currently more than 4,000 patents are available for license or sale.**

Currently more than 4,000 patents are available for license or sale. HP has always been interested in licensing technology. HP's revenue from licensing has quadrupled in less than three years, to over US$200 million this year. To develop and deploy a technology-licensing program and to secure IP licensing approval for out licensing, HP follows a six-step process:[28]

---

[28] Suzanne S. Harrison and Patrick H. Sullivan, *Einstein in the Boardroom: Moving Beyond Intellectual Capital to I-Stuff* (Hoboken, NJ: John Wiley & Sons, 2006), 64.

1. Evaluate technology readiness and competitive position to determine what can be licensed.
2. Evaluate organizational, ownership, partners, and technology transfer issues to determine who can help deliver the technology.
3. Organize patents and other IP.
4. Develop the licensee value proposition to determine who and why.
5. Evaluate carve-out with corporate development and selected Venture Capitalists.
6. Determine the technology valuation and financials.

MERCHANDISING

Merchandising is the licensing of publicly recognizable properties for use on or in association with products or services to promote sales of those products or services. It is traditionally used to promote and market the core products or services of the licensor. It has become well known in the fields of motion pictures, sport, and events.

Merchandising may be undertaken in a wide variety of fields. It now generates large income streams for licensors, which may exceed the revenue generated by the licensor's principal business activity. It is used in relation to an infinite range of merchandise (Figure 7.4).

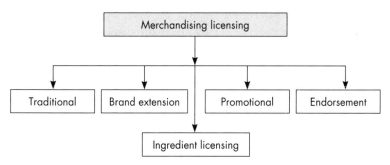

Figure 7.4 Types of Merchandising Licensing

1. Traditional merchandising: The licensor promotes its core products/services by licensing the IP that is incorporated in that product or service. For example, sports team apparels like caps and jerseys.

2. Brand extension: The licensor promotes its core product or service by licensing the IP that is incorporated in that product or service. Examples include the caricatures in Disney's "Lion King," uniforms of sports teams and associated clothing such as caps and t-shirts.

3. Ingredient: The licensor licenses its brand name to products and services that are related to its core product or service. This strategy depends upon having established a sound reputation in its core product or service. It enables the licensor to leverage off its existing IP portfolio with minimum investment in product development or distribution. Intel adopted this strategy way back in the early 1990s and was successful. Intel convinced manufacturers to place the "Intel inside" logo unit in their advertising and other marketing material. "The advertising results were stunning. For example, late in 1991, Intel research indicated that only 24 percent of European PC buyers were familiar with the Intel Inside® logos. One year later that figure had grown to nearly 80 percent, and by 1995 it had soared to 94 percent and continues at these high levels today."[29] Here it should be noted that the core product for Intel was and is the PC and the brand name, which it used on these PCs was "Intel Inside."

4. Promotional: Where the licensor provides its product or service to form part of a licensee's product or service and as a condition of that supply the licensee agrees to display the licensor's mark or logo on the licensee's product or marketing material for the licensee's service. Typical examples are short-term

---

[29] Stuart Whitwell, "Ingredient Branding Case Study: Intel", (November 2005), available at http://www.intangiblebusiness.com/Brand-services/Marketing-services/News/Ingredient-branding-case-study-Intel~466.html.

licenses taken by fast food companies like McDonalds in conjunction with a movie or other entertainment property.[30]

5. Endorsement: Where the licensor endorses a product and agrees to promote that product. This is a common strategy for well-known persons such as sports persons.

Merchandising helps the licensor in two ways:

1. It helps the licensor to expand the business into newer markets and product areas.
2. It helps the licensor to leverage off his existing customer base and cross sell its core products or service.

Under Indian law, merchandising is dependent on monopoly rights that derive from trademarks that are either registered or are protected under Tort Law (Common Law), copyrights and designs.

The core elements of merchandising are to generate revenue, achieve market penetration and maintain the integrity of the licensor's brand. The merchandising license must therefore address the following points:

1. A target should be set for production and for sales. The licensor must have the power to appoint an additional or alternative licensee if the goals are not achieved.
2. Proper guidelines should be given to the licensee on how to use the licensor's brand.
3. Quality standards should be put in place by the licensor on the merchandise produced or sold by the licensee.
4. The license should entitle the licensor to inspect samples and final items of the product or service and if not satisfied, require the samples to be remade.
5. The license should establish procedures for notification of infringements of the licensor's brands by third parties.

---

[30] Weston Anson, Donna P. Suchy et al., *Intellectual Property Valuation* (American Bar Association, 2006), 149.

6. Rules should be laid down for dealing with excess stock if the license were to end.
7. The license agreement should have a provision that prohibits the licensee from challenging the licensor's IPRs in the brands.

In relation to particular forms of merchandising the licensee may expect that the licensor will undertake steps to minimize the potential for ambush marketing and sale of counterfeit products.

ADVANTAGES AND DISADVANTAGES OF LICENSING

Licensing has some stunning advantages as a means of exploiting IP. IP Licensing is the excellent measure for different business organizations to work together to develop new products and services. Organizations licensing out their IP assets to others are earning substantial profits. Other advantages of licensing IP are as follows:

1. In many instances, there is no formal registration process (as is required for assignment of some forms of IP).
2. The greatest advantage for the "licensee" is that he need not have to spend money and time in the rigorous process of R&D.
3. The licensed technology will make the job of the "licensee" easier in getting the finance and cash in on the opportunities of commercializing the technology by introducing it at an appropriate time.

As it is said, a coin has two different sides; in the same way licensing also has a different side which is the disadvantageous side. Now you will ask, is there any disadvantage to IP licensing that has brought in revenue to most companies as would be seen in the later part of the chapter? The answer is yes!

The disadvantages are

1. Greatest danger is that the owner of the license, that is the "licensor" may lose control of his technology and risks it from

being exploited by unwanted third parties, who may exploit the technology through piracy.

2. For the "licensee," the danger is that the licensed technology may become superfluous in a short span, which would mean he would have to spend more to buy a newer technology.

3. Noninclusion of risk aversion clauses in the licensing agreement would mean that the licensee will be at a great risk of losing money.

The process of licensing an IP involves a mechanism of agreement in most of the cases. Normally, licensing agreement is a mode of promoting business ventures and it also marks the birth of a new relationship with a business entity. The crucial point that has to be noted is that the consent of the parties for the Agreement is necessary in all cases, except in the case of compulsory licensing. Though the terms and obligations of the parties are decided by themselves, they are always subject to the provisions of various laws.

8 Franchising—Understanding the Mechanism

After reading this chapter, you will be able to

- Understand the meaning of the term franchising
- Know the types of franchising
- Understand the elements of a franchising deal
- Understand the vital considerations to be made for entering into a franchising deal
- Understand the legal issues pertaining the franchising
- Advantages and disadvantages of franchising

INTRODUCTION

Commercialization of IP through franchising can take on other forms in addition to trademarks exploitation. Franchising can enable patented or copyright products to be wrapped up in a package that enables a business to be driven further.

Franchising is a form of licensing. The reason for not including this in the previous chapter is because of the fact that franchising in itself is a powerful tool to commercialize an organization's IP. In franchising, the "franchisor" licenses its IP such as trademarks, trade dress, copyright, know-how, trade secrets, and so on to the "Franchisee."

NATURE OF FRANCHISING

Franchising is one of the most effective means of exploiting one's IP. When properly structured and well run, franchising provides benefits and satisfaction to both parties. However, it is not an easy route to take, nor is it a remedy for the ills of a sick business. It takes skill, patience, and capital to establish a franchise. The time period for establishing a franchise system can be as long as three years.[1] It takes another three years before the franchisor earns profits and witnesses cash flow into the business.[2]

> **In a franchising arena it is important for a franchisor to have a strong trademark.**

In a franchising arena it is important for a franchisor to have a strong trademark. This is important because the franchisor is marketing the brand itself, so if there is no strong trademark, the ability to gain the fruits from a franchising agreement would be minimal. "Therefore from the Franchisor's perspective, the trademark becomes the key advertising component providing widespread recognition being sought by potential franchisees."[3]

Important

What does it take to establish a franchise?

1. Skill
2. Patience
3. Capital (Money)

---

[1] Kimberley Ellis, "The Franchise Timeline: Guidelines for How Long It Should Take to Open a New Franchise", (January 23, 2008) available at http://www.getentrepreneurial.com/franchise/the_franchise_timeline_guidelines_for_how_long_it_should_take_to_open_a_new_franchise.html.

[2] Jeff Elgin, "How Do I Start a Franchise?" (December 22, 2003) available at http://www.entrepreneur.com/article/66178.

[3] William A. Finkelstein and James R. Sims, *The Intellectual Property Handbook: A Practical Guide for Franchise, Business, and IP Counsel* (Chicago: American Bar Association, 2006), 49.

> **The Indian franchisees for McDonalds, Hardcastle Restaurants Pvt. Ltd. and Connaught Plaza Restaurant Pvt. Ltd., have benefitted immensely from using the famous McDonalds trademark.**

One of the most important benefits in a franchising agreement is that as a franchisee—you are able to trade under a well-known trademark. After obtaining a well-known trademark under a franchise agreement, the franchisee is rest assured that it would reap in huge benefits both in monetary and nonmonetary terms. The reason being that the public would associate franchisee with the trademark that the franchisee has obtained from the franchise agreement. The Indian franchisees for McDonalds, Hardcastle Restaurants Pvt. Ltd. and Connaught Plaza Restaurant Pvt. Ltd., have benefitted immensely from using the famous McDonalds trademark.[4]

It should be noted that the in a franchising arrangement, the franchisor grants a trademark license to the franchisor in return for a fee, which is a percentage of the total turnover. Most of the times, there is also a fee for a marketing budget to promote the licensed trademark. The granting of the trademark license to the franchisee does not mean that the franchisee has a free hand in using the trademark for any activity. The franchisor imposes certain requirements on the franchisee to act in accordance with a set of rules meant to preserve the value of the franchisor's IP and to deliver the best business results. The franchising agreement also has its negative side, as the franchisor could set stricter rules for the use of the franchisor's IP. This eventually leads to undermining the franchisee's own business creativity and activities.[5]

---

[4] http://articles.economictimes.indiatimes.com/2011-02-21/news/28617880_1_vikram-bakshi-mcdonald-s-india-jatia.

[5] "WIPO—KEPSA Seminar on Intellectual Property and Franchising for Small and Medium Sized Enterprises, Nairobi" (2006) available at http://www.wipo.int/edocs/mdocs/sme/en/wipo_kepsa_ip_nbo_06/wipo_kepsa_ip_nbo_06_3.pdf.

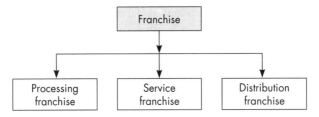

Figure 8.1 Types of Franchise

TYPES OF FRANCHISE

Before going into the detail about the elements of a franchising deal, it is important for us to know the types of franchise agreements that are prevalent in the market. Figure 8.1 shows the various types of franchise.

1. Processing franchise:[6] In other words, it is also known as "manufacturing" franchise. In this kind of an agreement, the franchisor supplies a certain ingredient or a technology to the franchisee. The franchisor would grant authorization to the franchisee to manufacture and sell products under the brand name and trademark of the franchisor. The franchisee in some instances may even be licensed to use trade secret information or patented technology held by the franchisor. The franchisee may also get training with regard to distribution and actual running of the service provided. This kind of franchise is mostly seen in the restaurant and fast food industry. Fast food giant McDonalds has applied the processing franchise model for its growth and expansion.
2. Service franchise: In this kind of a franchise, the franchisor develops a service that is to be rendered by the franchisee under the terms of the agreement. An example of a service franchise would be one involving the provision of automobile tuning or repair services. Madras Rubber Factory or MRF as it

---

[6] World Intellectual Property Organization, ed. *Introduction to Intellectual Property* (n.p.: Kluwer Law International, 1997), 289.

is popularly known has adopted the service franchise model to open various repair service centers for tires across India.

3. Distribution franchise: In a distribution franchise, the franchisor manufactures the product and sells it to the franchisees. The franchisees then sell the products to customers, under the franchisor's trademark, in their own geographical area. For example, the distribution of IBM computers from an electronic store.

ELEMENTS OF FRANCHISING DEAL

The substance of a franchising deal will vary significantly according to the parties involved, the industries in which they operate, and the territories in which they may be found. As part of the franchising deal, the franchisor will grant a right to use the trademarks that are registered in its name. Usually, the franchise agreement will detail the manner in which those trademarks are to be used and the controls that the franchisor has in place to ensure that the value of the mark is maintained.

The franchisor will also, depending on the nature of the business, supply products or ingredients or machinery that are sold on, or used, by the franchisee. A franchise agreement will set out the details of the supply of those products including arrangements for returns and ongoing technical support.

A franchisor will provide training and support to franchisees. The nature of that training and support might vary considerably and will depend on the model adopted and the philosophy of the franchisor. A central focus for the franchise will be the procedures manual established by the franchisor. This document will often become "a sacred text" for the franchisee as it sets out the processes that should be implemented in running the business and maintaining the "look and feel" that has become associated with the franchisor. Often this procedure manual will be closely guarded and its confidentiality maintained. Usually, this provides a competitive edge for the franchise. Of course, this need not always be the case.

Case Study

McDonalds and Franchising

McDonalds is one company that has benefitted immensely from franchising. When people think about the franchising concept, McDonalds usually comes up as an example. Brothers Dick and Mc McDonald opened the first "McDonalds" restaurant in 1940 on Route 66 in San Bernadino, California. Today, McDonalds franchise network is the world's leading food service retailer, with more than 30,000 franchise restaurants serving 52 million people in more than 100 countries. Of those stores, more than 70 percent are owned by independent operator franchisees. The most lucrative market for McDonalds is the People's Republic of China and India.

> **McDonalds franchise network is the world's leading food service retailer, with more than 30,000 franchise restaurants serving 52 million people in more than 100 countries.**

The name that will always be attached to the McDonalds franchising success is that of Raymond Kroc. It was in 1954, when McDonalds Restaurants caught the eye of Kroc because it was using eight huge multimixers to make milk shakes. He decided to visit the restaurants and was amazed at the full-fledged business operations within the restaurants.[7]

Kroc recognized the opportunity to sell lots of multimixers and made a proposal to the brothers to let him franchise restaurants outside of their home base in California. (Ray Kroc was not the only one impressed by the McDonalds restaurant, which was also visited by James McLamore, founder of Burger King, and Glen Bell, founder of Taco Bell.)

In 1955, Kroc launched "McDonalds Systems, Inc." as a legal structure to run his franchises, and by 1958, McDonalds had sold

---

[7] "The Marketing Genius Behind McDonalds Franchise Success", available at http://www.franchisedirect.com/foodfranchises/themarketinggeniusbehindmcdonaldsfranchisesuccess/14/25.

100 million hamburgers. In 1961, the McDonald brothers agreed to sell all the business rights to Kroc for US$2.7 million. The company went public in 1965, and 100 shares purchased then for about US$2,250 would have grown to 74,360 shares now worth over US$3 million.

The first McDonalds franchise opened outside the U.S. in British Columbia, Canada, in 1967. Since then, McDonalds has spread all over the world, with its largest franchise store featuring more than 700 seats opening in Beijing, China, in 1992.

One essential factor that contributes to franchise success is a consistent commitment to standards. McDonalds franchise restaurants became well known for the inspired and defining vision created by Kroc for his restaurant business. "Quality, Service, Cleanliness and Value" was the company's motto, and customers knew that no matter where they travelled, they could rely on those qualities at every McDonalds they visited.[8]

In India, the two companies that have a franchising agreement with McDonalds are Hardcastle Restaurants Pvt. Ltd. and Connaught Plaza Restaurant Pvt. Ltd. Connaught Plaza Restaurants owns the restaurants in North and East India and Hardcastle Restaurants owns the restaurants in West and South India.

Dominos and Franchising in India

Domino's Pizza started in 1960 as a single store. Now the brand has become a leading brand for pizza delivery across the world and at present Domino's Pizza serves more than 1 million people in 70 countries having more than 10,000 stores. Domino's Pizza is also famous for its delivery within 30 minutes at any place and these qualities are enough to establish a brand in any country. Domino's Pizza franchise in India can only be opened as partners of Jubilant Food Works Limited, which is the master franchisee of Domino's Pizza. Jubilant food works also constitutes another international fast food service franchise that is Dunkin Donuts. In 1995, Jubilant food product took the franchise of Domino's Pizza and started its

<hr>

[8] Supra note 3.

first store in Delhi in 1996. The promoters of the company, now Domino's Pizza, have about 552 Domino's Pizza stores in about 130 cities in India and holds a share of 62 percent of the pizza market and 72 percent share in pizza delivery in India.

Baskin-Robbins and Franchising

Baskin-Robbins is one of the diverse businesses of the Graviss Foods Pvt. Ltd., which is the master franchisee for Baskin-Robbins ice creams in India. It has an exclusive franchise for the SAARC region. A well-known name in the hospitality industry, the group has leading brands like RICH cream, The Intercontinental Hotel, Grand Mayfair, Banquets and Celebrations across various cities and Kwality ice creams (Middle East). Baskin-Robbins set up its operations in India in 1993 and then set up its own manufacturing plant in Pune, Maharashtra, the only of its kind outside North America. Late in the same year they opened their first outlet in Mumbai. Today, they are spread across the country with more than 400 outlets in 95 cities besides catering to other premium channels such as star hotels, leading airlines, malls, multiplexes, and top retail chains across India. Baskin-Robbins franchises offer the franchisee a license or right to sell its goods or services and/or use its business techniques. The franchisees usually pay an initial fee to acquire this right, and thereafter pay a percentage of their gross sales to the franchisor throughout the term of their franchise contract. In return for these payments, Baskin-Robbins franchisees gain privileges, including the right to sell a proven and recognized product or service, to use the franchisor's business practices, and to receive initial training and ongoing support.

Tips and Techniques

Elements required in a franchising deal:

1. Grant of right to use of trademark(s) by the franchisor
2. Supply of products, ingredients/parts sold on or used by the franchisor

3. Franchisee to contribute toward media campaigns, production of catalogues
4. Franchisor to provide training facilities and support to the franchisee

CONSIDERATIONS FOR ENTERING INTO A FRANCHISE

Securing the IP is fundamental to a successful franchise system. The franchisor should consider getting appropriate professional advice to identify what parts of its system can be kept secure including ensuring that it has adequate procedures for maintaining confidentiality of the critical elements of the system.

The franchisor needs to carefully consider establishing an appropriate fee structure that is within the ballpark so far as market rates are concerned but also provides for reasonable return of investment for the franchisor. An important element that can be easily forgotten is that the fee structure should also give the franchisee sufficient incentive to be committed to the franchise operation.

More often than not international franchising is implemented by establishing a master franchise for the particular foreign territory (e.g., Domino's and Baskin-Robbins). The franchisor needs to clearly establish how it wants the territory to be developed for the business. This will have an impact on the master franchisee's rights to grant subfranchises. For example, it may determine whether there should be a direct contractual relationship between the franchisor and subfranchisee, the degree of approval that is required from the franchisor and the conduct of the franchise businesses.

Of course, it is important to establish appropriate IP protection in the foreign markets wherein the franchising will occur. This is particularly so in light of the impact of the Internet where cyber squatting[9] has had some impact. The franchisor when establishing

---

[9] Unauthorized use of well-known trademarks as part of a domain name.

its franchise systems would be wise to look beyond the shores at an early stage in developing the franchise system and seek to protect its marks in possible future markets.

Important

Vital considerations to be made for entering into a franchising deal are as follows:

1. Sufficient capital to undertake the franchise
2. Securing IP protection, including trademark protection
3. Fee structure
4. Test and refine franchise operations
5. The product/service is worth generating revenue

Legal Issues Pertaining to Franchising

As discussed earlier, securing IP protection is fundamental to franchise's success in a particular jurisdiction. All franchising agreements involve certain provisions dealing with IP. Since franchising is a kind of licensing and India does not have a separate law for franchising, the laws governing IP licensing are considered to be the foundation for franchise laws in India. Here are the pertinent legal issues relating to franchising:

1. Due diligence: The franchisee before entering into a franchising agreement must ensure whether the franchisor has the authority to license the IP under the license agreement and whether the IP under the licensing agreement is violating any of the IP of any third party. This is very important because once the agreement is signed a violation can result in liabilities imposed on the franchisee.
2. Licensing: As noted in the beginning of the chapter, franchising is a kind of licensing. Since there are no specific laws dealing

with franchise in India, a franchise agreement is governed by the licensing laws of the land. One of the most important aspects of a licensing agreement is that it must be in writing, signed by both parties, specify the rights of both the franchisor and the franchisee, the rate of royalty, the term (duration) of the license, and the territory for which the rights are licensed.[10]

3. Misuse of rights: The franchisee must be prevented from using the IPR of the franchisor for the purposes outside the purview of the franchising agreement. Care should be taken in the language of the agreement to curtail the franchisee from using the IP after the agreement expires.

4. Protection of know-how and trade secrets: An essential aspect of the process licensing agreement (discussed before) is using the technology, know-how, and trade secrets of the franchisor by the franchisee. It is very must essential for the franchisor to decide what amount of technology, know-how, and trade secrets should be given to the franchisee.

ESSENTIAL FRANCHISING CLAUSES

It is important to note that there are a few essential franchise agreement clauses that should be a part of each and every franchising agreement, namely:[11]

1. **Training:** One of the most important aspects in a franchising agreement between two companies is the training clause. This clause is very important in franchising agreements involving two companies whose core business area for example is fast food. It is pertinent for franchisors to provide training to the franchisee on how to operate and make food in restaurants. The obligation to train must be solely with the franchisor and

---

[10] Sections 30 and 30A Copyright Act 1957.

[11] "Ten Key Provisions of Franchising Agreements", available at http://www.allbusiness.com/buying-selling-businesses/franchising-franchise-agreement/2193-1.html#ixzz2AzOl5f00.

that the role of the franchisor must not end at the initial training and should be a continuous process. This must be stated in the franchise agreement.

2. **Protection**: Under a franchise agreement, the franchisee pays for using the franchisors IP such as trade name, trademarks, copyright, and business system. The agreement should contain provisions highlighting the IP interests of the franchisor and the payment structure.

3. **Support**: Support by the franchisor to the franchisee during the duration of the agreement is an essential feature of franchise collaboration. The franchisor must support the franchisee in its operation of its franchised business. This should be stated clearly in the agreement on what kind of support would be provided by the franchisor and how long would there be such a support.

4. **Improvements in services:** Improvements happen in technology/services over a period of time. It is the responsibility of the franchisor to provide for improvement of services, products, and business system as and when they happen. This should be duly inserted as a clause in any franchise agreement.

5. **Assigned territory:** The franchise agreement must have an assigned territory in which the franchisee would operate.

6. **Duration of the franchise agreement:** The franchise agreement must have a start date as well as an end date until which time the agreement would apply to both parties.

7. **Dispute resolution clause:** This is the most important clause in any agreement and also important for a franchise agreement. There would be instances where the franchisee and the franchisor may have a dispute. Under such circumstances, it would be prudent to have a dispute resolution clause stating what kind of dispute resolution would the parties be ready and where would they want the dispute resolution to take place. It can either be a court proceeding or arbitration or mediation. But the choice and the location must be included in the franchise agreement.

ADVANTAGES OF FRANCHISING

Here are advantages of having a franchising arrangement:[12]

1. It allows companies (franchisors) to expand quickly in jurisdictions more quickly than they could have done alone without the franchisees.
2. Investment of the franchise can be thoroughly researched before any significant expenditure is made.[13]
3. It is cheaper for the franchisor to establish franchises as the franchisee will be provide the necessary capital and labor.
4. Franchisees face less risk through franchising a company than through starting a business from scratch, because the franchisor sells a defined proven business format to the franchisee.[14]
5. Franchisees get training from the franchisor for the business operations.
6. Franchisors help franchisees get financial help to start the franchise.
7. Franchisees can attract newer customers into the franchisees and gain financial benefits as well as good will for the franchisor's brand.

DISADVANTAGES OF FRANCHISING

Here are some of the disadvantages of having a franchising agreement:[15]

1. Franchisees have to spend a lot of money to open a franchise.

---

[12] "Franchising", available at http://www.referenceforbusiness.com/encyclopedia/For-Gol/Franchising.html#b.

[13] "The Benefits of Franchising in India", (January 2008) available at http://www.asialaw.com/Article/1988940/Channel/16958/The-Benefits-of-Franchising-in-India.html.

[14] Ibid.

[15] Supra note 11.

2. Franchisees have to pay a fixed royalty to the franchisor that can run into millions and can be a major expenditure.
3. Franchisee is bound by the franchising agreement; it cannot sell any of its goods or services under the franchisor's IP. It has to sell only the franchisor's goods or services.

9 Royalty and Intellectual Property

After reading this chapter, you will be able to

- Understand the various types of royalty determination
- Understand the factors that influence royalty rates
- Calculate royalties
- Understand the royalty payment structures
- Understand on how to manage royalties

The rewards for commercialization of IP can come in many forms. Ultimately, it is a matter for the parties to the transaction to determine what is most appropriate and reflects the needs and desires of each party. "Royalty" refers to a payment (a percentage of sales per unit) depending upon the productivity or use of the licensed IPR.

Royalty, in other words, is the return that an organization gets for licensing out its technology or assets to another organization. Companies like HP and IBM rake in billions of dollars through royalty agreements, as they license out a lot of their technology to various other companies worldwide. In fact, IBM more or less was in a state of financial bankruptcy when it decided to license out its patent portfolio to various startup companies and other well-established organizations.

> **Royalty, in other words, is the return that an organization gets for licensing out its technology or assets to another organization.**

There are various ways for determining a royalty rate that is acceptable

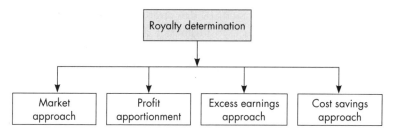

Figure 9.1 Royalty Determination

to both the licensee and the licensor. Here are a few approaches that were discussed in the Twelfth International Conference on Composite Materials—Marketing of Advanced Materials Intellectual Property. According to this discussion, there are four ways by which an organization can determine a royalty rate (see Figure 9.1).[1]

1. Market approach (comparables): In a market approach, the royalty rate is determined by comparing royalty rates of other royalty agreements. In simple terms, look at the royalties negotiated between independent parties for the exchange in a license agreement of similar a property. In the age of the World Wide Web, royalty rates can be easily accessed through web sites such as www.royaltysource.com and www.IPresearch.com.

2. Profit apportionment approach: As the name suggests, profits are shared between the licensor and the licensee. The popular 25 percent thumb rule is applied in this approach. The basic principle behind this rule is that the profit that is attributable to the IP asset should be split between the licensor and the licensee. The 25 percent rule holds that the licensor would get 25 percent of the profits while the licensee would get 75 percent of the profits.[2]

---

[1] Lecture delivered by Michael Martin available at http://www.wsurf.org/ValuationMethods.aspx.

[2] Gordon V. Smith and Russell L. Parr, *Intellectual Property: Licensing and Joint Venture Profit Strategies* (New York?: John Wiley & Sons, 2004), 221.

3. Excess earnings approach: In this approach, the royalty rate is derived by comparing two businesses directly, one which uses the IP asset (for which the royalty is determined) in its business operations with another that does not use that particular IP. The difference in the profits of the two businesses is then equated to the excess earnings that are derived by the use of the intangible asset (IP) for which the royalty has to be determined. The excess profit which is earned is then converted into a percentage of revenue that equals to the royalty rate the owner of the IP (licensor) would charge a licensee.[3]

4. Cost savings approach: This approach looks at the amount of savings enjoyed by the licensee by using the licensed technology. This approach assumes that the licensee would be willing to pay the amount that he or she has saved or an amount lesser to the licensor as royalty.[4]

FACTORS INFLUENCING ROYALTY RATES

There are various factors that influence the royalty rates.[5] Some of them are given below:[6]

1. Nature of protection: This is the most important factor while determining the royalty rate. If a technology or product has a strong patent protection then higher royalty rates are associated with it.

2. Utility over old modes and exclusivity: When looking at utility, a higher rate would be charged on a technology that is unique. "Utility over old modes can be interpreted to mean

[3] Jeffrey M. Risius, *Business Valuation: A Primer for the Legal Profession* (n.p.: American Bar Association), 170.

[4] Daniel Jonathan Slottje, *Economic Damages in Intellectual Property: A Hands-On Guide to Litigation* (New Jersey: John Wiley & Sons, 2006), 175.

[5] Paul McGinness, *Intellectual Property Commercialisation: A Business Manager's Companion* (Australia: Lexis Nexis Butterworths, 2003).

[6] Gordon V. Smith and Russell L. Par, *Intellectual Property: Valuation, Exploitation, and Infringement Damages* (New Jersey: John Wiley & Sons, 2005), 21.

that licensing executives will pay more for significant enhancements over the technologies of minor enhancements. The more unique or different the technology is, the higher the royalty rate."

Now if we look at exclusivity, if the licensor gives exclusive rights to the licensee, then it forgoes the opportunity of obtaining royalty revenue from any other third party, so a higher royalty rate is charged by the licensor.

3. Commercial success and territorial restrictions: A technology that has been proven successful in the laboratory as well as in the marketplace definitely deserves a higher royalty rate. If it can be demonstrated that the licensed technology already has established profitability in other markets or comparable products with less features have proven profitability streams, then the royalty rates for the target market may be able to be adjusted beyond the standards of the industry.

   Territorial restrictions play a significant role while determining rate of royalty. A large territorial limit provides a larger market to sell the technology. It is vice versa when the territorial restrictions are put in place.

4. Comparable licenses and duration of protection: As a common practice, parties to the royalty agreement while determining a royalty rate compare rates of several other royalty agreements (third parties) of similar technology. The duration of protection of a particular IP play an important role, the longer the protection duration, the higher is the royalty rate. The term of the license agreement and the life of the IP play an important part in the determination of the royalty. The licensor is not able to demand payment of royalty if a patent has expired. To some extent a hybrid license can overcome this where the license and royalties are dependent upon both patent and confidential information. However, once the formal registered IP expires, there is likely to be a decrease in the royalty payable by the licensee.

5. Commercial relationship: A situation may arise where the licensor and the licensee are competitors, it would be difficult

to decide a royalty rate, and therefore parties do not depart from the industry norm for deciding royalty rates. However, if the parties are in a kind of vertical relationship, where one is dependent on the other, then the royalty rate could be influenced. The party that has more market clout and has more knowledge would find it easier to negotiate a better deal.

6. Competitive technology: The range of technologies that can be used as substitutes to the licensed technology will have a negative impact on the royalty rate. The analysis of the market will ordinarily include an assessment of technology that is directly competitive to the licensed technology and technology that may be easily adaptable to compete with the licensed technology.

7. Cost of litigation: The costs of instituting proceedings to protect the IP in a particular market will have an important bearing on the royalty demanded by a licensor.

8. Investment by the licensee: Any amount of investment the licensee undertakes would impact the royalty it has to pay to the licensee. In other words, if the licensee invests money on testing procedures, clinical trials, and so on, it would be expected of the licensor to charge the licensee a lower royalty rate.

9. Fields of use: The scope of the license that relates to the field of use of the license technology will impact on the royalty rate. If it is narrow then a lower royalty rate can be expected.

Important

R&D: The Cost

The cost of R&D need not necessarily reflect the negotiated royalty rate. Essentially the cost of R&D will only be considered in the negotiated royalty when the following is included:

1. The cost of establishing work-arounds that enable alternative methods to be applied to achieve the same functionality as the license technology

2. Clinical trial costs
3. The costs of policing the licensing and IP protection

All of the above relate to post-licensing arrangements and effectively address the proposition of who carries the risk in the licensing relationship.

ROYALTY CALCULATION

The fundamental elements of calculating a royalty return involve a description of the (a) financial gain received by the licensee (such as gross/net sales or net profits); (b) the amount of the licensed technology exploited by the licensee (unit sales or manufactured); and (c) the identification of what has been exploited. This usually takes the form of a percentage of net sales for a licensed product or a fixed fee per input unit for a manufacturing process.

Net Sales

The most common form of basis for determining royalty rates is the net revenue or net sales price. The precise meaning of "net" with respect to sales or revenue or price is never clear. The only way to fully address the issue is to clearly set out in the license agreement those items that are to be deducted from the gross price revenue or sales received by the licensee. They may include taxes of some degree such as goods and services taxes or equivalent indirect taxes. They may expand to transportation costs and certain insurances. Depending on the nature of the technology it may include installation or maintenance costs.

It is not unreasonable for the licensee to be required to set out all items of costs that it expects to incur in exploiting the technology and that each of those elements be specified in defining the "net." If an item is omitted, deliberately or not, then the pie will be bigger for the licensor. From the licensor's perspective, the license agreement should clearly specify that the items of cost that determine the "net" result are exhaustive, otherwise there is a risk that the licensee may argue a cost item is implied into the agreement.

The use of "net revenue" base has a range of advantages. The licensee is more likely to be prepared to release information regarding sales or price rather than profit, which would otherwise entail a full audit of the licensee's business.

The net revenue base also accounts for any inflationary impact on the exploitation of the IP. The costs of the licensee already include the inflationary impacts.

The basis that relies upon the price or revenue, rather than profit, is advantageous to the licensor because the licensee must pay the royalty irrespective of whether the licensee is making a loss or not. Nevertheless, a royalty that relies upon a base of price or revenue can be vulnerable to bargains struck by the licensee with related parties. For this reason, the licensor must ensure that the definition of the basis for the royalty is confined to arm's length deals between the licensee and third parties. Of course, a royalty that relies upon a basis of price is at risk if the market is highly competitive which may force down the retail prices.

Where the licensed technology is in the form of a process the most common basis for a royalty is production volume. In manufacturing environments a fixed fee per unit is quite common. This formula gives certainty to the parties and is easily auditable. However, it does not allow for variations in a future production without a formula which often can be complex. This approach does avoid the need for enquiries into the confidential information of a licensee and the licensor is protected from a drop in profitability or price. The advent of inflation can be addressed by inserting a formula into the royalty rate that picks up a consumer price index.

A royalty basis that relates to sales of the license technology inherently relies upon the performance of the licensee. This will impact upon how the payment of the royalty is structured.

Description of the Licensed Technology or IP

Not only must the financial base for the royalty be clearly defined but also the nature of the technology or form of IP that will trigger a payment of royalty. This can present particular challenges in relation to patented technology. A patent will comprise a series of claims. Does the license apply to all of the claims that are the subject of the patent? If some of those claims are successfully challenged what will be the impact on the royalty payable by the licensee? In relation to software, is the royalty triggered by the number of copies of the software sold or distributed? The description of the software may be determined by reference to the functionality defined in the license contract.

Sublicensee Sales

The calculation of the royalties payable to the licensor should clearly state how sublicenses are to be treated. A threshold issue is whether the licensor should be entitled to receive any share of revenue generated by the generating of sublicenses. This will be influenced by the additional effort and risk that the licensee undertakes to market and generate sales.

The royalty calculation should address these tests:

1. Are sales of the technology by sublicensee included in the revenue figures that form part of the royalty calculation?
2. Are license fees payable by sublicensees to the licensee included in the revenue figures that form part of the royalty calculation?
3. What rights does the licensor hold to inspect and audit the records of the sublicensee? What must the licensee do to facilitate such rights?

PAYMENT STRUCTURES

After determining the appropriate rate of royalty and the basis for the calculation and the payments to the licensor, the parties will usually seek to structure the payments of the royalty in a way that reflects the following principles.

Milestone Payments

Where the development and exploitation of license technology is critical to the financial reward being achieved, it is common for the parties to provide for the payment to be made once those milestones have been achieved. This is particularly relevant in technologies that require regulatory approvals such as medical products or where the IP has not been fully registered.

Parties may allow for payment of royalties upon achieving pre-clinical goals or the filing of regulatory applications or receipt of regulatory approvals. This may in turn be structured to account for these events occurring in particular markets. For software, milestones may be linked to a testing regime to ensure that the promised functionality exists although this is usually relevant to the development stage.

Milestones may also be linked to

1. the filing of an application to register a form of IP;
2. the expiration of a statutory period for opposition to an acceptance of an application to register a form of IP;
3. the registration of a form of IP;
4. the lapse of a period of time in which no challenge has been made to registration of IP.

On the other hand, the royalty rate may well decrease if registration of IP is not renewed or is lost through a challenge to the IP rights of the licensor. The payment structures can be arranged to provide incentives in favor of the licensee. A sliding scale of a royalty rate as sales increase can give the licensee an incentive to earn greater profits as its cost structure reduces.

Advance or upfront payments may be appropriate. The advantages to the licensor are obvious as payment in advance reduces risk. However, this needs to be weighed against the fact that it can be treated by the licensee as a sunk cost. It could have a severe effect on cash flows for a startup venture.

Minimum Royalty

The licensor may require a minimum royalty to be paid no matter how the licensee performs in commercializing the license technology. In these circumstances, the licensee should place a qualification upon payment of a minimum royalty if such failure is due to poor performance of technology. Poor performance of the technology will almost certainly affect sales and result in returns for customers and complaints which can have a negative effect. The consequences for failing to meet the minimum performance obligations may include the right for the licensor to terminate the license contract, the conversion of the license from exclusive to nonexclusive, or a change in the royalty rate structure.

Timing for Payment

The parties should clearly state when the royalty becomes due and payable to the licensor. Is it upon shipment of the orders of the license technology, delivery to the customer, invoicing to the customer, or payment by the customer? The licensor's best position will be for the royalty to be payable only when the licensee itself has received payment from customers. Ultimately, this rests on whether the licensor or licensee bears the risk of bad debts of the licensee. Ordinarily that risk is borne by the licensee and royalties are usually structured on the basis of invoices issued.

Infringement Proceedings

It is common for the license contract to suspend the payment of a royalty if the licensee commences proceedings to assert the infringement by a third party to IPRs on which the license contract is founded. The licensee may be required to place the royalty sums into an escrow account until the result of the proceedings is known. At the very least, infringement proceedings may entitle the licensor to negotiate a license arrangement with the party that has allegedly infringed the IP. If the licensee is sued for infringing a third party's IPRs for an act that was within the scope of the rights granted by the licensor the license contract may enable royalty to be reduced or payment suspended until the dispute is resolved.

MANAGEMENT OF ROYALTIES

It is rare for a licensing deal to be struck where one party apprehends that the royalty will not be paid from the outset. Otherwise, the deal would not be struck in the first place. Nonetheless, the parties cannot foresee what may happen in the future or impact upon a licensee's ability to pay the royalty.

Nonpayment

It is accepted common practice for the license agreement to set out the consequences of the failure by the licensee to pay the royalty. The first sanction may be financial. Failure to pay may result in the licensee having to pay an additional amount over and above the royalty itself. Under Indian law, the licensee must be wary of imposing an additional amount that is characterized as a "penalty" under Section 73, Indian Contract Act, 1872. If the additional amount is more than a genuine estimate of the licensor's damage resulting from the failure of the licensee to pay a royalty, then a court will not enforce the contractual obligation to pay that additional amount. Essentially, the amount of damages that a licensor would incur in this case is a sum or interest rate that the licensee could have earned by investing those additional funds. For this reason, an interest rate is usually prescribed in the license contract and it applies to any unpaid amount of the royalty rate.

The licensee that is in breach of the license contract may also be required to pay the aggregate of any outstanding sums. The burden for the licensee in this situation is to bring forward all amounts payable by the licensee under the license agreement that can be a severe, if not fatal, blow to the licensee's business.

No prudent licensor should agree to sign a license agreement that does not enable it to terminate the agreement for failure by the licensee to pay the royalty agreed upon, in time, or at least within a specified period of being notified of the default.

Royalty Audit

Every licensor should ensure that the licensee is under an obligation to maintain proper records and accounts and retain to the licensor a right to undertake an audit of the royalties paid by the licensee including access to the accounts and records of the licensee. It is good practice to carry out royalty audits on a regular basis.

As royalty audits are the central mechanism for ensuring compliance with license agreements the licensor should retain the right to terminate the license agreement if the licensee fails to perform its compliance obligations.

The licensor should be able to nominate an independent auditor to undertake these tasks. The auditor may have to commit to maintaining the confidentiality of the licensee's records. The costs of the auditor are usually borne on the basis of the results of the audit and the degree of the discrepancy, if any, found by the auditor in payment of the royalties by the licensee. If the licensee is particularly concerned about a representative of the licensor inspecting its business records (especially where the licensor and licensee may be competitors) the licensee may insist upon the licensor relying upon a certificate issued by the licensee's own auditor.

Both the licensor and licensee need to put in careful consideration to the drafting of the audit clauses due to the potential long-term impact of the audit clause. Does the auditor have a right to assess whether the triggers for the payment of the royalty have arisen? For example, the licensee may claim that certain technology sold by it does not fall within the claims of the registered patent. Is this analysis the function of the auditor or is the auditor confined to exercising an accounting task in calculating whether all amounts have been paid? In these circumstances, the parties will need to be clear and in complete agreement about the scope of the task of the auditor and whether the appointed auditor has the appropriate skills and expertise to undertake the relevant analysis. The determination of whether royalties paid with respect to a technology come within the claims of a patent will usually involve both a technical and legal analysis rather than an accounting one.[7]

---

[7] *Fomento (Sterling Area) Ltd v. Selsdon Fountain Pen Co Ltd* (1958) 1 All ER 11.

10 Intellectual Property Valuation

After reading this chapter, you will be able to

- Understand the reasons for valuating IP
- Understand who conducts the valuation of IP and how to engage that person
- Understand the principles of valuation
- Understand the different methods to valuation
- Understand the meaning of a valuation report

Intellectual capital is recognized as the most important asset of many of the world's largest and most powerful companies; it is the foundation for the market dominance and continuing profitability of leading corporations.

Everyone involved with IP, whether for profit or not, needs to be able to measure what an IP asset is worth—in rupees or dollars! It has been noted that the valuation of intangible assets is "complex and widely misunderstood."[1] It is important to understand and visualize valuation concepts because the valuation of IP serves as a measure of its influence on a corporation or the wealth of a nation. Valuation is a crucial tool in the strategic management of IP.

---

[1] W. Lonergan, *The Valuation of Businesses, Shares and Other Equity*, 3rd ed (n.p.: Business and Professional Publishing, 1998), 257.

REASONS FOR VALUATION

There are wide ranges of reasons for valuation of IP the most crucial being the need to better deploy the IP asset. An organization may wish to value its IP or technology to determine licensing royalties, obtain financing, and establish potential damages for IP infringement proceedings or assist decision making of the organization.

Valuation of the Intangible Asset

A critical element to valuation is a clear understanding of what is to be valued. When addressing IP that may encompass the legal IPRs, reference is often made to the technology in which the IP subsists or the business of the organization that relies upon the IP or technology—the utility aspect. Commonly the utility of the IP will be embodied in a physical form or application and its value will be closely associated with that embodiment. The concept of embodiment is crucial, for example, to a patent. For this reason this chapter will refer to valuation of the IP and the associated technology in the same context.

In 1998, Sussanah Hart and John Murphy edited a book titled *Brands—The New Wealth Creators* (published by Interbrand, London, United Kingdom) because it was widely recognized that against the changing economic and financial background, commercial entities need to broaden their understanding of "what the assets of business are."

The methodology was developed by Interbrand in conjunction with Ranks Hovis McDougall and has since been used by, among many others, Grand Metropolitan, United Biscuits, Nabisco, BSN, and Lion Nathan. It has been used in a host of applications besides the balance sheet including mergers and acquisitions, fundraising, brand strategy development, and brand licensing. This methodology is by no means the only discourse available, others are detailed toward the end of the material as annexures.

VALUATION OF IP: PROFESSIONAL APPRAISERS

IP valuation is a matter of skill, experience, and the purpose for which the valuation is to be undertaken. If the valuation is required for a commercial transaction then the criteria for choosing the appraiser will be determined by the parties to that transaction. If the purpose is related to determining the financial status of the organization then appropriate accounting standards may impact who is able to perform the valuation.

As we will see from the discussion in this chapter an appraiser must have a grasp of a wide range of disciplines—economic, accounting, financial, legal, and management principles. An appraiser needs to be able to understand the market and the financial context in which the IP has appeal and the skill to dig out a wealth of information that everyone else in the industry wants to keep secret.

Aside from allowing for specific skills and standards relevant to valuation of IP, the engagement of an appraiser should not be any different from engaging any other adviser or consultant. The organization should seek referrals from other businesses that have used the services of the appraiser. The effort in appointing the appraiser should match the risk associated with the valuation. If the organization anticipates that the valuation is important to the future business operations, such as attracting venture capital or determining the preferred option between alternative licensees, the organization may wish to seek tenders or make detailed enquiries about the appraiser. At this stage, it is important to develop an internal common set of fundamental and basic approaches that are to be deployed in the valuation process.

A Contract Should Be Signed

There should be a written agreement between the organization and the appraiser—the starting point for the relationship. The services contract may be in the form of a letter. It is important that the contract clearly specifies the deliverable that is to flow from the performance of the valuation services. Under ideal circumstances, this is usually a valuation report. The appraiser will determine the form and style of the report but the contract should identify some fundamental issues and aspects to be addressed in the report that are enumerated as follows.

The Objective

A statement of the objective for the valuation

1. defines the IP that is to be reviewed and evaluated;
2. defines the legal rights relating to and emanating from the IP that is to be reviewed and evaluated;
3. identifies the financial, economic, and legal standards against which the valuation is to be determined;
4. identifies the time period at which or the period during which the IP is to be reviewed and evaluated.

The Purpose for the Valuation

A statement of the purpose for the valuation identifies

1. the reasons for the valuation;
2. how and when the valuation is to be used;
3. the organizations or institutions that are expected to rely upon and use the valuation.

Standard of Value

The purpose of the valuation will affect the standard that is to be applied in determining the valuation. If the IP is to be valued for the purpose of understanding an indication of the return or price that the organization can achieve by commercializing that IP, then the most common standard will be "fair market value." This standard applies to a scenario that there is a willing hypothetical transferee and transferor of the IP. The resulting valuation is therefore usually a hypothetical answer. The actual transaction will involve factors that were not envisaged in applying the fair market value standard.

Premise or Assumptions

The appraiser and organization should clearly understand the factual circumstances that are assumed to exist for the purposes of the valuation. One field in which brand valuation and the concept of brand value is beginning to have an impact is the area of trademark licensing. In the recent years there has been a marked increase in the attention given to the licensing of trademarks as well as other IP such as copyright, patents, and designs.

The premise should account for circumstances that are realistic for the specified purpose. If the premise reflects circumstances that are reasonably probable, the use of the IP is legal, physically possible, and financially feasible, and such use results in highest profit or other value (in present day terms) for the organization then the valuation will be based on the highest and best use of the IP.[2] The appraiser will apply his or her professional judgment to determine whether the circumstances required by the organization represent the highest and best use of the IP.

The Valuation Date

The date of valuation may be made as at a date that is before, at the same time, or after the time that the valuation is undertaken. The appropriate date will be determined by the purpose of the valuation or possibly to accord with a legislative requirement.

Appraisal Fees and Payment

The appraiser will usually perform the appraisal services on the basis of time spent in performing the task and seek to be engaged on a daily or hourly rate basis. The appraiser should also give an

---

[2] Robert F. Reilly and Robert P. Schweihs, *Valuing Intangible Assets* (New York?: McGraw Hill, 1999), 62.

estimate of the likely cost of the appraisal. It is in the organization's interest to lock in that estimate either as a fixed price or a
"fee not to be exceeded." The appraiser will often prefer not to
do so unless the appraiser can be relatively certain of the elements
of the task to be undertaken. For this reason, if the appraisal will
involve significant researching into a new market, the appraiser
may prefer to be engaged on a phased basis where the first phase
is a scoping study.

It is also usual for an appraisal firm to render its invoices on a
periodic basis, such as every month, and may delay delivery of the
final report until all prior invoices have been paid. The organization should seek to structure payments so that installments are paid
upon completion of specified milestones. The negotiation of these
issues will be determined by the relative bargaining strengths of
the parties.

Other Pertinent Requirements

The document engaging the appraiser should also specify the
following:

1. The milestones to be achieved in the appraisal process and the
   timing for completion of those milestones.
2. The specific individuals who are to perform the appraisal, particularly if the organization has selected the firm of appraisers
   on the basis that certain individuals will perform the appraisal.
3. The engagement document should clearly state that the
   appraiser must treat, as confidential, all reports prepared by the
   appraiser and all information provided by the organization.
   At the end of the engagement, the appraiser should return to
   the organization all information previously provided by the
   organization.
4. All IP created by the appraiser in the course of preparing the
   report (including the report itself and any earlier drafts) should
   vest in the organization. This will ensure that the organization
   legally controls the reports. The appraiser may wish to include

a provision that clarifies that the appraiser retains ownership of any templates used in the course of performing the appraisal.

5. It is also usual for a standard engagement document proposed by the appraiser to disclaim any liability if the organization were to use the valuation or the report for any purpose other than the purpose specified in the contract or for any liability arising from information provided by the organization.

6. The appraiser may wish to be indemnified for any claim made against the appraiser arising from anything other than the wrongful conduct of the organization. The organization may wish to consider placing a cap on such liability to the appraiser although that will be dependent upon the bargaining strength of the organization. Not surprisingly, the organization should seek to be indemnified for any claim made against the organization arising from the wrongful conduct of the appraiser as well as ensuring that the appraiser has appropriate and current professional indemnity insurance.

METHODS OF VALUATION

Acceptable methods for the valuation of identifiable intangible assets and IP fall into three broad categories. They are (a) market based, (b) cost based, or (c) based on estimates of past and future economic benefits.

Market Based

In a market-based approach, an expert would determine the market value of an asset by comparing comparable assets. This task is very difficult while dealing with physical assets as it is not always possible to find an asset that is exactly comparable. The task becomes even more difficult when dealing with intangible assets. What is the reason for this difficulty? It is because IP is not sold as a product but it forms a part of a larger asset or transaction that is to be sold and often at times many details of this IP asset is kept confidential. This is the main reason that stops experts to use method to value vital IP Assets.

Cost Based

In a cost-based approach, the assumption is that there is a relationship between cost and value of the IP asset. This cost-based approach can be better understood by breaking down this approach into three parts, namely, capitalization of historic profits, gross profit differential methods, and relief from royalty method.

1. The capitalization of historic profits: When you multiply the historic profitability of an intangible asset by a multiple that has been measured after measuring the relative strength of the IP in terms of its market value. In order to understand this concept, let us take an example of a brand named "X." In order to calculate the value of the intangible asset, the multiple is calculated after carefully looking at X under several factors which include (a) stability; (b) market share; (c) international acceptance; (d) whether it is showing any profitability; and (e) marketing and advertising support as well as (f) protection. On the face of it, this process looks at some important factors, but it has a major shortcoming, which is that it is associated with historic earnings and pays little regard to the future.

2. Gross profit differential method: As the name suggests it looks at the difference between the profits of products. This method is often associated with trademark and brand valuation. In this method, the difference between the margin of the branded and/or patented product and an unbranded or generic product is calculated.

3. The relief from royalty method measures the royalty an organization has to pay for licensing-in a particular IP from a third party. The royalty represents the licensing charge which would be paid by the licensee to the licensor. The method assumes that the value of the IP is defined as the licensing charge other

companies would pay to use it. In short, this method considers what the licensee could afford, or would be willing to pay, for an IP that it licenses in from a third party.

VALUATION APPROACHES VIS–À–VIS DIFFERENT FORMS OF IP

Knowing the various valuation methods places us in a better position to know what the appraiser is talking about. If we know how these methods apply to various forms of IP the organization can focus on factors that will assist the appraiser, hopefully derive a robust valuation and be well placed in contract negotiations with other parties to the commercial transaction.

In some cases, such as computer software, more than one form of IP will subsist in the technology. The purpose for which that technology is applied will have a bearing on the appropriate valuation method to be applied and the information to be gathered.

Copyright

Cost Approach

The cost approach is based upon the assumption that an investor wishing to acquire copyright will not pay more than the cost to purchase or construct a substitute property. Since the Copyright Act 1957 vests in the owner of the copyright monopoly rights in the copyright work, it is not legally possible to create a substitute version or "copy" of the copyright work unless the creation is done independently of the copyright work. The cost approach therefore can only provide the organization with an indication of the lowest possible value of the copyright work, being the cost incurred in creating that copyright work.

As balance sheets are traditionally drawn up on a historical cost basis, it was necessary to consider valuation systems based upon the aggregate of all marketing, advertising, and research and development expenditure devoted to the brand over a period of time. This approach was, however, rejected quite quickly; if the value of a brand is a function of the cost of its development, failed brands may well be attributed high values and skilfully managed, powerful, and profitable brands with modest budgets could well be undervalued.

The appraiser will need to account for any obsolescence relevant to the IP or technology. This will include considering whether the technology is maintained and enhanced. Technological obsolescence may occur in relation to software if the software is not written in up-to-date language or is reliant upon an outdated platform.

Market Approach (Comparables Approach)

Obviously much depends upon the nature of the copyright work. Software, for example, may have a ready market from which appropriate market information can be obtained to enable the market approach to be applied. In fair market valuation, the monetary value of an IP asset is based on a similar transaction involving similar assets. However, firm evidence of market transactions can be difficult to obtain because the parties seek to keep the transactions confidential.

Licensing of copyright works remains the most reliable form of market information that can be used to value the copyright.

Income Approach (Net Present Value or Discount Cash Value)

Any or all forms of the income approach methodologies (incremental analysis, profit split, or royalty income) may be applied depending on the nature of information available to the appraiser. The appraiser must form a view as to the useful life of copyright work for the purposes of determining the income stream and this will often be less than the legal life of the copyright work, particularly for computer software.

Information that is relevant to a copyright work includes the remaining legal and economic life of the work, which of the copyrights are being used and any known impediments to the use of the copyrights.

The appraiser may also refer to

1. information available from the copyright office;
2. decisions by the courts in which there may be a market for the copyright work;
3. professional societies such as Licensing Executives Society or International Licensing Industry and Merchandisers Association.

Trademarks, Brands, and Domain Names

The greatest difficulties in valuing trademarks and brands is separating other factors that contribute to the success of the product or business that is designated by the trademark or brand.

Valuation of domain names faces similar issues as trademarks and brands. The context of web pages and the Internet in general presents a special flavor for the appraiser. Any laws that prevent the use of the domain name by a regulatory entity will restrict the value of the domain name. The value of the domain name may be inseparable from the web site and its popularity will be due to the content.

Cost Approach (Sunk or Replacement)

What was the cost of acquiring the trademark? In a historical (or sunk cost) approach, the IP owner may add up the total costs incurred to create and protect the trademark or other IP asset. The cost of reproduction approach is possible if historical data is available concerning the creation of the brand. Interestingly and most crucially, the cost of replacement approach would not usually be applicable because the brand will be unique and so theoretically, the brand cannot be recreated in some other form.

The drawback is that the cost approach would usually be expected to indicate a low valuation which would not truly represent the market value of the brand. The brand may be the result of the use of a name, an informal brainstorming session, or have involved the engagement of experts, designers, and market analysts. The actual and historical monetary costs incurred in the development of the brand may be small or significant.

Market Approach

The market approach may be useful if the appraiser has data of assignments of brands that are comparable to the brand that is being assessed. It is possible to resort to the subtraction method although many businesses will have more than one brand and unless discrete figures are known for each brand it may be difficult to reliably deduce the valuation applicable to the comparable brand.

The brand can be valued on the basis of the royalty income that it could generate by licensing to others. An important factor is the assessment of the remaining useful life of the brand. A registered trademark may be registered forever by maintaining appropriate renewals of registration. The market value of the brand, however, may be less if the goodwill associated with the brand is diminished due to poor performance of the organization or the industry in which the organization carries on business.

If the market information is available, a brand may be valued by reference to the premium price payable for the branded article compared to generic goods of the same type.

Income Approach (Net Present Value or Discount Cash Value)

The difficulty with the income approach is establishing the link between income projected and the brand because the brand is a means to attract clients whereas organizations will apply a range of strategies to attract clients. The projected life of a brand depends upon a broad range of factors such as the support to the maintenance of the brand, the performance of the organization itself, and fluctuations in the market.

Data Required for Valuation of Trademarks and Brands

The appraiser may refer to

1. the influence of the umbrella brand on the sub-brands;
2. the attention and support provided by management to the maintenance, marketing, and development of the brands;
3. advertising and promotional expenses as reported in the financial statements and accounts;
4. historical revenue received that relates to the trademark or brands;
5. brands of competitors;
6. the market share enjoyed by the products or services that are marked by the brand and the ability of that brand to influence the market;
7. the level of demand for the branded products and the trend for that demand over a specified period of time;
8. the retail price of the branded products or services and the retail price of generic forms of the same types of the goods or services;
9. evidence of transfers of brands of other companies in the same or similar industries;
10. development and maintenance costs concerning the brands;
11. information related to the strengths and weaknesses of the brands;
12. whether the brand is registered as a trademark, the jurisdictions in which it is registered, the degree of infringement activity, and the response of the organization;
13. decisions by the courts in which there may be a market for the brand or similar brands;
14. specialist texts or external data resources concerning trademark licensing.

Patents and Confidential Information

All three standard valuation approaches can be applied to the valuation of patents. However, the usefulness of the approaches varies according to the integrity of the information available. The legal life of a patent will often outlast its economic value as new innovations cause the target patent to be superseded. Whether this is so will depend upon the scope of the claims within the patent and the breadth of the potential applications.

The significant costs associated with developing patent-related technology and applying for and maintaining patents are an incentive for an organization to understand the value of the patent and related technology as early as possible. In this context, "rules of thumb" may be of assistance where a qualitative methodology has greater influence than a quantitative analysis that may be associated with the three standard approaches.[3]

Similar issues apply to confidential information except that the potential legal life of this form of IP is limitless. Confidential information is often linked with people who have the know-how and the secrets. The scope for those people to leave the organization will need to be considered by the appraiser. The appraiser will also consider the procedures applied by the organization to prevent unauthorized disclosure of the confidential information.

Cost Approach

Application of the replacement cost method will result in a valuation of technology that has the same utility as the target patent and related technology. The appraiser will need to account (or discount) for the fact that greater utility may have been achieved because contemporary creation methods are assumed to be used in the development of the technology. Allowance must also be made for obsolescence.

---

[3] Robert S. Bramson, "Rules of Thumb: Valuing Patents and Technologies", *Les Nouvelles* XXXIV, No. 4 (December 1999), 149.

The appraiser will need to tread carefully to distinguish between R&D expenses that led to the patented technology and those expenses that were indirect to it or led to a separate form of technology. The lapse of time between the incurring of costs of early research and the time of valuation may prevent identification of the relevant costs.

Market Approach

The market approach is often used for patents because there will usually be an existing market for a comparable product. Of course, there will be occasions when the "next big thing" arrives where the innovation has no obvious market demand. In these circumstances, the market approach may be inappropriate.

Income Approach

Projection of income derived from patents can be estimated by having regard to the premium in pricing of the patented article that would be lost if the patent expires and generic articles are able to be legitimately produced. This can be witnessed in relation to pharmaceutical products when the patent of the drug expires. In some instances, a pharmacy company may develop its own generic drug to develop a brand allegiance before the expiry of the patent. In those circumstances, the price differential between the two drugs will be a reasonable basis for valuing the patent. The appraiser will need to consider the factors that may prevent direct comparison between the goods such as increased branding and marketing costs for the generic product.

The IPRs associated with patents are interlinked with the product or process that is to be sold. This means that the market approach will be a useful check against projected income. The income approach can be used to assess savings from greater efficiencies in a manufacturing process that is the subject of a patent.

The expense associated with developing innovation (particularly in the biotechnology fields), participating in clinical trials, and prosecuting multijurisdictional patents are well known. However,

R&D costs will not be relevant to determining valuation on the basis of the income approach.

The portfolio of products or technology that the organization has in the pipeline will influence the risk factor that the appraiser applies. In relation to the development of drugs, only one in 5,000 compounds that enter into the preclinical trial testing graduate to human testing and after that, only one in five are approved.[4] Even fewer are actually marketed. So the organization that relies on one patented product will bear a greater degree of risk.

Other factors that will affect the risk discount applied to determine the value of patent include

1. the likelihood of the patent being granted;
2. whether the patent is standard or innovation;
3. the period of time in which the patented product will be in demand once it reaches the market;
4. the position that the technology will achieve in the market;
5. the degree of control that the organization can exercise to prevent competitor products.

Data Required for Valuation of Patents

The appraiser may refer to

1. financial statements, accounts, and budgets;
2. payroll, time recording, and laboratory records;
3. details of technology licensed-in;
4. descriptions of trade secrets and other confidential information used by the organization;
5. the stage of development of the technology;
6. the legal and economic life of the patent;
7. market opportunities;
8. competitor technologies;
9. barriers to entry into the market.

[4] V. W. Bratic, P. Tilton, and M. Balakrishnan, "Navigating through a Biotech Valuation" available at www.pwcglobal.com.

VALUATION REPORT

The valuation report is the primary outcome or deliverable that the organization expects to receive from the appraiser. The final report presented by the appraiser to the organization be expected to

1. Conform with relevant professional standards applicable to the valuation of intangible assets.
2. Provide a clear statement, free from jargon, of the estimated value of the IP or technology and the reasoning behind that conclusion. This description should be sufficient to reflect the complexity of the task and the impediments that were found in undertaking the appraisal.
3. Have an analysis of the market conditions that influenced the conclusion and an analysis of known trends that might affect future income that may be earned from the IP or technology.
4. Include appropriate documentation supporting the conclusion and analysis.
5. Incorporate any assumptions made in the course of preparing the report that should have been cleared with the organization before the task was commenced, or at least, before the final report is submitted.
6. Include a statement of contingent and limiting conditions and any professional qualifications responsible for the valuation.
7. Explain the reasons for any decision not to use any of the standard methodologies and any reconciliation of differences arising from the application of the different methodologies.
8. Explain any adjustments made to financial information provided by the organization.

Intellectual Valuation Report Certification

Standard Rule 10-3 of the USPAP states that each appraisal report must contain a certification by the appraiser that conforms to a particular content. The appraiser confirms while some of the methods described earlier are widely used by the financial community, it is important to note that valuation is an art more than a science and is an interdisciplinary study drawing upon law, economics, finance, accounting, and investment. It is rash to attempt any valuation adopting so-called industry/sector norms in ignorance of the fundamental theoretical framework of valuation. When undertaking an IPR valuation, the context is all-important, and the valuer will need to take it into consideration to assign a realistic value to the asset.

Glossary

Abstract: A brief summary of an invention, book, or periodical to help in quickly identifying its key features.

All Rights Reserved: Refers to a notice which indicates that all rights granted under copyright law are retained, including the rights to take legal action, if there is any infringement.

Anticipation: Refers to when Prior Art discloses each and every element of a claimed invention. In India, Chapter VI of the Patents Act, 1970 talks about anticipation.

Basic Application: A basic application is the priority document in any country where patent protection is sought in another country. An applicant who files a basic application for patent in a convention country can make application in India within 12 months from the date of basic application.

Business Method Patents: Class of patents that reveal new ways of doing business; they are the most recent iteration of patent types and have come under scrutiny by the courts over eligibility issues.

Certificate of Registration: Official confirmation that your design, copyright, or trademark has been registered.

Classes: Patents, trademarks, designs, and plant variety rights each have an internationally recognised classification system that divides their respective applications into different technology groups, classes of services or goods, or plant varieties. India uses these classification systems to assist with searching our databases of patents, trademarks, designs, and plant varieties. Classes for patents are determined by the International Patent Classification system; trademarks by the NICE International Classification; designs by the Locarno System of Classification; and plant variety rights by the International Union for the Protection of New Plant Varieties (UPOV).

Clearly Descriptive: A mark that clearly describes a feature of a ware or service and therefore, cannot be registered as a trademark.

Co-inventor: Refers to an inventor who is named with at least one other inventor in a patent application, wherein each inventor contributes to the conception (creation) of the invention set forth in at least one claim in a patent application.

Collective Mark: A mark used in the course of trade by members of an association. An association is an unincorporated body and includes any organization of people with a common purpose and a formal structure such as a society, club, trade union, or other body. The association of persons, who own collective marks may compose of the manufacturers, traders, producers or professional bodies such as Institute of Chartered Accountants, Patent Agents, Trade Mark Agents, Board of Cricket Control, or alike.

Collective Works: A work, such as an issue of a magazine, an anthology, or an encyclopedia, in which a number of contributions, constituting separate and independent works in themselves are assembled into a collective whole.

Complete Specification: This is the basis for your patent. It must describe your invention fully, detail the best way of putting your invention into effect, and include at least one claim.

Computer Program: Refers to a set of statements or instructions to be used directly or indirectly in a computer to bring about a certain result.

Concept: An idea or design.

Copies: Refer to material objects, other than phonorecords, in which a work is fixed by any method now known or later developed, and from which the work can be perceived, reproduced, or otherwise communicated, either directly or with the aid of a machine or device. The term "copies" includes the material object, other than a phonorecord, in which the work is first fixed.

Copyright Infringement: Violation of copyright through unauthorized copying or use of a work or other subject matter under copyright. In *R.G. Anand v. Delux Films,* the court held that copyright does not subsist in an idea and hence cannot be infringed.

Counterfeit Mark: Refers to a spurious mark that is identical with, or substantially indistinguishable from, a registered trademark.

Country Code Top-level Domain: It is an Internet top-level domain generally used or reserved for a country.

Domain Name: A domain name is the unique name that corresponds with an Internet protocol address. It is often easy and intuitive to remember. For example, Law Wire™ is located at www.lawwireonline.com.

Dramatic Work: Includes any piece for recitation, choreographic work, or entertainment in dumb show, the scenic arrangement, or acting form of which is fixed in writing or otherwise but does not include a cinematograph film.

Drawings: Drawings (or photographs) disclose the industrial design and are a basic requirement of a design application.

Examination Trademarks: The process through which the Trademarks Office determines whether an application for trademark is registrable.

Exception: A provision in a copyright law permitting the use of a work by defined user groups without the consent of its creator or without the payment of royalties, conditions that would normally constitute an infringement of copyright. Examples of user groups benefitting from exceptions are educational institutions, libraries, museums, archives, and persons with a perceptual disability.

Fair Dealing: Use of works for purposes of private study, research, criticism, review, or news reporting that does not constitute infringement of copyright.

First to File: A patent system in which the first inventor to file a patent application for a specific invention is entitled to the patent. In India and in most other countries, the first person to file has priority over other people claiming rights for the same invention.

Fixed: When a work is set in a tangible medium of expression. It occurs when a work's embodiment in a copy or phonorecord, by or under the authority of the author, is sufficiently permanent or stable to permit it to be perceived, reproduced, or otherwise communicated for a period of more than transitory duration. A work consisting of sounds, images, or both, that are being transmitted, is "fixed" for purposes of this title if a fixation of the work is being made simultaneously with its transmission.

Generic Top-level Domain: Refers to one of the categories of top-level domains (TLDs) maintained by the Internet Assigned Numbers Authority (IANA) for use in the domain name system of the Internet. It is visible to Internet users as the suffix at the end of a domain name. For example, Law Wire™'s domain name is www.law-wireonline.com and the gTLD is .com.

.INDRP (.IN Dispute Resolution Policy): The INDRP has been formulated by the National Internet Exchange of India (NiXI), and has laid down terms and conditions to resolve domain name disputes between the registrant and the complainant concerning the use of the .in Internet domain name.

Joint Application: An application in which the invention is presented as that of two or more persons.

Joint Inventor: An inventor who is named with at least one other inventor in a patent application, wherein each inventor contributes to the conception of the invention set forth in at least one claim in a patent application.

Joint Work: Refers to a work prepared by two or more authors with the intention that their contributions be merged into inseparable or interdependent parts of a unitary whole.

License: Refers to a legal agreement granting someone permission to use a work for certain purposes or under certain conditions. A license does not constitute a change in ownership of the copyright.

Licencing an Invention: Allowing a business or individual to manufacture and sell an invention, usually in exchange for royalties.

Licensee: If an entity is licensed by or with the authority of the owner to use the mark, and the owner has direct or indirect control over the character or quality of the wares or services with which the mark is used, then the licensee's use of the mark or a trade name including the mark is deemed to have, and to always have had, the same effect as use by the owner.

Literary Work: Refer to work consisting of text such as novels, poems, song lyrics without music, catalogues, reports, tables as well as translations of such works. It also includes computer programs.

Logo: A graphic representation or symbol of a company name or trademark, usually designed for ready recognition. The term has no legal significance in the law of trademark.

Moral Rights: Rights an author retains over the integrity of a work and the right to be named as its author even after sale or transfer of the copyright. This view was upheld by the court in *Mannu Bhandari v. Kala Vikas Pictures Ltd.*, AIR 1987 Delhi 13.

Notice: A formal sign or notification attached to physical objects that embody or reproduce an intellectual property right.

Novelty: To be patentable an invention must be "new." It is one of the three conditions that an invention must meet to be patentable. Novelty is present if every element of the claimed invention is not disclosed in a single piece of prior art.

Obviousness: A condition of nonpatentability in which an invention cannot receive a valid patent because a person with ordinary skill in that technology can readily deduce it from publicly available information (prior art).

Patent Office: India's patent granting authority and disseminator of patent information.

Patent Pending: A label sometimes affixed to new products informing others that the inventor has applied for a patent and that legal protection from infringement (including retroactive rights) may be forthcoming.

Patent Thicket: A dense web of overlapping IPRs that a company must hack its way through to actually commercialize new technology.

Patent: An exclusive right to exploit an invention commercially, granted for a limited term in return for public disclosure of the invention.

Piracy: The act of exact, unauthorized, and illegal reproduction on a commercial scale of a copyrighted work or of a trademarked product.

Place of Origin: A word or depiction that designates the origin of a product or service and that therefore may not be registered as a trademark.

Plagiarism: Using the work (or part of it) of another person and claiming it as your own.

Plant Variety Rights: Plant variety rights are used to protect new varieties of plants by giving exclusive commercial rights to market a new variety or its reproductive material.

Preliminary Search: The search of Trademarks Office records that one should undertake before submitting an application for trademark registration. The search may turn up conflicting trademarks and show that the application process would be in vain.

Prior Art: All information that has been disclosed to the public in any form about an invention before a given date.

Priority Date: A priority date is a concept in IP law whereby the first to take a particular action is entitled to a right that excludes others who may have innovated later. For example, in most countries, if two people apply independently for a patent on the same invention, the earlier application has priority and so can prevent the second succeeding. Also public disclosures made before the priority date are relevant for determining whether an invention is new and inventive for patents and new and distinctive designs.

Private Copying: Copying of prerecorded musical works, performers' performances, and sound recordings into a blank medium, such as audio tape or cassette, for personal use.

Provisional Application: A provisional application is an interim document in patent actions. It does not form the basis of the grant of the patent but is a document that precedes the complete application upon which the grant is based. A provisional application establishes a priority date for disclosure of the details of an invention and allows a period of up to 12 months for development and refinement of the invention before the patent claims take their final form in a complete application.

Publication: Refers to the distribution of copies or phonorecords of a work to the public by sale or other transfer of ownership, or by rental, lease, or lending. The offering to distribute copies or phonorecords to a group of persons for purposes of further distribution, public performance, or public display constitutes publication. A public performance or display of a work does not of itself constitute publication.

Punitive Damages: These are damages intended to reform or deter the defendant and others from engaging in conduct similar to that which formed the basis of the lawsuit. In simple words, these are damages exceeding simple compensation and awarded to punish the defendant.

Search: The act of searching through IP records in order to verify whether a patent, trademark, or industrial design has been previously filed or registered.

Service Mark: Service mark is a trademark used in some countries to identify a service rather than a product.

Sound Recordings: Refer to works that result from the fixation of a series of musical, spoken, or other sounds, but not including the sounds accompanying a motion picture or other audiovisual work, regardless of the nature of the material objects, such as disks, tapes, or other phonorecords, in which they are embodied.

Trade Name: Refers to any name used by a person to identify his or her business or vocation.

Uniform Domain–Name Dispute–Resolution Policy: ICANN requires that all registrars in the .biz, .com, .info, .name, .net, and .org TLD follow the Uniform Domain–Name Dispute–Resolution Policy (UDRP). Under the UDRP, many trademark based domain name disputes must resolved by agreement, court action, or arbitration before a registrar cancels, suspends, or transfers a domain name. Ownership disputes alleged to originate from cyber squatting or other "bad faith" registration practices may be addressed through expedited administrative proceedings, initiated by the trademark holder through an approved Dispute Resolution Service Provider (DRSP). To initiate proceedings under the UDRP the trademark owner must either file a complaint in a court of proper jurisdiction against the domain name holder (e.g., an in rem action concerning the domain name) or submit a complaint to an approved DRSP.

Utility Patent: It is granted to anyone who invents or discovers any new and useful process, machine, article of manufacture, or compositions of matters or any new useful improvements thereof.

WIPO: World Intellectual Property Organization (WIPO) is one of the United Nations specialized agencies created to encourage creative activity, to promote the protection of IP throughout the world in 1967.

Word Mark: Refers to a form of trademark comprised of text.

Index*

* The letter *t* following a page number denotes a table, letter *f* denotes a figure, and letter *n* denotes a note.

About the Authors

Rodney D. Ryder is a leading technology, intellectual property, and corporate lawyer. He is the founding partner at Scriboard®. He is presently Advisor to the Ministry of Communications and Information Technology, Government of India on the implementation of the Information Technology Act, 2000.

Mr. Ryder has been nominated as a "Leading Lawyer" in intellectual property, technology, communications, and media law by Asia Law, Who's Who Legal, Asia Legal 500, among other international publications. He was named as one of Indian Lawyer 250's "40 under 45" last year in recognition for his work.

His second book, *Intellectual Property and the Internet*, published by LexisNexis is perhaps the only one of its kind in Asia. The text has been acknowledged to be an authoritative work by the Hon'ble Supreme Court of India and has been quoted in the first and only judgment by the Hon'ble Supreme Court of India on domain names. He is advisor to the National Internet Exchange of India (NiXI) and a member of the panel of independent and neutral arbitrators with NiXI.

He has authored the following books:

*   *Guide to Cyber Laws (E-commerce, the Information Technology Act, 2000, Data protection and the Internet)* (LexisNexis Butterworths Wadhwa Nagpur, India).
*   *Intellectual Property and the Internet* (LexisNexis, 2002).
*   *Brands, Trademarks and Advertising* (LexisNexis, 2004).
*   *Internet Law and Policy* (Oxford University Press, 2010).
*   *Drafting Corporate and Commercial Agreements: Legal Drafting Guidelines, Forms and Precedents* (Universal Law Publishing, 2005; Reprint 2007).

- *An Introduction to Internet Law and Policy: A Course Book on Cyber Law* (LexisNexis Butterworths Wadhwa Nagpur, India, 2007)

Ashwin Madhavan is Co-founder and Director of Enhelion Knowledge Ventures Pvt. Ltd., heading the Strategic Alliances and Operations team. He is also a lawyer at Scriboard—Advocates and Legal Consultants, where he advises clients on intellectual property, management, and information technology issues. He completed his law from Gujarat National Law University and an LLM in Technology Laws and Intellectual Property Laws from Dalhousie University, Canada. He is a founding member of Enhelion. His areas of expertise are domain names and cyber squatting, trademarks, copyrights, and information technology laws. He is a former member of the Canadian Bar Association. He has advised various Fortune 500 companies on various aspects of India's technology and IP laws. He has written several articles for various journals, national, and international publications. He was a member of the Editorial Board of *Journal of Legal Research*, GNLU, and also a member of Law Wire's Editorial Board.

Mr. Madhavan loves to read books related to history, business management, and foreign policy. He has travelled extensively to different parts of the globe. He has taken part in discussions pertaining to India's foreign policy matters at Jawaharlal Nehru University. He has conducted workshops on intellectual property and management in Indian law schools and universities. He recently was an instructor at a training program on "Intellectual Property and the Plant Varieties Act" organized by the Ministry of Agriculture—Government of India for scientists. Very recently he was invited to be a speaker at the U.S.–India Business Council summit on intellectual property held in Gujarat National Law University. During his spare time, he practices yoga and plays the piano. This is his first book. He can be contacted at madhavan.ashwin@gmail.com